THE **COLLIGNON BROS. MANUFACTORIES**

WAREROOMS 181 CANAL ST. N.Y.

T FOLDING CHAIRS NEAR CLOSTER, BERGEN CO. N.J.

ILLUSTRATED CIRCULARS MAILED FREE.

Innovative Furniture in America
From 1800 to the Present

Participating Museums

Cooper-Hewitt Museum, The Smithsonian Institution's
    National Museum of Design, New York

Grand Rapids Art Museum, Grand Rapids

The High Museum of Art, Atlanta

Los Angeles County Museum of Art, Los Angeles

The Lowe Art Museum, Coral Gables

Museum and Library of Maryland History
    Maryland Historical Society, Baltimore

Minnesota Museum of Art, St. Paul

Musée des Arts Decoratifs, Le Château du Fresne, Montreal

Museum of Art, Carnegie Institute, Pittsburgh

The Saint Louis Art Museum, St. Louis

Museums at Sunrise, Charleston, West Virginia

Innovative Furniture in America
From 1800 to the Present

David A. Hanks

INTRODUCTION by RUSSELL LYNES

With essays by Rodris Roth and Page Talbott

Horizon Press   *New York*

To my mother

Contents

Index to Illustrations

Figures refer to illustration numbers. Patent models are indicated by asterisks (*), patent drawings by daggers (†).

Acknowledgments

The Smithsonian Institution Traveling Exhibition Service (SITES) is pleased to make possible the tour of "Innovative Furniture in America." It is our hope that the exhibition will increase public appreciation of this important aspect of American design by enabling the participating museums to present objects from the Smithsonian in relation to innovative furniture in their own collections.

We would like to acknowledge the cooperation of other offices and bureaus of the Smithsonian in this endeavor. Dr. Richard H. Howland, Special Assistant to the Secretary, who has encouraged so many innovative projects, gave support and help at every stage from inception to completion. His assistant, Barbara Russell, helped greatly in carrying out many details of organization and, along with the Office of Membership and Development, in securing funding. Gail Prensky and James M. Goode of Dr. Howland's office have also contributed their time and invaluable advice.

Among the SITES staff, all of whom lent their talents to the exhibition, special mention is due Marjorie Share, education coordinator; Eileen Harakal, public information officer; Andrea Stevens, publications coordinator; Emily Dyer, registrar. In the Office of Exhibits Central, we thank William Jacobs, the exhibition's designer, and Karen Fort, editor. The loans from the collection of the National Museum of History and Technology were particularly important in making the exhibition possible. Dr. John N. Hoffman of the National Museum made available the Warshaw Collection of Business Americana. Rodris Roth, Curator of the National Museum's Division of Domestic Life, provided enthusiastic support in all phases of planning, shared her research generously, and wrote the pioneering essay on patent furniture for this book.

Craig Miller and Marilynn Bordes of The Metropolitan Museum of Art gave liberally of their time and expertise. Virginia Strauss spent many days doing directory runs and the general research so necessary in preparing the text. The Cooper-Hewitt Museum, and in particular Dorothy Twining Globus, Christian Rohlfing, and Lisa Taylor, contributed to the successful realization of the project by arranging for the opening of the exhibition in New York. The exhibition would not have been possible without the generous financial assistance of Herman Miller Inc., Steelcase Inc., the American Society of Interior Designers, and The MacDonald Stewart Foundation.

We also gratefully acknowledge the assistance of Kenneth L. Ames, Winterthur Museum, Winterthur, Delaware; Lee Anderson; Geoffrey Bradfield; Mark A. Clark, Chrysler Museum at Norfolk; Angela D'Antuono; Sharon Darling, Chicago Historical Society; D. J. De Pree, Herman Miller Inc.; Jessica S. Goss, Worcester Memorial Museum, Massachusetts; Catherine Hager, Greenfield Village and the Henry Ford Museum, Dearborn, Michigan; David Parker; Pat Hop, Herman Miller Inc.; Gary Kingsley; Richard McGeehan; Donald C. Peirce, The High Museum of Art, Atlanta; Elinor Reichlin, The Society for the Preservation of New England Antiquities, Boston; Jan Seidler, Museum of Fine Arts,

Boston; Lynn E. Springer, The Saint Louis Art Museum; Doris Stephens, Amos Memorial Library, Sidney, Ohio; Irma Strauss, Chicago Historical Society; Sandra Tatman, The Athenaeum of Philadelphia; Neville Thompson, The Joseph Downs Library, Winterthur Museum; Linda Wagenveld, Herman Miller Inc.; Gillian Wilson, J. Paul Getty Museum, Malibu, California.

Page Talbott deserves special thanks for her part as collaborator in this book, which also serves as a catalog for the exhibition. (Her entries are indicated by the initials P.T.) Our gratitude also to publisher Ben Raeburn, editor Ruth Misheloff, and the Horizon Press staff; and to Craig Miller, David McFadden, and Rodris Roth, who checked the manuscript for accuracy.

Nancy Davis
Exhibition Coordinator, Smithsonian Institution Traveling Exhibition Service

David A. Hanks
Guest Curator

Introduction / *Russell Lynes*

We are likely to gloss over our innovative genius in matters of comfort and convenience, though we are properly awed by the Wright brothers and the tinkerers who harnessed the power of the atom. Does any one of us know who invented the electric refrigerator, the shock absorber, or the revolving door, all of which have contributed so much and so differently to our comfort? To call such innovators "unsung heroes" puts the case too strongly, but to collect the work of some of their counterparts in a book such as this is not only to give credit where credit is overdue but something of an act of academic heroism in itself. Let me invite you to look with me from the point of view of a consumer and, most particularly, a consumer of comfort, at what David Hanks has assembled and explained.

There are, it seems to me, two kinds of furniture: one kind on which we impose our wills in order to derive the greatest degree of comfort suitable to the place and circumstances under which it is used, and the other kind which imposes its will on us and makes us behave as it dictates. One, such as the rocker or the easy chair, might be called passive (or friendly) furniture, the other active (or disciplinary) furniture, like schoolroom desk-chairs. Both sorts have their uses, both sorts have called forth a great deal of inventiveness over the last two centuries in their design.

By and large, "innovative furniture," as the term is used here, is of the first kind. Some was designed primarily for convenience, some primarily for comfort; sometimes they overlap. Comfort has many definitions; it is not only a matter of physical relaxation, it is also a matter of appropriateness. One can be physically comfortable in an easy chair and socially *un*comfortable in it if the circumstances are not such as to condone or promote informality. Victorian ideas of physical comfort probably were little different from our own, since the basic shapes of the human body do not vary from era to era, but Victorian dress, manners, and concepts of what was suitable relaxation were very different from ours, and the furniture of the mid-nineteenth century and the mid-twentieth shows the distinction. It would be difficult for a lady in a bustle to be comfortable in the same chair as a lady in a bouffant skirt or one in the fashionable "wasp waist" corset of the time when buxom Lillian Russell was regarded as the apotheosis of what was then called feminine pulchritude. Different costumes require different chairs or chaises longues and different postures to satisfy different standards of acceptable behavior. A lady in a bustle in a sling chair is as unthinkable as a man in a frock coat in Saarinen's "womb" chair (Figs. 137 and 89).

The design of furniture has often both catered to concepts of comfort and at the same time tried to make amends for the strictures of manners. By contrast, many designers, especially since the influence of the Bauhaus, which began to make itself felt in the 1920s in America as well as in Europe, have been convinced that they know better than we do what is good for us, and have applied principles of "functionalism" to furniture which tell us how we ought to relax or how we ought to sit up straight, whether we like it or not. This is disciplinary furniture with the customary overtones of morality. One might call it "health food" furniture.

It may not suit your taste, but "it's good for you."

I believe that as you look at *Innovative Furniture in America* you cannot but be convinced that a great deal of ingenuity and research has been devoted to reconciling comfort with manners and the whims of changing taste. There are pieces—tables, beds, chairs, "convertibles," which are several kinds of furniture at the same or alternative times—about which we can only say that this is Victorian or this is Modern, but there are also some that would fool us, pieces designed in the nineteenth century that seem to be made for our own time. The Belter chair (Fig. 39), for example, with its elaborately carved ornament, is ineffably Victorian. The Isaac Cole bentwood chair of 1874 (Fig. 41), on the other hand, might, except for its understated ornament, have come out of Finland or Sweden in the 1920s or 1930s (there was *no* ornament on Scandinavian furniture then). The same may be said of Thonet's bentwood furniture of the 1850s and 1860s, the principles of which were converted into metal tubular furniture in the 1920s by Mies van der Rohe and Marcel Breuer. Some furniture, like the Belter pieces, is best considered in the context of the prevailing taste at the time it was made, in Belter's day a taste for fringe and lambrequins, Brussels carpets and bell glasses filled with wax flowers or stuffed birds. But under the ornament, the laminated rosewood of the Belter chairs and the bentwood of the pieces by Thonet (Fig. 33) have a marked affinity with the fashionable taste of the present and the recent past.

Neither the Belter chair nor Cole's bentwood laminated one appears to have been designed for comfort. They seem to be showing off the ingenuity of their designers and suggest that whoever sits on them must make the best of it. They are not going to let their occupants down or make them uncomfortable socially, and they are not going to pitch them forward as the cantilevered chair designed by Alvar Aalto in the 1930s had a way of doing. (I owned several and retired them to the attic when they proved to be dangerous to my children. I did so reluctantly; they were handsome pieces.) It would appear that high style and comfort are commonly at odds, though this is by no means always the case.

The rocking chair sometimes attempts to bridge the gap and take on a formal, stylish appearance as it did in Hunzinger's 1882 platform rocker (Fig. 108), but in general, for rocking chairs, comfort came first and style second. The rocker, an American invention, or so it is said, was not the sort of furniture one would have found in an eighteenth- or nineteenth-century parlor. Benjamin Franklin had one in his library, a "great armed chair, with rockers, and a large fan placed over it, with which he fans himself, keeps off flies, etc., while he sits reading, with only the small motion of his foot." One might call this a rocker with extras. (It wasn't until after the middle of the nineteenth century that fly screens for windows were marketed, a simple device that benefited mankind more than air conditioning ever has!) The earliest rockers were not built as such; they were vernacular chairs to whose legs were attached the kinds of rockers used on cradles. They had an obvious appeal to Americans, a restless people who found it difficult to sit still, a people for whom mobility was part and parcel of freedom—and still is.

"You will recall," President Kennedy is recorded as having remarked, "what Senator Dirksen said about the rocking chair—it gives you a sense of motion without any sense of danger." The primary function of the rocker has always been to provide ease and comfort (Kennedy, you will remember, relied on one because he suffered from a bad back), and nineteenth-century designers of patented furniture produced a great variety of "platform rockers" in which the base of the chair stood still and solid on the floor and the seat rocked on or with the aid of springs. If Hunzinger's chair would have been quite at home with Belter's pieces, the same cannot be said of Heywood Brothers' charming and simple 1873 design (Fig. 107).

Andrew Jackson Downing, quite probably the most influential tastemaker of his day, wrote in 1850 in *The Architecture of Country Houses*, "Much of the character of everyman can be read in his house." By the same token, much of the character of Americans can be read in the kinds of furniture with which they have furnished their dwellings, whether they are substantial houses or log cabins or the modern equivalent of the cabin, the one-room apartment. Americans like gadgets—and much patented furniture satisfied that taste—and perhaps especially gadgets that abet their restlessness or, if you prefer, their need for mobility both physical and social. We not only travel, most of us, the minute we have a vacation, we also move from house to house as we prosper, or from city to city if opportunities for jobs and advancement beckon us. The basis of our national economy (and at present of our national headache) is "wheels," which are also the *sine qua non* of our leisure.

So it is not surprising that mobility was at the root of a great many pieces of innovative furniture besides the rocking chair. The designers who patented them reflected the concerns of the Americans they hoped would find them congenial. The most extreme example here is the "wearable chair" designed by Darcy Robert Bonner Jr. in 1976 (Fig. 149). Since it is strapped to you, it goes where you go and assumes that you do not intend to stay anywhere for very long. (It looks monstrously uncomfortable in the photograph! An earlier and more humane version of this sort of chair was the "shooting stick," a cane with a handle that opened into a small seat and a metal disk that could be attached to its ferrule to keep it from sinking into the ground. It was common in Edwardian times not just for shooting but for watching field trials.) The various folding camp chairs—like the sling chair (Fig. 137) designed in the late nineteenth century (the prototype of the "Hardoy" chair both for indoor and outdoor use that was so fashionable in recent years), and the folding camp chair of 1880 (Fig. 132) and its predecessor of circa 1860 (Fig. 125) which is the prototype of the modern "director's chair"—all bespeak people on the move. The ultimate mobile chair is the pilot's seat that can be ejected from an airplane in flight, though tremendous ingenuity was devoted in the nineteenth century to the design of seats and berths for railroad cars to assure the comfort, a relative matter, of long distance travel in the days before we were scrunched into airplanes.

If we are restless, we are also gregarious, and designers of furniture have invested resourcefulness in making chairs that can be folded and stored, or stacked so that a dozen may take up more air space but no more floor space than a single one. B. J. Harrison's chair of circa 1866 with its carpet seat (Fig. 130) becomes as flat as a sandwich when folded; Charles Eames's 1955 side chairs of molded polyester and steel tubing (Fig. 143) fit as tidily on top of one another as poker chips. The folding chairs and stackable ones are active chairs. They are disciplinary. In them one can only sit up straight with hands clasped in the lap or squirm. Even when they are used at card tables (Fig. 131), another kind of furniture that has received the attention of innovators, they are not for relaxation but are intended to make their occupants alert and attentive. In this respect they have a good deal in common with side chairs and chairs designed for use at dining room tables and in cafés or, when I was young, in drugstores—the steel rod chairs (Fig. 68). They are less for comfort (they dictate posture and one does not spend long periods of time in them) than for the ease with which they can be moved.

It is obvious that adaptability has played a motivating role in the design of many of these innovative pieces—furniture designed to serve not just one but several purposes. Sometimes the subsidiary purpose is, literally, an extension of the primary one—a table, for example, that by the addition of leaves can comfortably seat ten or twelve persons instead of two or four. Sometimes it is merely a matter of a table top that tilts to an upright position so that it can be put against a wall. Sometimes a flat top becomes an angled easel to make it a drafting or writing table or to hold papers or a heavy book at a readable angle (Fig. 165). There are library tables and chairs (Figs. 160 and 156) that unfold into library steps. The "folding lounge" and "chest-bed" (Figs. 162 and 124) are artifices for concealment very familiar in the nineteenth century when large wardrobes turned into double beds so easily that advertisements depicted small children opening them, just as Castro Convertibles did until recently. George Nelson's storage system (Figs. 169–71) had its prototype in a remarkable book called *The American Woman's Home* (1869) by Catherine E. Beecher and her better remembered sister, Harriet Beecher Stowe. The Beechers recommended a high storage unit on rollers that could be set against a wall or rolled out to divide one bedroom into two. One of the most amusing and ingenious of convertible pieces (if perhaps the most hideous) is the baby's highchair that becomes a pram and another that is highchair, folding table, baby carriage, and rocker depending on which shape it is manipulated into. Its complexities must have made mothers and nursemaids frantic (Fig. 31).

I have suggested that comfort is not only a matter of physical ease but of social ease, a matter of time, place, and circumstance. Essentially, all furniture is designed for comfort if not primarily for relaxation. Chairs get us off our feet, tables get our games and work and food off our laps, beds support us in many kinds of physical and emotional needs. When we speak of a comfortable chair or sofa or bed, we mean one that accommodates itself to our pleasure at a particular time and under particular conditions. (A tree stump can be a wonderfully comfortable chair for a weary hiker in the woods.) An "easy chair," on the other hand, is an indulgent chair whose function is only for relaxation, like Eames's wonderful "lounge chair" (Fig. 1) or the classic "Morris chair" (Fig. 117) which turned up in many manifestations, each intended to relax its occupant more satisfyingly than its competitors. The same cannot be said for all reclining chairs which determine the posture of your relaxation whether you like it or not. I do not like them (I'm a restless sitter) though there must be many who do. I want the furniture that is meant to relax me to be passive, to yield to my whims, not to be active and tell me how I ought to relax.

I am not alone in admiring and sometimes being awed by the ingenuity that designers of furniture have exhibited in trying to make that curiously constructed mess of bones and flesh which is you and me comfortable, socially at ease, and fashionable in the spirit of the times as they interpret them or, if they are influential enough, order them so to be. I am sure that I am also not alone in my gratitude to those who conceived this collection of inventive devices to make life pleasanter to endure, when enduring is necessary, and to enjoy when it is not.

Author's Preface

Innovative Furniture in America concentrates on the inventive genius of this country in furniture design for almost two centuries.

The scope of the subject is immense. It embraces the possibilities for design and production during that period in terms of technological changes, new materials, approaches to comfort, and concerns for portability, multiple functions, efficiency, and cost. Imagination and creativity are essential to the design of virtually every kind of innovative furniture, but it is the functional aspect of the design that is our chief focus here.

The groundwork for this study was laid by the pioneering, although not exhaustive, work of Siegfried Giedion, who in *Mechanization Takes Command* divided his material into themes of comfort, movability, multiple functions, the nomadic, and twentieth-century designs by both craftsmen and architects. To the themes of comfort and multiple functions, *Innovative Furniture in America* has added technique, portability, and materials. Within each category, the chronological arrangement emphasizes the continuity of inventive design and indicates that much twentieth-century technology is rooted in the nineteenth century. One example of early pathbreaking designs is Samuel Gragg's "elastic chair," patented in 1808 (Fig. 35), which may be seen as a forerunner of such twentieth-century pieces as Peter Danko's molded plywood armchair of 1978 (Fig. 53).

American furniture in the nineteenth century was characterized by revivals of the classical, rococo, Renaissance, and Gothic, among the most popular. Concurrent with the production of this high-style furniture was the manufacture of another type which anticipated the functionalism so important in the twentieth century.

Giedion characterized these two categories as the "transitory" and the "constituent." High-style revival furniture, an outgrowth of fashion, serving what he termed the "ruling taste," was transitory and lacked the creative force and inventiveness which marked the constituent forms. Nineteenth-century patent furniture, in contrast, addressed the "popular taste" and "called forth all the constituent powers of the century as it liked to relax when wearing none of its masks. This patent furniture tackled problems in a manner completely new to the century."[1]* (A thorough and practical guide to the various aspects of patent furniture is supplied by Rodris Roth's study, "Nineteenth-Century American Patent Furniture," below.) Also in Giedion's constituent category was "vernacular furniture"—the simple and the functional, not governed by short-lived styles or fashions—such as the enduring Windsor chair (Fig. 32) and Shaker furniture, important throughout the nineteenth century.

In Giedion's scheme, the work of the "anonymous engineer" responsible for patent furniture was identified with the "popular taste"—a constituent category. "In America," he wrote, "inventive fantasy and the instinct for mechanization were the common property of

---

*Footnotes begin on page 191.

the people. There, the furniture of the engineer was created in glorious unconcern. It is the absolute opposite of the ruling taste."[2] The work of the nineteenth-century upholsterer he associated with the "ruling taste"—a transitory category. Yet in tracing the development of upholstered furniture in the eighteenth and nineteenth centuries, he also describes the innovation of the spring, revealed by the numerous patents taken out for spring chairs and mattresses.

We find, moreover, that some known manufacturers of high-style furniture—such as John Henry Belter and George J. Hunzinger, who considered themselves cabinetmakers—were also responsible for important patented pieces (Figs. 36 and 128).[3] Conversely, while American patent furniture is today regarded as "protofunctionalist," historic-revival styles may be found, contemporaneous with simpler designs, among the hundreds of patents taken out from 1850 to 1900. We may say, therefore, that both the "anonymous engineer" and the high-style craftsman were often innovators.

Although innovation implies originality, it does not always imply discovery or invention of an entire form. The concept of the folding chair, for instance, can be traced back to ancient times. Yet the form may be considered innovative in the period we are surveying, having been discovered anew (rather than merely revived) in the nineteenth century; as Rodris Roth tells us, the first U.S. patent for a folding chair was granted in 1855. Moreover, a form that is not innovative in an overall sense may nevertheless incorporate a special new device or technique or "improvement" not always apparent from merely looking at the piece of furniture. So many folding chair patents were issued in the nineteenth century that the choice of a specific example was difficult. The question of patents aside, wholly new furniture forms are in fact rare. As George Nelson has pointed out, designers inevitably build on the work of their predecessors and contemporaries. The famous and seemingly unique Eames chair, he notes, would not have been possible "without the earlier work of [Alvar] Aalto and [Bruno] Mathsson in Finland and Sweden, which is the way design has always developed."[4]

The objects in the exhibition were chosen to illustrate the themes around which it was organized rather than to represent specific designers.[5] Many important pieces could not be included. Certain classics, however, such as Thomas E. Warren's patented spring chair (Fig. 101) and Charles Eames's side chair (Fig. 51), will be found here, juxtaposed with less familiar examples. In some instances, an object might have fit equally well into more than one thematic category. The Warren chair, for example, is presented under "Comfort" because of its spring seating device, but its innovative use of iron would also have warranted placing it in the section on "Materials."

Technological innovation has not, of course, been the sole criterion in the choice of objects. "Pure technology," Reyner Banham has remarked, "would probably bring furniture to an end, or at least render it invisible."[6] Beauty of form, the concept of furniture as art,[7] also guided the selection. The simple, functional forms of inexpensive factory-produced patent chairs of the nineteenth century stand up to modern aesthetic scrutiny, as do the distinctive twentieth-century designs of a Charles Eames or a George Nelson. Objects both innovative and aesthetically satisfying claimed consideration over the merely inventive, although it is important to recognize that technological innovation has often provided the basis for outstanding aesthetic achievement.

Innovative Furniture in America appears at a time of noticeable decline in American technological and aesthetic innovation. In many fields today, it is Japan and Germany which are making the technological advances, and it is Italy which is today pre-eminent in design. Frederick Andrews, writing on the relation between technology and productivity (*New York Times*, January 31, 1979), observed that the American inventive genius "is running down, no longer producing the starbursts that have spurred and sustained industrial productivity for a century or more." To a large extent, the decline of innovation in American furniture design is due to an industry which, with a few notable exceptions, feels that technological and design

Note on Dating, Measurements, and Furniture Collections

The dates assigned to furniture here are either patent dates, design dates (e.g., "designed 1946"), or dates of manufacture (e.g., "design introduced 1950").

Captions to the photographs of patent furniture in the Innovative Furniture in America exhibition use the date the patent was issued, although commercial production of the design—or of the particular example shown—may have occurred several or many years later (it is often difficult to determine the production date of any given example). Prior to 1861, the term of patent was fourteen years; since then it has been seventeen years. Presumably, production of objects labeled or stamped as patented began before the expiration of the patent.

In other cases, primarily more contemporary ones, the date given is either that of the design plans (for items never, or not yet, commercially produced) or the date the item was introduced for sale by the manufacturer. For objects about which no specific information is available on patenting, designer, or maker, approximate dating is based on style.

Working dates of designers or patentees are based on directory listings.

The measurements should be interpreted as follows: overall height x width x depth in inches, followed by centimeter equivalents in parentheses.

Important collections of innovative furniture may be found at the National Museum of History and Technology, Smithsonian

Institution, Washington, D.C.; Greenfield Village and the Henry Ford Museum, Dearborn, Michigan; The Metropolitan Museum of Art, New York; and the Cooper-Hewitt Museum, the Smithsonian Institution's National Museum of Design, New York.

innovations are unrelated to profits. This may have been true in the nineteenth and early twentieth centuries as well, of course; perhaps there were merely more exceptions to the rule then. Even in the nineteenth century, American innovative furniture was sometimes more appreciated in Europe than at home. At the great Crystal Palace Exhibition in London in 1851, for example, American ingenuity in two patent chairs was admired: "In [American] chairs, the best is an arm-chair [see Fig. 101], in which, by the motion of the body, without the aid of any complicated machinery, the seat and back can be made to assume and retain a number of forms, from that of a flat couch intermediately to that of a straight back. . . . There are a set of chairs arranged on four C springs, which are new to us, and would seem to be rather pleasant for study or library use, because they give way to the motion of the body in writing, and afford a sort of lounging chair without reclining. They are rather dear."[8]

Several American institutions have been instrumental in encouraging innovation in furniture design in the twentieth century. The Institute of Design in Chicago and The Museum of Modern Art in New York are two of many that deserve special mention. From its founding in 1937 by Laszlo Moholy-Nagy, the Institute of Design has consciously sought to develop educational methods "for the training of artists, industrial designers, architects, photographers and teachers. . . ." Moholy-Nagy's idea was that the Institute should be based on the principles and educational methods of the Bauhaus, modified by the needs of America. According to Bauhaus principles, information about old and new materials was to be combined with a knowledge of the means of expression, as well as the principles and practices, of industry. Designing experimental furniture was an important part of the curriculum. Some of the innovative designs in this exhibition were created by Institute students or emerged from its experimental courses.

The programs and exhibitions sponsored by The Museum of Modern Art in the 1940s and 1950s were a great encouragement to innovative furniture design. These exhibitions, many of them organized by Edgar J. Kaufmann Jr., resulted from a shared concern by museum curators, designers, manufacturers, and retailers about the general quality of furniture design. Specific reference to the exhibitions will be found throughout the book.

David A. Hanks

1. Technologically innovative American furniture was manufactured in the nineteenth as well as the twentieth century. The two periods are poignantly juxtaposed in this tongue-in-cheek photograph by Charles Eames, showing his famous lounge chair and ottoman of 1956 in the setting of a Victorian parlor. The Eames chair looks quite at home because, although not possible without twentieth-century technology, it was designed for comfort, as was the Victorian upholstered easy chair. Photograph courtesy of Herman Miller Inc.

2. This 1935 interior of a humble country store at Ewen Avenue, Spuyten Duyvil, N.Y., shows wire chairs, popular in America from the late nineteenth century to the present. Important when first produced because of their innovative material, which combined strength and lightness, these chairs were also inexpensive and thus accessible to rich and poor alike. Photograph by Berenice Abbott, October 11, 1935, Federal Art Project, "Changing New York." Courtesy of the Museum of the City of New York.

3. Although innovative patent furniture was generally intended for the needs of ordinary people, it appealed to the rich as well. Light, portable furnishings were particularly popular with the affluent for leisure-time pursuits, as seen in this portrait of the Vanderbilts on their yacht. Photograph courtesy of the Preservation Society of Newport County.

4. Display in The Work of Charles Eames exhibition, The Museum of Modern Art, January 1946. Eliot Noyes, then director of the Department of Industrial Design, described Eames's pieces as "the most important group of furniture ever developed in this country." MOMA's exhibitions in the 1940s and 1950s influenced consumers as well as designers and manufacturers, helping to make innovative furniture and "good design" appreciated by a new generation of Americans. Photograph courtesy of Herman Miller Inc.

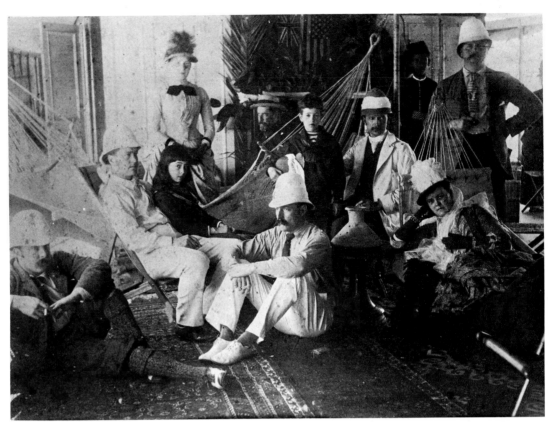

3

4

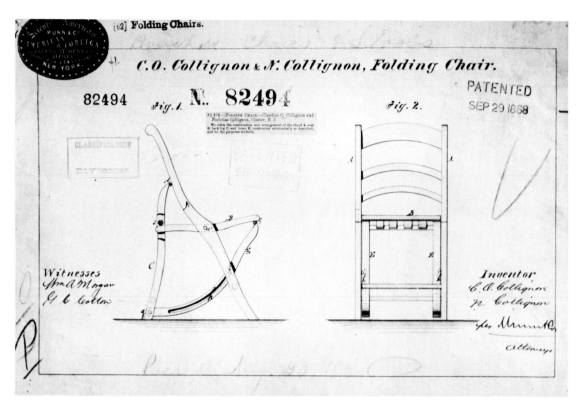

5

Nineteenth-Century American Patent Furniture/Rodris Roth

5. Patent applications must be accompanied by a drawing of the invention. This one of a folding chair was submitted by Claudius O. and Nicholas Collignon of Closter, N.J. As is customary, the drawing was signed by the inventors and witnesses. Applications were often also signed by the patent attorney, in this case "Munn & Co.," whose stamp, as well, is affixed at the upper left. Various written and stamped notations were added at the Patent Office, including the printed abstract of the patent from the *Annual Report*, here pasted in the center below the patent number. The National Archives.

6. Until 1880, a working model had to be submitted with the patent application. This one of a folding chair was prepared by the Collignons. When patent 82,494 was issued, the model was tagged with the pertinent information: patent number, patentee's name, invention, and patent date. Then it probably was put on display in the "Museum of Models" in the U. S. Patent Office building. Smithsonian Institution, transfer from U. S. Patent Office, 65.260.

Patent furniture is any piece covered wholly or in part by a patent. In the United States during the nineteenth century, virtually every kind of object was incorporated in some way into a patent covering some aspect of form, shape, design, or function. We are made aware of the inventors' scope from the range of surviving examples, and from brochures, advertisements, popular publications, and the patent records themselves. It was an age when Yankee ingenuity flourished in tinkering and mechanical dexterity. Promotion stimulated desire for the latest styles and gadgetry and immediate use was found for innovations in the expanding mass production of furniture. At international expositions—those great trade fairs of the second half of the nineteenth century—American innovations in mass-produced articles were also gaining favorable recognition.[1]

Believing that people should be rewarded for new ideas and new ways of doing things, the framers of the Constitution provided innovators with some means of protecting their "inventions." The patent system embodied in Article 1, Section 8, gives Congress the power "To promote the Progress of Science and Useful Arts, by securing for limited times to Authors and Inventors the exclusive Right to their respective Writings and Discoveries." We will examine the process and resources of the Patent Office in detail later in order to trace the use of patent furniture and to understand its place in nineteenth-century American life.

The American patent system simplified the submission of applications. To the public the patented object perhaps suggested the latest if not the best in its field; it had something none of its competitors had, and was so "valuable" that it was "protected" by patent. Advertisements in the 1870s and 1880s stressed that certain products were so protected, though in truth it was rare that the catalog and advertising material was specific about what, exactly, the patents were or did. Mixed in with a tremendous amount of gadgetry, however, were truly innovative ideas. It might even be suggested that to buy a patented article was to share in America's progress. Moreover, the appeal of the "exclusive feature" should not be overlooked; patent furniture suggested the new, the novel, and at the moment of purchase the buyer could feel he had risen to the level of the Joneses.

There was a touch of folk wisdom in all this. If it is worth protecting, an idea must be an improvement, and since a patent prevents copying, one feels certain that the original must be the best. The pleasure of having the best goes with each patented piece. Patent furniture was not just a nineteenth-century novelty, however; it was an instance of the innovation that went with mass production and industrial expansion. "Inventiveness" and "ingenuity" seemed a part of the air Americans breathed.

As we noted earlier, the Constitution made the patent system a law of the land. On April 10, 1790, President Washington signed the act which created the Patent Office. Congress had also acted to separate copyright, which pertained to "writings," from patents, which pertained to "discoveries." Today copyrights are registered with the Copyright Office, which since 1870 has been under the custodianship of the Library of Congress. The Patent

Office is responsible for inventions, designs, and trademarks. Originally in the Department of State, the Patent Office was transferred in 1849 to the newly established Department of the Interior and then moved in 1925 to the Department of Commerce, where it now remains.

It should not be assumed that the patent system was a startling innovation. Before 1790, patents had been granted by some American colonies and states, but in each instance a special act of legislation was required. In Europe, the granting an inventor the exclusive right to his or her idea for a specific period is recorded as far back as 1420, and became more common in the 1500s. The Maritime Republic of Venice is credited with adopting the first patent law in 1474. The Netherlands began granting privileges encouraging inventions in 1581. In England, the Statutes of Monopolies of 1624 extended "letters patent and grants of privilege for the term of 14 years . . . to the true and first inventor or inventors of new manufactures." The English law served as the model for some of the North American colonies; so it seems that in creating a patent system the Americans were neither revolutionary nor innovative, but merely following normal procedures. The significant difference, however, was that the American system democratized what had once been a privilege by simplifying a long, tenuous, and uncertain procedure. Thus instead of depending on

---

United States Patent Office.

CLAUDIUS O. COLLIGNON AND NICHOLAS COLLIGNON, OF CLOSTER, NEW JERSEY.

Letters Patent No. 82,494, dated September 29, 1868.

IMPROVED FOLDING CHAIR.

The Schedule referred to in these Letters Patent and making part of the same.

TO ALL WHOM IT MAY CONCERN:

Be it known that we, CLAUDIUS O. COLLIGNON and NICHOLAS COLLIGNON, of Closter, in the county of Bergen, and State of New Jersey, have invented a new and useful Improvement in Folding Chairs; and we do hereby declare that the following is a full, clear, and exact description thereof, which will enable others skilled in the art to make and use the same, reference being had to the accompanying drawings, forming part of this specification.

This invention relates to improvements in folding chairs, whereby they are made more durable and substantial than those heretofore known.

And the invention consists in the construction and arrangement of parts, as hereinafter described, but more particular reference to the use of a brace, which is so arranged that, while it may act as a back leg to the chair, it is a supporter to the front part of the seat.

Figure 1 represents a side elevation, showing the construction of the chair.

Figure 2 is a front view.

Similar letters of reference indicate like parts.

A represents the principal stands or supports of the chair. They form the front legs and back, and are the principal supports of the seat.

B is the seat, which is attached to the stands A by pivots, as seen at *a*.

C represents the back legs. These legs are hinged to the stands A, as seen in the drawing, at *d*.

E represents braces, which are hinged to the front part of the seat, as seen at *f*, at one end, and jointed to the back leg by a pin at the other end, as seen at *g*.

The braces have a slot, *k*, in their outsides, and the stand A is provided with pins, *i*, which work in the slots as the chair is folded.

With the parts thus arranged, it will be seen that by raising the seat, the chair will fold together so as to occupy a space but little larger than the stand A alone. The side-pins of the seat may extend back, so as to bear upon the cross-round J, and be supported thereby, if desired, but it is not deemed important.

Having thus described our invention, we claim as new, and desire to secure by Letters Patent—

The combination and arrangement of the stand A, seat B, back leg C, and brace E, constructed substantially as described, and for the purposes set forth.

The above specification of our invention signed by us, this 22d day of July, 1868.

CLAUDIUS O. COLLIGNON,
NICHOLAS COLLIGNON.

Witnesses:
WM. DEAN OVERELL,
ALEX. F. ROBERTS.

7

7. Printed specifications are available for all numbered patents issued by the U. S. Patent Office. After the Collignons were granted a patent for their folding chair, an abstract of the specifications appeared in the *Annual Report* for 1868.

8. The printed patent also includes a drawing. A comparison of this printed drawing of patent 82,494 with the original (Fig. 5) shows how closely they correspond. The particular invention claimed by the Collignons was "the use of a brace, which is so arranged that, while it may act as a back leg to the chair, it is a supporter to the front part of the seat." The brace is "E" on both the printed drawing and the original. It can be examined on the patent model as well (Fig. 6).

sovereign grace or special legislation, an opportunity limited to a privileged few, the American patent system was governed by general laws and open to all: anyone who applied, submitted proper drawings, and paid the necessary fee could secure a patent.

European countries quickly followed the Anglo-American system of enacting general patent laws; France was first, Austria was next in 1810, and fourteen other countries, including German and Italian principality states, followed between 1810 and 1843. This was only one consequence of the Industrial Revolution; as new ideas produced innovations, it became necessary to develop general laws.[2]

The Act of 1836 re-established the "American" (examination) system of granting patents, which had been in force for the first three years of the office, 1790 to 1793, and remains pretty much the system today. Each application is examined to determine whether it is novel, "sufficiently useful," and "important"; and a search is made for "prior art," that is, for previous instances of the same invention's publication or use. If "prior art" is found, the invention is not patentable. When applying for a patent, the applicant files a specification, a drawing, and, when pertinent, a model (Figs. 5 and 6). The latter requirement was waived in 1870 and discontinued in 1880, although the Patent Office may in certain instances request a model. The present numbering system of patents is consecutive since it started in 1836;

8

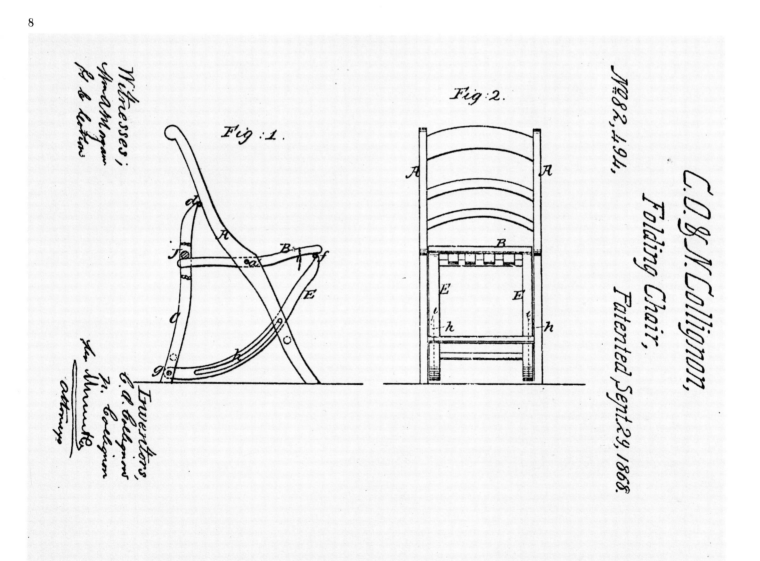

patents issued before that are not numbered. Moreover, a disastrous fire on December 15, 1836, completely destroyed the Patent Office, so early records are incomplete. Funds were appropriated by Congress to replace a portion of the lost records, which was done in the next few years, with the result known as the "reconstructed patents."

Some provisions of later acts are worth noting. The term of a patent was changed in 1861 from fourteen to seventeen years, the same term as today. Designs were made patentable by the Act of 1842. By the Act of 1870 the Patent Office began registering trademarks, which it still does.

Information about patents is readily accessible. The *Annual Report of the Commissioner of Patents* contains an index of patentees listing name, residence, invention, and patent date and number; it also contains indexes of patents by subject, reissues, designs, extensions, disclaimers, and trademarks. Patent specifications and drawings until 1872 are also summarized in the *Annual Report* for the year the patent was granted. After 1872 the summaries are published weekly in the *Official Gazette of the United States Patent Office.* The patentee and subject indexes continue to appear in the *Annual Report* in addition to the *Annual Index;* and copies of the *Annual Report, Annual Index,* and *Official Gazette* are usually available in larger and most state libraries. In addition, complete specifications with the drawings of the numbered patents are reproduced for distribution (Figs. 7 and 8). Referred to as "printed patents," these, along with the pre-1836 restored patents, are now available in microform.[3] Copies of individual printed patents can be obtained for a small fee by sending the patent number to the U.S. Patent and Trademark Office, Washington, D.C. Original patent drawings and specifications up to 1870 are at The National Archives, Washington, D.C.; those dated after 1870 are still under the jurisdiction of the U.S. Patent and Trademark Office.

The patent models were sold at auction in 1908 and 1923. Prior to both sales the Smithsonian Institution made a selection of models for its collections. In 1964 another group of models was transferred to the museum from the Patent Office. Other institutions, such as the Greenfield Village and Henry Ford Museum in Dearborn, Michigan, and the Hagley Museum in Greenville, Delaware, also have patent models in their collections. Many individuals have acquired examples as well.[4]

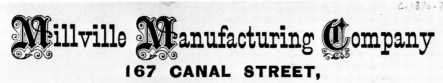

9. Patent furniture seems to have been favored by the Millville Manufacturing Company, which featured it on both the obverse and the reverse (Fig. 10) of this advertising card from the early 1870s. Smithsonian Institution.

9

A few subject indexes have been compiled by the U. S. Patent Office. The major one is the *Subject-Matter Index of Patents for Inventions Issued by the United States Patent Office from 1790 to 1873 Inclusive.* Originally published in 1874, this was reprinted in 1976 as *America in Two Centuries: An Inventory.*[5] It also includes subject indexes of patents reissued, designs, extensions, disclaimers, and trademarks. As in the *Annual Report* and *Annual Index,* the patentee's name, residence, invention, and the patent date and number are listed. The main difficulty in tracking down a patent in the *Subject-Matter Index . . . 1790 to 1873* is determining the correct subject or knowing what the patent was to be used for or how it was identified. The importance of this is illustrated by the case of John Henry Belter, whose name appears only once under the heading "chairs" as inventor of "Chairbacks, Machinery for sawing arabesque." (The listing is misspelled as "J. H. Better.") Yet we know that Belter patented another process that could be used for chair backs, for "dishing pressed work" as he called it. What he was patenting was an "Improvement in the Method of Manufacturing Furniture." The listing in the *Subject-Matter Index . . . 1790 to 1873* is "Furniture, Method of Manufacture." No comprehensive name or patentee index has been published. To find a name, the *Annual Report* and *Annual Index* must be checked.

Where to search for a patent is determined by the data one may have come across. With a patentee's name and the patent date, the *Annual Report* or *Annual Index* for the appropriate year will provide the patent number. If the patent dates before 1872, a summary of the specifications and drawing will be found by the patent number in the same *Annual Report* in which the name is listed. If the patent dates after 1872, it will be found by its number in the

10. The reverse side of the Millville advertising card. Case's patent bed and settee, made of canvas and wood, could be "folded into a compact form for transportation." The foot of the bed served as the seat to form a stool; when the "head-piece" was "turned-up," the result was a settee or chair. Although Case's name was associated with the piece as part owner of the patent, its inventor was actually Joseph H. Greenleaf of New Haven, Conn.

August Liesche of Syracuse, N. Y., was granted at least three patents for improvements in combined chairs and stepladders. The first, 106,067, August 2, 1870, was for a side chair like the one seen here. Hinged near the front edge, the seat folded over so the top of the chair back rested on the floor and the ladder was ready for use. "By these means a useful article of ordinary household use is readily converted into a stepladder for fixing up stove-pipe [*sic*] and window-curtains, or for washing the wood-work and for various like purposes, and a more useful article of stepladder is obtained for use in stores, etc."

10

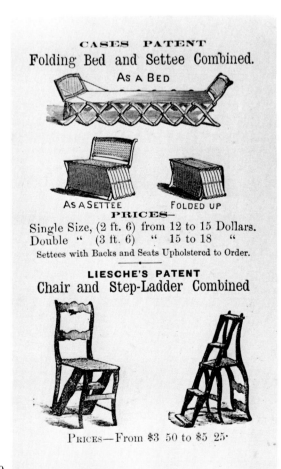

issue of the *Official Gazette* for the appropriate date; or, if the set of printed patents in microform is available, one can immediately locate the patent by its number. Sometimes only the date of a patent is known, in which case all patents of that date—many are granted on any one date, which is always a Friday—will have to be scanned in either the *Annual Report*, the *Official Gazette*, or the printed patents in microform to determine the proper one. This is not always easily done; as an example, in the 1870s an average of about 250 patents was issued on a specific date. If the patent was for a hinge, or mechanical device not obvious on the original piece of furniture, it may at first be overlooked.

To determine how many furniture patents were put to actual use is virtually impossible: the patent records show only what was patented, not what was used. Nevertheless, they chart the trends in furniture then current and perhaps some of the fads as well. When patents are issued fairly regularly over a period of years for one type of attachment or specialized part or kind of furniture, that item must be a focus of attention. It may fill a need (or seem to), it may have been rediscovered, it may appeal as a novelty, it may be saleable. Each inventor must have thought he had a better way to solve a problem or present a new approach or improve an existing combination. For various reasons—perhaps as simple as pride in obtaining a patent and being a patentee—people seek to have their inventions patented and submit an application with drawing, specifications, and model to the Patent Office.

For one citizen, at least, an improvement in bedsteads apparently was ready for submission almost as soon as the U. S. patent system was operating. Such a patent was issued

11. Ornamented with an inlaid wood floral motif and gilt-engraved lines, this combined cabinet and stand incorporates patent 212,695, February 25, 1879, granted to George W. Hessler of Moosic, Pa. In the patent specifications, Hessler described his stand "as a repository for sheet-music, and provided with compartments for preserving papers, books, or other articles of like nature." The patent drawing (Fig. 13) shows a stand with two cabinets, the upper one a "tilting compartment" of pockets, the lower one containing shelves and partitions. The single cabinet of the stand seen here tilts out to reveal what Hessler described as a "fan-shaped receptacle" of "triangular-shaped pockets." Smithsonian Institution, Anonymous Gift Fund R, 1980.125.1.

11

12

12. This small brass-colored metal plaque on the inside front of Hessler's cabinet provided the clue to the inventor's name. Of the patents issued on that date, only one had features, such as the tilting "triangular-shaped pockets," which matched the stand. By this process of elimination, the patent and patentee were identified.

13. Drawings of the two-cabinet stand in printed patent 212,695, with inside views of the tilting compartment on top and the shelf section below. Hessler was not seeking a patent on the tilting compartment, which was "old," he stated in the specifications, meaning that the form had long been in use and, as an instance of "prior art," could not be patented. Nevertheless, what Hessler claimed as "new" and desired "to secure by Letters Patent"—and what he in fact received a patent for—was a music stand with a tilting compartment "provided with triangular-shaped pockets."

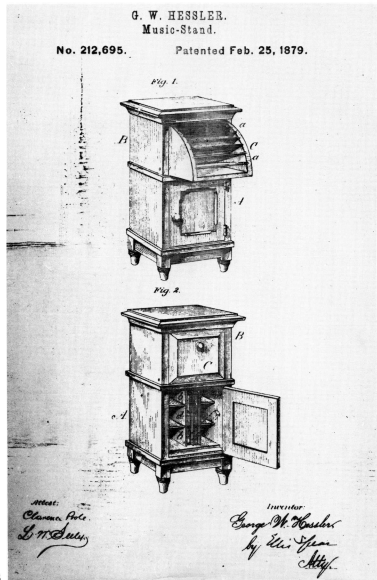

G. W. HESSLER.
Music-Stand.

No. 212,695.   Patented Feb. 25, 1879.

13

14

15

14. The seat and back of this patent rocking chair manufactured by E. W. Vaill of Worcester, Mass., are made of pile fabric like carpeting. Colorful as well as durable, the material was available in a variety of designs. Besides florals, Vaill offered landscapes (e.g., New York harbor), figures (e.g., stag's heads), and monuments (e.g., Daniel Webster's birthplace). "In carpet designs I defy competition," he announced with justifiable pride in his *Fortieth Semi-Annual Catalog of Fine Folding Chairs, Spring and Summer 1882.* Originally, the front seat edge may have been trimmed with fringe, a popular upholstery treatment at the time which Vaill also used (Fig. 22). The frame, painted to imitate wood graining, is ornamented with brass-colored metal bosses across the top of the back, on the tips of the finials, and the curved side braces. Smithsonian Institution, 259580.1.

15. Printed on green paper, this label is pasted on the underside of the front seat rail of the folding rocking chair shown in Fig. 14. Patent 179,979, July 18, 1876, pertained to the combination of parts "so that the seat-frame will fold the seat up against the back, and the chair will occupy but a small space while being transported." The frame was one of Vaill's standard forms and in fact is seen on five of the nine chairs in his advertisement of 1881 (Fig. 22). While Vaill held patents for inventions of his own, as clearly stated on the label, for this patent he was an "assignee." The inventor was John H. Wakefield, who had "assigned"—transferred ownership of—his invention to Vaill.

August 10, 1791, to L. C. Kuhn. The entries for bedsteads continue throughout the nineteenth century with a sizable listing under this subclass and its various sections. An examination of the *Subject-Matter Index . . . 1790 to 1873* shows that patents began to be issued with regularity for sofa bedsteads in the 1840s, folding bedsteads in the late 1850s, and wardrobe bedsteads in the 1860s. While considerably fewer in number, patents were also being issued regularly for bureau bedsteads beginning in the late 1850s, cabinet bedsteads in the late 1860s, and lounge bedsteads in the 1870s.

Convertible furniture was not entirely new, of course. Fold-up beds, table-chairs, chair-ladders, and so on had been in use for centuries.[6] In the nineteenth century, however, especially during the second half, multipurpose furniture was new to the mass market buying it for the first time.

Patent applications were submitted by women as well as men and in practically every class. Some women followed their own bent and invented agricultural implements, street-lights, and railway appliances such as car coupling and spikes, among the kinds of inventions not traditionally associated with women but for which they in fact obtained patents. Most inventions by women, however, were related to clothing and the household, areas in which a woman inclined to invent might be expected to obtain a patent. Understandably, furniture and furnishings were an area in which women had ideas and experience. A Patent Office compilation by class for the three-year period from 1892 to 1895 reveals 55 patents for furniture and furnishings granted to women. In a ranking of patents by the quantity issued, this followed the 132 for wearing apparel and 102 for culinary utensils, and preceded the 52 for washing and cleaning. The predominance of household inventions continued between 1790 and 1888, judging from a cursory examination of the chronological listing of women patentees published in 1888 by the Patent Office. During that time nearly 2,500 patents were issued to women.[7]

Whether the inventor was a woman or man, the search for a better bedstead, chair, or table seems never to have abated; judging from the addresses of the patentees, the need existed in every part of the country.

The *Subject-Matter Index . . . 1790 to 1873* further reveals a growing specialization of forms. By 1873 there were sixty-eight kinds of chairs listed, from "accouchers" to "wall-wainscott," about half the entries relating to the household. In that same year tables follow a parallel pattern, with seventy entries ranging from auxiliary to work tables, of which, however, only about one-third were related to domestic use. Patents began to be issued for extension tables with some regularity in the late 1840s and for folding tables in the 1860s. A handful of patents was issued for self-waiting tables in the 1850s and entries for revolving tables started to appear in the late 1860s. (Self-waiting tables had trays or containers moved by wires, chains, and so forth, as described by their inventors, to facilitate self-service at hotel and boarding house tables—a comment on nineteenth-century America.) There was also a growing demand for specialized chairs, patents being issued for both folding and reclining chairs with regularity in the 1860s. Entries for rocking chairs were sporadic until the late 1860s, when they appeared regularly, signaling the popularity of the platform rocker.

Then as now, applying for a patent did not mean that it would be granted. John Henry Belter's application for "Improvement in the Method of Manufacturing Furniture" was twice rejected. When the Patent Office stated that the "dish form" was not patentable and that "pressed work" or laminated wood was a "prior art," Belter responded that it was not those features that he was seeking to patent but rather the arrangement and method of joining the staves or pieces of pressed work to obtain the dish form. In due course, on February 23, 1858, patent 19,405 was granted. His satisfaction seemed to be that he had triumphed over the Patent Office, for as far as we know he seldom applied the method in production[8]; the rose-wood chair seen in Fig. 36, attributed to him, may be one of the exceptions.

16

17

16. Of simple but sturdy construction, this walnut folding side chair was one of a variety patented and produced by the Collignon family at their manufactory in Closter, N. J. The shaped slats in the back and the turned stretchers between the legs provide the only ornamentation on an otherwise plain, utilitarian piece. The same slat seat and turned stretchers were used by the Collignons for the model submitted with their application for yet another folding chair patent (Fig. 6). Smithsonian Institution, gift of Edith H. Fetherston, 307707.4.

17. Gold lettering on blue paper distinguishes this label pasted under the front seat rail of the chair in Fig. 16. From their manufactory in Closter, not far from the Hudson River, the Collignons transported their products a short distance downriver to their warerooms in New York City. From the late 1860s to the late 1890s, the firm manufactured chairs incorporating the many patents issued to various members of the family.

For many years following the return to the examination system in 1836, the Patent Office examiners became stricter in interpreting what was patentable. From 1842 to 1853, the necessity for proof of originality, novelty, or utility was rigorously enforced. Then a more lenient faction prevailed, increasing somewhat the number of applications and patents in the remaining years before the Civil War. A note of caution: patent statistics as a basis of trends must be used with care.[9] Nevertheless, trends suggested by furniture patents seem to be confirmed by what we know of patent furniture and the companies producing it. Folding chairs, for example, seem not to have been made or used in this country much before the middle of the last century; the first patent for one was issued in 1855. In the next decade patents for folding chairs began to appear regularly, some companies beginning to specialize in them in the 1860s, more appearing in the 1870s, a few expanding into international trade. As the market for folding chairs waned in the late 1880s and the 1890s, several companies shifted to the manufacture of stationary chairs (one concentrated on invalid and wheelchairs) or went out of business.[10]

The role of the Patent Office is to grant patents, not to keep records of what is manufactured, and one must turn elsewhere to discover which patents were applied to the market. Two major sources of information are surviving pieces and pictorial materials such as catalogs, magazines, and advertisements.

Most patent furniture since 1842 may be identified because it is marked "patented," with the date, to meet requirements; for noncompliance a fine of $100 was imposed, and false marking of an article as patented was also fined. In 1861, however, the penalty for failure to mark patent articles was withdrawn. Examples predating 1842 were sometimes marked: the "elastic chair" patented August 31, 1808, by Samuel Gragg of Boston (Fig. 35) usually has impressed under the front seat rail or divided between the front and back rails "S. GRAGG/BOSTON./PATENT." A patent mark might be impressed on the furniture, cast in a metal part, or applied with a paper label, metal plaque, or stencil. On chairs, marks are often found on the underside of the seat or seat rail, occasionally elsewhere—on a back leg, brace, stretcher, or frame. On tables they are usually on the underside of the top or in a drawer. Patent marks may also be located on mechanisms for folding, extending, rocking, tilting, or what have you. Without a mark or label, a piece loses its patent identity; there is no way of knowing it is patented. If an unmarked piece matches a patented one, then an attribution may be considered. A patent infringement may account for a look-alike piece of furniture, or some part of it, but instances of this are negligible, and franchise abuse also seems rare. If patented features of two pieces match, an attribution of the unmarked object on the basis of the marked one seems safe, at least until more work is done on the history of patent furniture.

Patent furniture can date any time after its patent date, and the word "patent" probably continued to be applied to the piece long after the patent expired. Since the term of patent was fourteen years up to 1861, when it changed to seventeen, presumably this is the date range of most patented objects. As an example, O. F. Case was granted patent 65,072, May 28, 1867, for a combination bed and settee (Figs. 9 and 10). Fifteen years later "Case's Pat. Folding Bed and Settee Combined" was given a full page in the 1882 catalog of Hall and Stephen, a New York wholesale firm specializing in beds and bedding. Once obtained, a successful patent continued to be promoted by its manufacturer for years. Apparently Case's patent bed filled a need or it wouldn't have been stocked by this large and active wholesaler. The patent term still had two years to run.

One should be aware that a few instances of a reissued patent do occur, when the original patent is inadvertently defective. The reissued patent completes the unexpired term of the original and does not extend it. Reissued patents have their own number series, as do design patents. Since there have been fewer in these two categories, the numbers are much lower than for the standard invention patents. One should not confuse the categories. For

18

19

18. "Elastic arms" is how Theodore J. Palmer of New York described the ingenious feature of his rocking and reclining chair, identified on the pivot as his patent (Fig. 19). The chair won an award at the 1876 Centennial Exhibition in Philadelphia, commended by the judges for "originality in principle." Made of spring steel, the arms provided the tension for a back-and-forth or rocking motion by pulling the tilted chair, which rested on a pivot or hinge, into an upright position. Here was an innovative use of material. While the metal could have been disguised or upholstered, this seems not to have been done. Only arm pads were used. While perhaps a concession to the coldness and hardness of the metal, they were a common treatment of the period, regardless of the material used in the arms. In fact, Palmer recommended pads, noting in the patent specifications, "these spring-arms . . . may be cushioned, as the arms of rocking-chairs usually are." Aside from the spring-steel arms, the chair is conventional. The walnut frame has burl veneer panels, a shaped crest, applied bosses, and incised decoration. The chair has been reupholstered. Smithsonian Institution, 1979.605.1.

19. Stamped metal plate attached to the pivot of Palmer's rocking chair (Fig. 18).

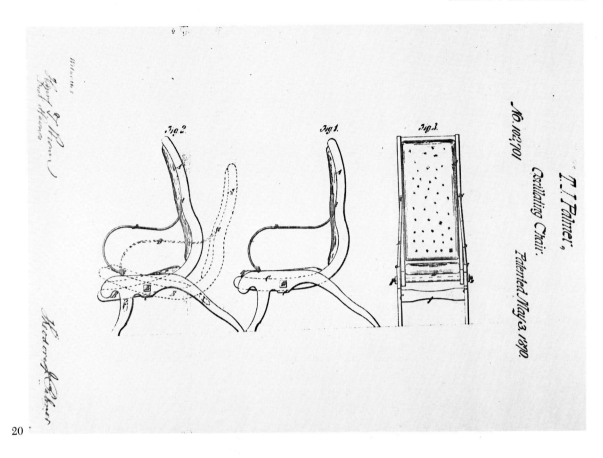

20

21

20. Theodore J. Palmer was granted patent 102,701, May 3, 1870, for the "Oscillating Chair" seen here in the printed patent drawing. As stated in his specifications, "this invention consists in providing for the rocking or the adjustment of the inclination of the back and seat of a chair relatively [sic] to the base to which they are pivoted by means of arms composed of springs." The base frame (C) was stationary. The back (A) and seat (B) were suspended in the frame on a hinge or pivot, allowing them to tilt. The spring-steel arms were attached at the front end to the base frame and at the other end to the chair back. When the seat and back of the chair were tilted back or forward, the metal springs or arms were stretched. When the pressure was released, the "elastic" arms pulled the seat and back into their original position, "thus facilitating the easy rocking of the chair to the person sitting therein." The chair could be converted to a reclining position "by means of suitable clamps applied thereto."

21. Palmer's patent rocker and reclining chair in an upholstery treatment favored at the time, including fringe-trimmed arm-rests. Palmer described the chair as "upholstered with a fine broche stripe inserted in Terry and puffed sides, spring seat and back, price $29.33." This view is from Kimball's Book of Designs: Furniture and Drapery, a catalog illustrating the work of various American manufacturers, published in Boston in 1876. Photograph courtesy of the Winterthur Museum.

example, while the first patent issued in 1853 was number 9,512 for invention, it was only 540 for design and 229 for reissue.

Some labels on patent furniture are advertisements in themselves. They may, in fact, have served both as label and leaflet. An example is in the drawer of the adjustable table made by the Clowes and Gates Manufacturing Company of Worcester, Massachusetts (Fig. 164). Besides the name and locality of the manufacturer and the patent date, June 19, 1877, the label lists the uses and advantages of the table and features a picture of it in the center.

The other extreme is the minimal label: "PATENTED/FEBRUARY 25,/1879." This is the only information embossed on the metal plaque attached to the cabinet or music stand incorporating the patent granted to George Hessler of Moosic, Pennsylvania (Figs. 11–13). Concise yet informative paper labels were used by Edward W. Vaill of Worcester, Massachusetts, on his folding chairs. Often found pasted on the underside of the front seat rail, they may read, as does one example, "E. W. VAILL,/Patentee and Manufacturer,/ Worcester, Mass./Patented July 18, 1876. No. 94A" (Fig. 15). ("No. 94A" was the model number of the chair, seen in Fig. 14.) Another example of this type of label, also on a folding chair, is "Collignon's Patent,/March 10, 1868 and November 16, 1869/Closter, Bergen Co., N.J." (Figs. 16 and 17). Usually the name of the manufacturer is included in the label or mark. On most of his furniture, George J. Hunzinger impressed his name, location, and the patent date. An example on an armchair is "HUNZINGER/N.Y./PAT. MARCH 30, 1869" and "PAT. APRIL 18, 1876" (Fig. 64). Theodore J. Palmer did the same on his platform rocker (Figs. 18–21). He used an oval metal plaque, embossed "PALMER'S/PATENT/ROCKING CHAIR/NEW YORK./PATENTED MAY 3, 1870."[11]

In one way or another, the manufacturers implied that among their wares the "best" products were patented. Besides marking the furniture "patented," "patent," or "pat." and identifying themselves as "patentee," many manufacturers also laid further claim in advertisements in trade journals and popular periodicals to the superiority of the patent products. One example is Edward W. Vaill. Like many manufacturers, he was a frequent advertiser in *The Trade Bureau*, a weekly magazine for the furniture industry which periodically featured a page summarizing pertinent patents with a drawing and abstract of the specifications. His June 29, 1878, advertisement blazoned "VAILL'S PATENT FOLDING CHAIRS" in a bold headline (Fig. 22); a display of chairs with their model numbers is arranged around a folding table whose patented status merited its own caption. Vaill was sufficiently proud of the patent aspect of his furniture to publicize it not only in advertisements and, of course, on the labels applied to his chairs, but on stationery and invoices, and in the city directories of Worcester, where his entrepreneurial success may be traced. First listing himself in 1861 as "furniture dealer and auctioneer, 1 Flagg's block," he soon began to specialize, and the entry in 1864 was "patent folding chair dealer and auctioneer, 150 Main" and finally in 1871 "patent folding chair manufacturer." The following year he moved to 310 Main and in 1877 to 15 Union, where his business remained until 1891, the last year it was listed. The only change came in 1889 when the word "folding" was dropped from the firm's name, suggesting a modification of the product.[12]

During his three decades in business, Vaill was credited with running "the largest folding chair factory in the world." Certainly, his patent folding chairs came in a seemingly endless variety of shapes, sizes, upholsteries, finishes, and prices. According to a report in *The Trade Bureau* of February 26, 1881, "Mr. Vaill attends personally to every department of this immense business, and it is no child's play for even as energetic a man as he is." Besides being the largest manufacturer of folding chairs, he was also an exporter. In his catalog for 1882, he claimed "Branch Houses: New York . . . Melbourne . . . London." With justifiable pride, he used a picture of his multibuilding factory in his advertisements and on his stationery, invoice forms, advertising cards, and catalogs.

At the 1876 Centennial Exhibition in Philadelphia, Vaill exhibited "patent folding chairs,

22. A "Patent Folding and Revolving Table," shown both fully extended and compactly folded, was the centerpiece of E. W. Vaill's advertisement in *The Trade Bureau*, June 29, 1878. Vaill claimed that the table "when folded occupies a space of only three and one-half inches in depth." Besides folding, revolving, and tilting, it boasted a device for adjusting height. The table had multiple uses: in addition to being "readily converted into an easel," it was recommended for drafting, sewing, and card playing. Also pictured is a sampling of Vaill's specialty, folding chairs. Most were patented. Photograph courtesy of the Library of Congress.

VAILL'S PATENT FOLDING CHAIRS.

98

111

116

Patent Folding and Revolving Table.

104A

105A

117

This Table can be varied in height seven inches, and adjusted at any angle. The size of the top is 26 x 33, and the Table when folded occupies a space of three and one-half inches only in depth. It is easily adjusted, can be used as a drafting, sewing or card table, is readily converted into an easel, and is altogether the most desirable Folding Table ever offered to the public.

118

109

114

in great variety." His display won an award, and patents were among the reasons why. The judges' report notes specifically that "the great number of patents applied deserve consideration."[13] By that date Vaill had at least six patents in his own name pertaining to improvements in folding chairs and nine assigned to him by other inventors, for which some read "J. E. Wakefield assignor to E. W. Vaill."

Also a resident of Worcester, John E. Wakefield was listed in the city directories first as a "packer" in 1875 at 310 Main, then in 1877 at 15 Union, and after 1879 as "Supt. 15 Union." The addresses are those of Vaill's patent folding chair manufactory where Wakefield worked until 1888, a year before the business changed from folding chairs to chairs. Although he had already sold, given, or turned over his patent to Vaill, Wakefield wanted to be recorded as the inventor, so he had himself listed as the "assignor" to Vaill, the latter holding the patent.

Another example of an "assignor" occurs in the already mentioned patent 65,072, May 28, 1867, for a folding bed and settee combined (Fig. 10). The heading on the printed patent reads "Joseph H. Greenleaf, of New Haven, Connecticut, Assignor to Himself and O. F. Case of same place." Case seems to have considered the patent his; as the assignee he was the owner or, more correctly in this instance, the joint owner of the patent. The combination piece was identified as Case's patent for at least a decade, from the early 1870s when it was pictured on the Millville Manufacturing Company card (Fig. 9) to the early 1880s when it was listed in the 1882 catalog of Hall and Stephen, the New York wholesale bedding firm. Case was not claiming the invention. That was listed for all the world to see as Greenleaf's, as the designation "assignor" made clear. If Case prepared the patent application and eventually acquired all the rights to the invention, both of which seem likely, then in a sense he was the patentee, or at least the owner, and the patent was his.

Another name associated with patent furniture is George J. Hunzinger. Practically every piece he manufactured incorporated a patent and was so marked, an indication of the importance this enterprising businessman and inventor attached to patents. A German immigrant of the 1850s, he was living in Brooklyn when his first patent was issued in 1861, for a reclining chair. Five years later, he was granted another patent, also for a reclining chair that folded as well (Fig. 127). The same year, 1866, he opened his own business in New York at 192 Laurens Street, selected two examples of his most recent chairs, pictured them in a quarter-page advertisement in *Baldwin's Consolidated Business Directory [of] New York, Boston and Philadelphia* for 1867–68, and identified himself as "Manufacturer of Patent Folding, Reclining & Extension CHAIRS."[14]

In all, Hunzinger obtained twenty patents for furniture during his more than thirty years

23. There need be no question about the patent employed in the extension table manufactured by A. W. and S. D. Ovitt and Company. In this advertisement in *The Trade Bureau*, July 16, 1881, it is clearly identified on the underside of the drop leaf as "BENT'S PAT^D/AUG. 17 1875." The number is 166,679. The problem with other extension tables, according to Chicago inventor John W. Bent, was the folding rails and sliding extensions. The parts "are liable to sag and move unevenly," he noted in his patent specifications, "owing to the fact they have not been sufficiently supported." He proposed "to remedy this defect" by employing "sliding extensions, supported by a central leg or support, in connection with folding rails."

Besides Bent's table, Ovitt and Company also featured a "Pat. Pillar Extension" table, and offered numerous styles suitable for use in homes, saloons, restaurants, and offices. The table on the left side of the advertisement is presumably one of the fifty styles and sizes of "Centre and Parlor" tables the company produced. Photograph courtesy of the Library of Congress.

23

A. W. & S. D. OVITT & CO.,
MANUFACTURERS OF
Bent's Pat. Fall and Folding-Leaf
EXTENSION TABLE.

6 Styles and sizes of Pat. Pillar Extension.
16 Ditto, Common Extension,
8 Ditto, Breakfast Extension,
4 Ditto, Kitchen Extension,
2 Ditto, Saloon,
3 Ditto, Restaurant,
3 Ditto, Office,
50 Ditto, Centre and Parlor.

SEND FOR CATALOGUE AND PRICE LIST.

Cor. Lake and Peoria Sts., CHICAGO, ILL.

24

24. The model submitted by Julius Werner of New York City with his application for a patent on an invention pertaining to sofa beds. His name is misspelled "Weaver" on the Patent Office's tag but the patent number and date are correct. The model is a working one, as required by the Patent Office, and demonstrates the invention of pivoting or flipping over the back and seat to form the mattress. Werner's specifications noted that "when the back is folded down in line with the seat . . . , the seat having been turned to bring the mattress side to the top, a large double bed is produced." The sequence is pictured on Werner's circular (Fig. 25). The frame of the model is mahogany and the upholstery is beige color with a woven diamond pattern. Smithsonian Institution, transfer from U.S. Patent Office, 65.523.

25. The method by which Werner's piece was converted from sofa to bed was ingenious. In this circular from the early 1870s, it is shown first as a sofa, then half open, then as a bed. The back and seat were inverted by pulling the back forward and swinging out the frame to support the matfress. As known from the two patents for the devices involved, the parlor sofa bed also had arms that converted to bolsters and footrests. Flipping over the cushions separated the sitting and sleeping surfaces and permitted the bedclothes to remain in place "ready for use." Smithsonian Institution.

25

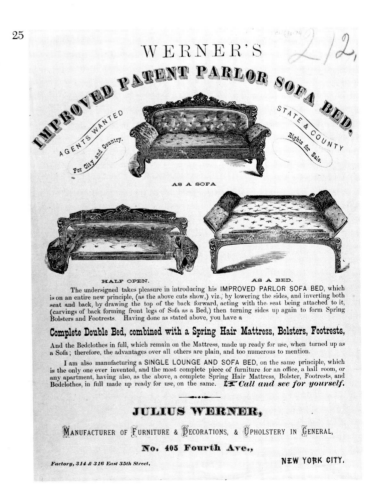

of prosperous business. Most of the inventions were for chairs. So far as is known, Hunzinger's furniture incorporating patents is always marked "patent." He also tried out some of his inventions before patents were granted for them. An example is a side chair in the Smithsonian collection, of ebonized wood with gold-color metal molding fitted over a ridge at the edge of the back uprights, seat side rails, and front legs. As was customary with Hunzinger's work, the chair has an impressed mark on the back leg. It does not say "patented" as we might expect but "PAT. APP. FOR/HUNZINGER."

"Patent applied for" means just that. "Patent pending" is the same thing and means no more than it says. In either case, we assume that the inventor has submitted his application for a patent and is awaiting action. Such a term has no significance in relation to either the patent or the Patent Office. For the inventor, however, it may serve to protect his claim. In addition, such a statement also connotes some of the status of a patent. Although apparently without legal standing, "patent pending" or "applied for" must have a popular appeal, too, as one or the other appears frequently on a variety of objects. While the inventor has applied for a patent, in a sense he has already begun to use it although he has yet to receive it. In the case of Hunzinger, he was granted a patent for the invention used in the side chair.[15]

Vaill and Hunzinger, like so many in nineteenth-century America, obtained a number of patents and applied them, announcing the fact through advertisements, cards, catalogs, leaflets, and stationery, invariably noting on their furniture that it was patented, which suggested that such pieces were all better than other goods. To put it another way, the furniture, or some feature of it, was worth patenting. They continued to mark their pieces "patented" although not strictly required to do so. The word had status.

It is interesting to note that certain companies seemed to specialize in patent furniture. They continued to find better or innovative ways of solving problems of manufacture and function. Hunzinger, for instance, was granted patents for pieces such as reclining and folding chairs (Fig. 127), a platform rocker (Fig. 108), a diagonal side brace for a chair (Fig. 128), metallic strips for seating (Fig. 64), a folding bedstead, and a game table.

Certain names, often of manufacturers or assignors to them, turn up regularly as patentees in the *Annual Report*. Some people we recognize as having had their patents put into production; others may never have had more than a farfetched idea or an impractical whim. Among the furniture manufacturers, some of the frequent patentees were Collignon, Doremus, Gardner,[16] Hardy, Heywood, and, of course, Hunzinger and Vaill. All manufactured chairs. Specializing in folding and extension or steamer chairs, the Collignons of Closter, New Jersey, were granted at least eight patents between 1868 and 1873. Two of these are incorporated in a simple slat-back folding chair, according to the label on the underside of the front seat rail (Figs. 16 and 17). Patent 75,373, March 10, 1868, was granted to Claudius O. for an improvement in a cottage chair. Patent 96,778, November 16, 1869, was granted to Nicholas and Claudius O. for a folding chair.

The manufacture of patent folding chairs was a Collignon family business, involving Adam, Claudius O., Nicholas, and, later, Peter C. The Closter factory probably was well into operation by the late 1860s; showrooms were opened in New York City in 1871 and maintained until 1896.[17]

As the Collignons continued to acquire patents, they featured them in their advertisements, leaflets, and catalogs, and, as we have seen, on the furniture they produced. "Original Inventors and Patentees" is how the Collignons identified themselves in a leaflet distributed at the 1876 Centennial Exhibition in Philadelphia where they displayed "folding rocking chairs, settees, chairs." A lithograph of their multibuilding factory in the *Atlas of Bergen County*, published in 1876, is captioned in bold letters, "COLLIGNON BROS' MANUFACTORIES PATENT FOLDING CHAIRS CLOSTER BERGEN CO., N. J.," and the print's four corners feature pictures of Collignon patent products—one extension chair and three rocking chairs. The popularity of these patent folding chairs, which extended over a quarter

26

27

26. A page from the catalog of George Knell, the Philadelphia manufacturer of this sofa bed. The catalog may have been distributed at the Centennial Exhibition of 1876 where Knell exhibited examples of his patent furniture. These views show how the piece was converted from sofa to bed by "turning down the lever H" and lowering the back and the metal legs attached to it to form the mattress; "the arms extend themselves for head and footboard." Smithsonian Institution.

27. Enumerating the advantages of his patent sofa bed in a *Trade Bureau* advertisement, September 24, 1881, Henry F. Hover alluded to some of the problems with this form of furniture. His invention eliminated the need for "props, hinged-feet and iron ratchets," which are "unsafe and liable to get out of repair." Moreover, the piece featured a place to store the bedclothes and could be taken apart and cleaned, "keeping it free from insects." The superiority of Hover's product apparently included the fact that it was "Patented in France, England and America." Photograph courtesy of the Library of Congress.

HOVER'S WORLD-RENOWNED SOFA BED.

Patented in France, England and America.

As a Parlor Sofa.   As a Bedstead, with Hair and Spring Mattress.

This Sofa Bed is considered by experts to be the most complete article of the kind ever invented. It is so arranged that, by simply turning out the ends, you have a neat bedstead with a luxurious Hair and Spring Mattress complete; or, by closing them, it presents an elegant Parlor Sofa. All props, hinged-feet and iron ratchets are dispensed with in this patent, which every cabinetmaker knows are unsafe and liable to get out of repair. It has the conveniences of a Bureau for holding clothing. The mattress is made to take off, and the bedstead to unscrew. This gives greater advantage over all other sofa beds, in keeping it free from insects. Orders for frames or upholstered solicited.

H. F. HOVER, 230 South Second St., Below Dock St., Philadelphia, Pa.

of a century, may have fostered pirating by competitors, yet another sign of their success. Here was where a patent could truly serve its purpose of protecting one's invention. A rival manufacturer seems to have produced a folding rocker that infringed on the Collignon patents. A notice in *The Trade Bureau* of June 11, 1881, points out that "Collignon Bros. have obtained a temporary injunction against L. S. Hays, of Cortland, N. Y., restraining him from manufacturing folding rockers. If this is sustained, and Collignon Bros. feel positive that it will be, it will be an important decision."

The table was another form that attracted inventors throughout the nineteenth century. Patents were issued for tables that would fold, revolve, tilt, expand, and contract, among other things. Vaill, for example, produced patent tables that folded (Fig. 22), a nice complement to his patent folding chairs. The Clowes and Gates Manufacturing Company, also of Worcester, produced folding tables, too (Figs. 164 and 165).

But, among tables, perhaps most attention was focused on the extension type, suggesting that there were problems with the form, or at least that a great many people thought they could improve on the existing designs. One inventor, Thomas C. Ellison of Albany, New York, explaining the need for his device in his patent specifications, described some of the major defects of extension tables: "[They] require two persons to effect the extension or contraction of the length of the table, and generally more or less labor is required to effect an extension table in a true line of direction, especially when any of the sliding pieces are in the least warped, or work any way binding." Ellison's solution was a cranked screw mechanism that would "render an extension table capable of being extended or contracted in its length by a single person with ease and accuracy of the several parts."[18] We have no record of it being marketed.

Some further difficulties with extension tables are revealed in other patent specifications. One problem was what to do with the leaves. A number of patents dealt with methods for storing leaves in the table. As one patentee noted, this was a "very important consideration, as with the common extension-table a separate box or rack must be provided." This inventor's solution was to have the leaves hinged crosswise "for the purpose of reducing their length" so they could be folded and stored in the bed of the table.[19] Devices were likewise proposed to prevent the warping of leaves and the warping, shrinking, and swelling of slides, to extend or contract the table as needed, and to lock leaves and slides in place. On some tables there was a need "to draw the parts of the table together," wrote another patentee, whose spring drum and band would make the table "firm and substantial and not as loose as extension tables usually are."[20]

Extension tables had a tendency to wobble and sag as well. A number of patents dealt with these defects. The solution proposed by John W. Bent of Chicago was a central support in combination with the slides and rails, for which he was granted patent 166,679, August 17, 1875. This was one patented concept that went into production. How it looked can be seen in the advertisement of A. W. and S. D. Ovitt and Company, which mentions Bent's patent twice (Fig. 23). At both ends of the table were drop or, to use the manufacturer's term, "fall" leaves. In between were a series of hinged leaves that folded under the top when not in use. To enlarge the table, the ends were pulled away from the center and the leaves unfolded and set on the sliding extensions and folding rails. As a remedy against sagging and sticking, Bent's patent form would provide "a very firm support for the supplemental leaves" and take the "strain" off the rails so "all parts work smoothly together."

Parlor sofa bed: by its very name we know something of its use and placement. The Patent Office's subject indexes took no notice of the adjective "parlor," listing the form simply as "sofa bed" or "bed, sofa." But the furniture manufacturers and dealers were quick to use the term. Perhaps they felt it added a touch of elegance to their products and sanctioned the placement of convertible furniture in the parlor.

While the sofa appears to have belonged primarily in the parlor in the nineteenth century, it also turned up in the library and occasionally the hallway. After the late 1860s, however, it was seldom encountered in either the dining room or the bedroom, which were usually the domain of the lounge. The patents for lounge beds, which, as already noted, began to appear with some regularity in the 1870s, showed a couch for reclining which was raised at one end. Sofa beds had backs of the same height at both ends, and they customarily had arms.

The great usefulness of these convertible forms was discussed by that mid-nineteenth century arbiter of taste, Andrew Jackson Downing, in *The Architecture of Country Houses* (where, however, he did not mention lounges): "*Sofa-beds*, which may now be found in a variety of forms, at most of the modern upholsterers, are pieces of furniture, having externally the exact appearance of a sofa, ottoman, or divan, but which are so contrived, that the seat draws out, so as to form a comfortable bed in a moment, and with very little trouble. They are particularly convenient in a house where the number of bed-rooms is limited—or as seats for dressing-rooms, enabling the mistress of the house, when her hospitality is severely taxed, to turn a dressing-room into a bedroom at a moment's notice."[21]

The need for the sofa bed continued and in fact persists to this day.[22] Almost a quarter of a century after Downing described the usefulness of the form, an inventor summed up in his patent specifications the reasons for a combined sofa, lounge, and bed: "The object of my invention is to produce a neat, compact, and convenient piece of furniture which . . . will, when folded, occupy but a small space in a room of limited dimensions, which would not accommodate the three large pieces separately."[23]

In many households, it is clear, space was at a minimum. Convertible furniture which filled two and sometimes three functions was desirable.

Of the three patent parlor sofa beds pictured here (Figs. 24–27), two were converted from sofa to bed by letting down the back to form the mattress, and the third by bringing the back forward to turn it and the seat over. The last method was the invention of New Yorker Julius Werner, for which he was granted patents 76,570 and 118,994, dated April 7, 1868, and September 12, 1871. The conversion of his piece from sofa to bed was based, Werner claimed, on an "entire new principle." He manufactured both singles and doubles, recommending them for use not only in parlors but in offices, "hall rooms," indeed "any apartment."[24]

Patent was a key word in George Knell's business. The cover of his catalog announced "GEORGE KNELL, INVENTOR AND PATENTEE OF PARLOR SOFA BEDS, ALSO DIFFERENT KINDS OF ADJUSTABLE CHAIRS. MANUFACTORY NO. 155 North Fourth Street, PHILADELPHIA, PA.," and one of the inside pages is headed "GEORGE KNELL'S PATENTED FURNITURE" (Fig. 26). The patent for the parlor sofa, 120,283, October 24, 1871, pertained to

28. Levi C. Boyington identified himself as the "Pat[entee] and Sole Mfr." of these "Patent Automatic Cabinet Folding Beds," one of which is shown open at the center of this advertisement from *The Trade Bureau,* July 9, 1881. Flanking the bed are some of the guises for it manufactured by Boyington in his Chicago factory and sold in the New York City warerooms of E. H. Norton: a "dressing case" (No. 22), sideboard (No. 34), writing desk (No. 36), bureau (No. 10), and another sideboard (No. 28).

Boyington received two patents for his design, 219,342, September 9, 1879, and 230,397, July 27, 1880. Hinged at midpoint, the bed was opened by separating the front and back of the cabinet. Next, the legs, concealed as pilasters at the corners of the cabinet, were pulled down. At the same time, metal rods were extended in a cross-brace support under the bed. The top and sub-top of the cabinet became the headboard and footboard, respectively. In appearance the cabinets conform to the taste of the day for the Renaissance-revival and Eastlake styles. Photograph courtesy of the Library of Congress.

28

29

"strengthening the hinged joints between the said back to be retained in a vertical or inclined as well as horizontal position." Here, as on the two other sofa beds pictured, the upholstery was tufted, adding texture and dimension to the surface while controlling the upholstery and springs. For storing the bedclothes, Knell offered an ottoman "made so as to hold pillows and blankets" for $5. The sofa bed "Covered with All Wool Terry" sold for $65.[25]

The George Knell and Son exhibition of patent furniture was an award winner at the 1876 Centennial Exhibition. The judges' commendation specified the "originality of design and multiplicity of changes provided for in the construction of the various exhibits." The "changes" were the convertible and adjustable features of Knell's patented furniture.

The patent parlor sofa bed manufactured by Henry F. Hover worked on the same principle as Knell's sofa.[26] The back was let down to convert the sofa to a bed. In his *Trade Bureau* advertisement, September 24, 1881 (Fig. 27), Hover stated this was done "by simply turning out the ends" and that there were no parts on his sofa bed "to get out of repair." Hover received an award at the Centennial, too—for his "Magic Folding Lounge and Bed," which the judges commended for combining "all the qualifications needful for the uses intended."

While Hover's and Knell's backward extension of the sofa to form a bed seems simple by comparison with Werner's inversion maneuver, there was a problem. The Hover and Knell beds had to be moved out from the wall, or space had to be left to let down the back. By using a forward extension, Werner's piece did not have to be moved.

Inventors were well aware of the difficulty. One patentee, citing the advantages of his stationary-back sofa bed with a pullout frame at the front to support the mattress, explained that "it will not be necessary to move the sofa from the wall, the inconvenience of which is

30. Concealed within the desk shown in Fig. 29 is this bed with a woven-wire mattress. The paper label on the underside of the hinged top (which forms the headboard when turned down) reads, in part: "NOTICE DIRECTIONS/ ATTENTION:/How to Open and Close Folding Beds Easily, Without Damage,/ . . . /PAINE'S FURNITURE CO.,/48 CANAL STREET,/ BOSTON, MASS." Paine, like Andrews, manufactured furniture for church, school, lodge, and library, as well as for the home. Since Paine also had a retail store, it may be that the bed was manufactured by Andrews and sold by Paine.

30

thereby avoided." The inventor called special attention to the design of the seat cushion, which was hinged in front and flipped open to form the bed. Since the mattress itself was not used for sitting, "a fresh sleeping-surface is presented, the advantages of which, for health, comfort and cleanliness, are apparent."[27]

During the more than forty years he was in business, Henry Hover obtained not only a U.S. patent for his sofa bed, but French and English patents as well.[28] According to the 1881 *Trade Bureau* advertisement, Hover's sofa bed was "Patented in France, England and America." If this was in fact so, then his invention was, as he claimed, "HOVER'S WORLD-RENOWNED SOFA BED."

Other American furniture was patented and sold abroad. For example, the cabinet secretary desk invented by William S. Wooton of Indianapolis, Indiana, patent 155,604, October 6, 1874, and manufactured by the Wooton Desk Company, was available throughout the world (Fig. 168). During the late 1870s and the 1880s, the Wooton patent desk was sold by dealers in England, Scotland, Canada, Europe, South America, and the Far East, and Francis and James Smith, the London and Glasgow cabinetmaking firm, "took out the British patent for Wooton's desk."[29] As noted earlier, Edward W. Vaill's patent folding chairs were distributed through branches in London and Melbourne, besides New York. The metal-frame, adjustable lounge/invalid/easy chair manufactured by the Marks Adjustable Folding Chair Company of New York City (Figs. 111–113) is another example of American patent furniture sold in England.[30]

The status of American patent furniture in England is revealed by one correspondent's report of the First Annual Furniture Trades Exhibition at Agricultural Hall, London, in 1881. About a "Ladies Rocker" he commented: "the Americans are great at 'spring rockers,' but this version is certainly the most simple and perfect we have seen in this country. It is protected by the vendors by an English as well as an American patent, and after a glance at its qualities, the old style English rocker would not be thought of."[31]

Also admired were American extension tables and folding furniture of every sort. The London-based correspondent was of the opinion that extension tables "are made over there in greater variety than here," and noted: "Folding chairs are also shown of every conceivable kind, at from a crown upwards, and marvels in other folding furniture sustain the Yankee reputation of 'doubling up' almost everything."[32] "Other folding furniture" most likely meant beds, tables, and sofas. While patent systems were in force in most European countries, the number of patents put into production appears to have been greater in the United States than elsewhere, at least for furniture. It seems safe to say that patent furniture, if not unique to the United States, was certainly an American phenomenon during the second half of the nineteenth century.

With patent furniture, we move from the special-order and limited-edition pieces created for the privileged few to mass-produced everyday furniture bought by ordinary people. The emphasis is on the functional, although many pieces reflect the fashionable styles of their period, such as the Renaissance-revival and Eastlake. The impulse that motivated the development of all these novel ideas—if we accept the inventors' claims in their patent specifications—was to make furniture more "durable and substantial," "simple and inexpensive in construction," "convenient to use," "cheap to manufacture," and "easier to operate," of "lighter weight," "stronger," "firmer," "securer," and "compacter." Surprisingly, we still do not know how extensively this furniture was manufactured or how widely it was distributed: we know only that there were many factories turning out and marketing huge quantities of furniture.

As we probe into America's material and technological history, patent records are one fixed point of reference for establishing the date of popular acceptance, if not the actual use and distribution, of the objects examined. They reveal the multiplying effect of one idea spawning many others and in that sense make us more aware of some of the trends and problems of home furnishing for the common people. Patent furniture also provides a valuable vantage for studying the development of furniture in its totality.

31

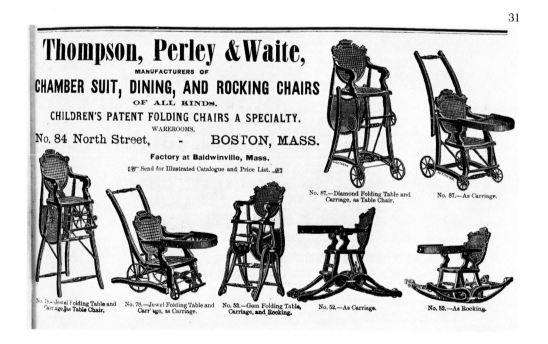

31. When furniture of the combination and convertible type is patented, it usually is for a specific invention. One exception is this child's folding chair, several versions of which are pictured in this *Trade Bureau* advertisement, January 1, 1881. The patent is for the design of the back, seat, and arm portion of the chair—design patent 9,111, February 29, 1876, issued to Charles A. Perley, assignor to Thompson, Perley and Waite of Baldwinville, Mass. Extant examples are clearly marked, often twice on the back of the frame, "DESIGN PAT FEB 29 1876." This combination high chair, carriage, and rocker met several needs of child care—feeding, transportation, amusement. It presumably was a money-saver as well as a space-conserver, important considerations for a family of moderate means with limited room. Photograph courtesy of the Library of Congress.

TECHNIQUE: BENDING AND LAMINATION

Bentwood is perhaps best known from its use in the famous Windsor chair (Fig. 32), developed in England and America in the eighteenth century. The chair's bow was shaped by steaming or boiling the wood and then pegging it in a plate over a mold. Found in taverns as well as in fine parlors of the time, Windsors are still popular today.

Not until the nineteenth and early twentieth centuries, however, was the potential of bentwood exploited to its maximum. Samuel Gragg, a Boston chairmaker in the early 1800s, was one of the first to produce significantly new designs using the bending technique. But it is with the name of Austrian manufacturer Michael Thonet, whose sales outlets in America were extensive, that bentwood has most often been associated. His designs, first produced around 1840, were achieved by means similar to those employed in the Windsor chair. But the Thonet aesthetic, with its simple but striking *tour de force* curves, was revolutionary. Equally important was the fact that his new forms were composed of mass-produced "knock-down" parts. Attractive, inexpensive, easily transported, Thonet furniture continued to be sold in the United States and Europe throughout the nineteenth century and beyond. In the 1920s and 1930s it inspired designs by Le Corbusier and others, and it retains its appeal in the 1980s. The present popularity of bentwood, in fact, represents the survival of a style rather than a conscious revival.

As Nikolaus Pevsner has pointed out, lamination—the technique of plying together layers of veneer with the grains running crosswise for strength and resilience—has its origins in the eighteenth century. Thomas Chippendale's dining room chairs for Osterley Park, for example, designed by Robert Adams circa 1773, have back splats of "three-ply" mahogany.[1] In the nineteenth-century development of the technique, as Pevsner has also pointed out, Michael Thonet is again a key figure. His experiments with lamination, in fact, antedate his work with bentwood. As early as 1830 he began making chair parts, and subsequently whole chairs, from narrow, thick strips of veneer bent in heated molds and glued together. It was not until the 1850s that he abandoned his experiments with plywood to concentrate on the equally innovative bending of solid wood for which he became famous.

That plying techniques were also known in the United States in the 1850s is indicated by John Henry Belter's patent application for a bedstead (patent 15,552, August 19, 1856) which explicitly notes that the techniques of glueing veneers with their grains at right angles had "been long in use," and by his description of plying in another patent application two years later. Improvements in the process continued to be patented, for example by John K. Mayo in 1865 and 1868.

Other early patented designs include the plywood chairs of Gardner and Company (Figs. 44 and 46). According to Pevsner, the designs for plywood chair seats and backs of the American manufacturer Frost and Peterson (later Frost Patent Veneer Company) were used by the Thonet chair factories in Europe. An article by T. D. Perry in the May 1932 issue of *Hardwood Record* shows that several American firms used a primitive plywood for cabinetwork, among them the Indianapolis Cabinet Company for desk tops (1883) and the Sauer Company of New York for doors and dining table tops. Pevsner dates the European manufacture of plywood panels for cabinet and joinery work in the early twentieth century, with Central and Eastern Europe apparently leading before World War I. It was only later that English designers used plywood to achieve their aesthetic goal of flush surfaces. In America in the twentieth century, under the leadership of Laszlo Moholy-Nagy, the Institute of Design in Chicago included extensive experiments with plywood furniture as part of the course work. Students began with a piece of flat plywood, manipulating it to raise its elasticity and resilience.[2]

Some technical notes on laminated or plied wood will enhance appreciation of its aesthetic in furniture design. Wood is, of course, an organic material whose vitality, even after seasoning and fabrication, causes warping with changes in humidity—a fact which leads a good cabinetmaker to season his wood and to construct his furniture in such a way that it can move without breaking. The advantage of lamination or plying is that the composite construction tames the wood so that it can be worked as if it were a different material. Plywood is not necessarily a cheap substitute for fine woods, but an entirely different material with different properties: three or more layers of wood glued together, the grain in each layer lying at right angles to that of the one underneath it. Since the fibers in each layer counteract movement in those above and below it, the stretching and shrinking of the wood is reduced to one-tenth that of solid wood. Rotary cutting of the veneers or layers makes plywood twice as hard as ordinary timber, since the annular rings are left intact in the surface of the veneer. Thus the strength of plywood is inherent in the position and strength both of the veneers and the glue, with movement hardly a problem.

Briefly, the manufacturing process consists of the following steps (Fig. 34). 1) The logs are cut to length, barked, and soaked in water to make them pliable. 2) If the logs are to be rotary-cut, they are put on veneer lathes to remove the rough outer wood; then the veneer is peeled off in a continuous ribbon, as in peeling an apple. 3) The sheets are trimmed to size and passed on rollers through drying machines. 4) The core sheet is covered with adhesive as it is passed between rollers and dipped into glue. 5) The sheets are pressed together in a hydraulic press. 6) The sheets are left to dry for a few days and then scraped and trimmed.[3]

32

32. Windsor armchair, New England, early nineteenth century. Windsor chairs made use of wood bent under the pressure of steam to form the graceful bow back, as seen here. The stiles and crest are made of a single piece, which holds the spindles, creating the elegant functional structure which is so admired today. National Museum of History and Technology, Smithsonian Institution.

33

34

33. Bentwood furniture in the Austrian section of the Philadelphia Centennial Exhibition, 1876, showing the work of Thonet Brothers and Joseph and Jacob Kohn. Thonet's designs, shipped all over the world, have been popular in the United States for over a hundred years. From *The Masterpieces of the Centennial International Exhibition.* Photograph courtesy of the Philadelphia Free Library.

34. Top left: front view of a rotary cutter with the veneer being "unpeeled." Top right: back view of cutter, with fixed vertical knife and side cutters to trim the veneers to width. Bottom left: "peeled" veneers passing forward to the "clipper" which cuts the sheets to size. Bottom right: large bandsaws converting logs into boards to make cores for block boards. From *Architectural Review Supplement,* September 1939.

SAMUEL GRAGG (1772–?1855)

According to Patricia E. Kane,[4] Samuel Gragg was born in Peterborough, New Hampshire, the son of a wheelwright who turned to farming. It is not known where the younger Gragg learned his trade. At the age of twenty-one he moved to New York State, where he remained for four or five years. By 1801, after the death of his wife, Lucinda Campbell, he had moved to Boston; the Boston marriage records list his second marriage, to Elizabeth Hopkinson, on September 10 of that year. In 1802 twin sons were born, and later a daughter. Kane has surmised that Gragg started a chairmaking business in Court Street as soon as he arrived in Boston, probably in partnership with William Hutchins, who married Gragg's sister Elizabeth in 1806. The Gragg-Hutchins partnership is listed in the Boston directories between 1805 and 1807, and in 1808, the year he patented his "elastic chair," Gragg announced he had moved his "fancy chair factory from No. 25 Hanover Street to The Furniture Warehouse, near the bottom of the mall—where he has taken a shop, and calculates to make and have constantly on hand, all kinds of Fancy and Bamboo CHAIRS, of the newest fashion . . ." (*Independent Chronicle*, February 25, 1808). The Boston directory of 1813 lists Gragg as a chairmaker on Tremont Street, where he remained until at least 1822. He is not listed with a business address after 1830, and the last year for a house address is 1855, possibly the year in which he died, at the age of eighty-three.

Side Chair, 1808

Although this fancy chair (Fig. 35) is not branded by its maker, it is identical to the marked side chair by Gragg in the Winterthur Museum. Apparently Gragg, who is also known to have produced Windsors, was the only chairmaker of the time to create these unusual and technologically innovative designs, for which he was issued a patent on August 31, 1808, for an "elastic chair."[5] In place of the traditional dowels, mortise, and tenon of stile and rail construction, Gragg has substituted a continuous bentwood form that combines stiles, seat rails, and front legs in a single piece—a startling innovation in its day and an early example of the exciting possibilities of bending wood. Although some Windsor chairs (Fig. 32) had made use of bentwood, it was limited to the hoops; moreover, the curves had to be maintained by the spindles after bending.

Gragg's unique achievement in the early nineteenth century anticipated by many years the use of bentwood by Michael Thonet and John Henry Belter (see Figs. 33 and 36). Few examples of bentwood furniture branded by Gragg are known to have survived; usually the light, thin curved elements were cracked or broken. As in the Gragg chair at the Winterthur Museum,[6] the original surface of this side chair was decorated with painted leaves, banding, and, in the center of the crest rail, an exotic peacock plume.

35. Side chair, Samuel Gragg, Boston, Mass. Ash, oak, maple, beech (repainted). 33 x 17¾ x 27 (83.8 x 45.1 x 68.6 cm.). An American classic, Gragg's "elastic" chair stretches the imagination as well as the boundaries of design in wood. Bent under steam pressure to the wood's furthest point, the stiles, seat rail, and front legs comprise one continuous graceful movement, anticipating the furniture of Michael Thonet by more than thirty years. Patented August 31, 1808. Lent anonymously.

35

JOHN HENRY BELTER (1804–1863)

Born in 1804 in Ulm, in the province of Württemberg in southern Germany, Johann Heinrich Belter was apprenticed in Württemberg and, according to family tradition, emigrated to the United States in 1840.[7] Four years later his name appeared in *Doggett's New York City Directory* as a cabinetmaker at 40½ Chatham Street (now Park Row). From 1846 until 1852 Doggett listed him at 372 Broadway. In 1853, he exhibited an "ebony and ivory table" in the New York Crystal Palace Exhibition, and was listed in *Trow's New York City Directory* at a new address, 547 Broadway. In 1854 J. H. Belter and Company was listed for the first time and the opening of his factory at Third Avenue near East 76 Street was recorded. In 1856 the directory noted the shop's move to 552 Broadway and the entry of John H. Springmeyer, a brother-in-law, into the business. In 1861, two more Springmeyers, William and Frederic, joined the firm, now at 722 Broadway, and after Belter's death from tuberculosis in September 1863, continued it under the name of J. H. Belter and Company until 1865, when they changed it to Springmeyer Brothers. In 1867 bankruptcy forced them to close the factory.

Belter's technological innovations were protected by four U. S. patents:

1) Patent 5,208, July 31, 1847, "Machinery for Sawing Arabesque Chairs," for a jigsaw and vise to hold and cut chair backs into openwork designs. The device was so constructed that the saw could be adjusted to compensate for the curved back.

2) Patent 15,552, August 19, 1856, "Bedstead" (Fig. 40), whose innovation was a bed without posts that could be made in two pieces for easy assembly. Belter's process for laminating sheets of veneer was outlined here.

3) Patent 19,405, February 23, 1858, "Improvement in the Method of Manufacturing Furniture" (Fig. 37), which perfected Belter's process for "dishing pressed work," making possible the manufacture of furniture which curved in two directions.

4) Patent 26,881, January 24, 1860, "Bureau Drawer," which used pressed work for the drawer sides. A locking mechanism secured all the drawers with one turn of the key.

Side Chair, 1858

Innovative bending and lamination enabled Belter to transcend the normal limitations of wood. He abandoned the traditional method of constructing chairs with rails and stiles in favor of a bent and laminated back to support the elaborate pierced and carved rococo-revival decoration. The design is an unusual combination of discreet ornament and innovative form.

His patent drawing for an "Improvement in the Method of Manufacturing Furniture" (Fig. 37) demonstrates his new technique. As may be seen, the back of the chair is composed of four vertical laminated panels (staves), A, B, C, and D. Belter's specifications note: "As veneers are not capable of being extended or compressed except to very slight extents, it has not been heretofore practicable to manufacture pressed work in any dishing forms. Pressed work has consequently been curved only in one plane, so that each part forms a portion of a hollow cylinder or cone; but by my invention each portion of the pressed work, when completed, forms a portion of a hollow sphere or spheroid, so that a section thereof in every possible plane exhibits a curved figure."

This chair (Fig. 36), which illustrates what he meant by "dishing," conforms to the profile shown in the patent drawing, as does the patent model in the Smithsonian Institution (Fig. 38).[8] Both the S-curve and concave shapes (bending in two directions) are achieved here.

36

36. Side chair, John Henry Belter, New York. Laminated rosewood, twentieth-century upholstery. 36 x 18¼ x 17½ (91.4 x 46.4 x 44.5 cm). This chair is one of at least five known examples of Belter's "dishing," through which the back is bulged, as specified in the patent application. The bulge is obtained by bending the wood in two directions, an important innovation used in the Eames-Saarinen chair designs of 1940 (Fig. 50) which achieved the aesthetic result of a new sculptural form. Patent 19,405, February 23, 1858. Lent by Dr. and Mrs. Milton L. Brindley.

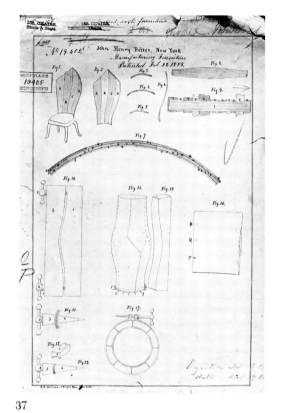

37

38

39

37. Patent drawing of Belter's side chair, an illustration of what Belter referred to as "dishing pressed work" (plywood) to manufacture furniture which curved in two directions. The process used stavelike pressed veneers, molded in "cauls" (diagram, Fig. 10) to form barrel-shaped cylinders (diagram, Fig. 14). When dry, the cylinders were cut apart into chair backs (diagram, Figs. 1 and 2). The National Archives.

38. Patent model of Belter's side chair. Made of laminated, bent, and carved rosewood, this is Belter's only known patent model. The "dishing pressed work" produced a bulge at the center of the back. National Museum of History and Technology, Smithsonian Institution.

39. Side chair (slipper chair), attributed to John Henry Belter, 1850–1855. The traditional construction of rail and stile is replaced by a perforated sculptured back. The elaborate carving in a pattern of intertwined grapevines and oak leaves was made possible through Belter's technological innovation in laminating and bending wood. The Metropolitan Museum of Art, gift of Mr. and Mrs. Lowell Ross Burch and Miss Jean McLean Morron, 1951.

40. Patent drawing of an "Improved Bedstead," John Henry Belter, New York. Belter's patent specifications indicate two laminated pieces held together by an internal frame. As with Belter's chairs, the stile and rail construction is replaced by a "wraparound" form which could be easily set up and dismantled. The drawing also illustrates the "pressing" of veneers, or plywood, although this was not Belter's invention. Patent 15,552, August 19, 1856. The National Archives.

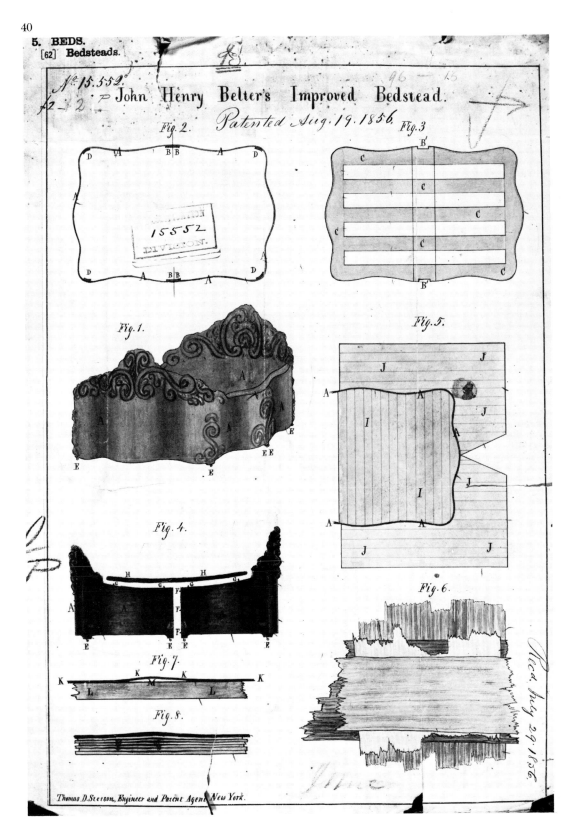

ISAAC I. COLE (working 1870s)

That little information has been discovered about Isaac Cole supports Siegfried Giedion's theory of the anonymity of patent furniture inventors. No city directories were published in Bergen County, where he lived, in the nineteenth century and Cole is not listed in the Paterson, New Jersey, directory in 1874, the year he patented his veneered chair.

There was an Isaac Cole who emigrated to this country in 1631 from England, settling in Mahopac, New York. Page 110 of the *Walker Atlas Map of Bergen County, New Jersey (1786–1886)*, shows a substantial property, with residence and stables, on the corner of Summit Avenue and Serpentine Road in Hillsdale (Washington Township), owned by Isaac I. Cole, who is probably the inventor. The catalog *Early Furniture of New Jersey* lists an Isaiah Cole as a cabinetmaker circa 1860, who may be a relation. Interestingly, a town near Hillsdale had a furniture factory called Collignon Brothers Patent Folding Chair Manufactory which was in business in the 1870s (with a wareroom at 181 Canal Street in New York City).

Patent Model of Plywood Chair, 1874

As described in Cole's patent specifications, the layers of veneer for his "new and improved veneer chair" (Fig. 41) were so used that "the grain of the middle one runs crosswise to that of the outer layers, and so alternately in similar manner if a greater number of veneers are used." The chair was made of three sections, as identified on the patent drawing (Fig. 42): the back part (B); the brace part (C); and the front or seat part (D), which extends up over the upper part of the back for additional strength. The sections could be attached at the connection points either by gluing or by means of rivets or clasps. Ornamentation could be achieved by cutting through the outer darker veneer to the lighter veneer below (alternatively, the lighter veneer could be on the outside).

Acquired by The Museum of Modern Art in 1943, the patent model was of great interest to the Design Department because of the bending of laminated wood so important in the experimental design of Alvar Aalto as well as in the work of Charles Eames and Eero Saarinen. The Cole chair was seen as a prototype, which the Eames chair (Fig. 51) developed further by bending in two directions, thus achieving a significant sculptural form. Bending in two directions, as we know, had been accomplished by John Henry Belter (Fig. 36) prior to Cole. Cole's chair, however, represents an important experiment in a simple, direct form of laminated bentwood with ornament integral to its structure. While Belter's chairs replaced the traditional stiles and crest rail with a single sculptural back, in the Cole chair the traditional stiles and legs are supplanted by a single piece of bent and laminated wood which served as back, seat, and leg sections. It is not known whether any of these chairs were actually manufactured.

41

41. Patent model of plywood chair, Isaac I. Cole, Hillsdale, N.J. 7⅞ x 4⅛ x 3¾ (20 x 10.5 x 9.5 cm). Cole's chair is admired today because of its advanced technology and design. Its back, seat, and front support are made of a single continuous piece of bentwood, anticipating the designs of Alvar Aalto in the next century. Patent 148,350, March 10, 1874. Lent by The Museum of Modern Art.

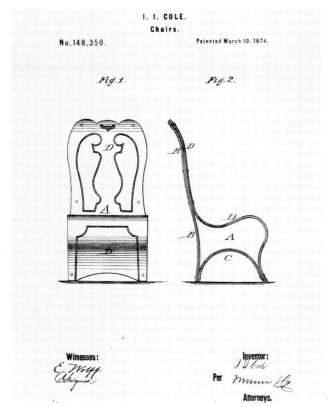

42

43

42. Patent drawing of Cole's plywood chair (front and side elevations), 1874. Ink on paper. 18½ x 14 (47 x 34.6 cm). Identical to the patent model, the drawing seems particularly daring and innovative when viewed in the side elevation. Lent by the U.S. Department of Commerce, Patent and Trademark Office.

43. Side chair, Thonet Brothers, Vienna, c. 1880. Probably constructed as an experiment, this molded wood chair, made from one continuous piece, bears a remarkable similarity to the Isaac Cole patent model (Fig. 41). According to Christopher Wilk's dating of it as c. 1880, the Thonet chair was produced later than Cole's model. Technical Museum, Vienna.

GARDNER AND COMPANY (working 1863–1888)

The history of this firm (which has been outlined by Kenneth Ames[9]) begins around 1863 when five Gardner brothers—William, Oliver, George, John, and Joseph—moved from New York City to Clarksville, New Jersey, where they began to manufacture picture frames. In their honor the name of the town was changed in 1871 to "Glen Gardner."

The dwindling demand for frames encouraged the company's changeover to the manufacture of three-ply veneer chair seats. George Gardner had been granted a number of patents, the most important and commercially successful one for a veneered and perforated chair seat (Fig. 45), which won a number of awards, including a bronze medal at the Franklin Institute in Philadelphia in 1874. Sales increased so much that the firm maintained an office at 110 Bowery in New York and retail agents in Philadelphia and New York. In 1874, the Gardner brothers (except for one who remained in New Jersey) moved to New York City. Gardner and Company's greatest recognition came in 1876, with its exhibit at the Philadelphia Centennial Exhibition; and in 1878, exhibiting at the Paris Universal Exposition, the company again received much praise. A number of catalogs have survived which indicate the popularity of the firm's products. Among the first to exploit the potential of bent and veneered wood for seating furniture, Gardner and Company was also innovative in the development of theater seating. By the 1880s a number of competitors (such as C. N. Arnold and Company, Poughkeepsie, New York) were producing similar items.

Platform Rocker, 1872

In May 1872, George Gardner was granted a patent for a three-ply veneer chair seat (Fig. 45). As described in the patent and in Gardner and Company's catalogs, the seats were "made by gluing veneers together, so that the fibre of each layer crosses the other at right angles. . . ."[10] Gardner's intention was to replace the popular cane seats with a cheaper, stronger material. This armchair, an innovative example of the firm's work, is noteworthy not only for its use of a single piece of perforated plywood for the back and seat but for its iron and spring supports, thus combining metal and plywood as Charles Eames was to do in the twentieth century.

According to the company's 1884 catalog, the veneered seats were "manufactured square and can be cut to fit any chair." It also warned: "Be sure that each seat has our trademark stamped on it. All others are imitations." The perforations create an appealing design of a star with circles on the seat, and of Gothic arches on the back.

44. Platform rocker, Gardner and Company, New York. Walnut, plywood, cast iron. 34¼ x 20¼ x 25 ⅜ (87 x 51.4 x 64.5 cm). Gardner and Company's perforated plywood seats were sometimes combined with the back in a single continuous piece of wood. The technically advanced use of plywood here is embellished with an appealing perforated design. Patent 127,045 (issued to George Gardner), May 21, 1872. "Gardner's/Patent/May 21, 1872" stamped on rear of plywood back. "Patented/May 1872" impressed on both iron spring supports. Lent anonymously.

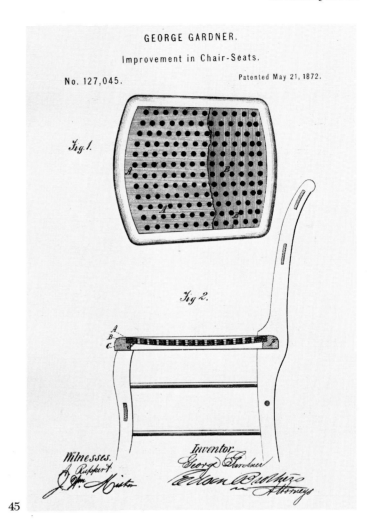

45. Patent drawing of "Improvement in Chair-Seats," George Gardner, Glen Gardner, N.J. The patent was for the chair seat, not for the chair itself. Gardner's veneers, like Belter's, were placed so the grains would run crosswise, thus adding greater strength. Whereas Belter used from five to sixteen plies for carving, Gardner used three for perforation. His "new and useful" design provided an inexpensive, more durable substitute for caned seating. Patent 127,045, May 21, 1872. U.S. Patent Office.

46. Advertisement, Gardner and Company, showing examples of the firm's perforated plywood seats. Private collection.

Rocking Chair, circa 1900 (designer unknown)

This remarkably exuberant rocking chair (Fig. 47) takes advantage of the nature of its simple material—fresh green willow branches. Cut, and most likely soaked to enhance their inherent flexibility, these branches made possible the chair's vigorous curvilinear forms. Probably influenced by the sturdier furniture of Michael Thonet, which was widely distributed in the United States, the intricate interweaving of the more delicate willow is necessary for stability. Each branch is an integral element of the overall structure, yet in itself creates a fanciful form. The decorative nature of the raw twig is emphasized, adding to the informal and picturesque feeling of the design.

Rustic furniture, casual and romantic, was extremely popular in the late nineteenth century; found in great quantities in remote vacation regions such as the Adirondacks, it became fashionable front porch furniture at home.[11] Firms across the country manufactured rustic furniture, but this elaborate example was probably made by an individual craftsman or in a small shop. (P.T.)

47. Rocking chair, designer unknown, c. 1900. Bent willow, painted. 42½ x 25¼ x 39 (108 x 64.1 x 99.1 cm). The use of bent twigs creates a graceful design of overlapping curves and circles, echoing the chair's rockers. In contrast to the steam-bent wood of Windsor chairs, these natural twigs were bent by soaking. Lent by the National Museum of History and Technology, Smithsonian Institution, gift of Mrs. Emmy Lou Packard.

48. Twig and rattan armchairs in use in a relaxed outdoor setting, late nineteenth century. Placed in a tête-à-tête position, the chairs provide a pleasant counterpoint for the focus on the newspaper and the lady's terrier. Photograph courtesy of The Society for the Preservation of New England Antiquities.

48

GILBERT ROHDE (1894–1944)

Born in New York City, Gilbert Rohde was the son of Max Rohde, a cabinetmaker who had come to the United States from East Prussia in 1888. The son was educated in New York public schools and attended the Art Students League and the Grand Central School of Art. After his first job as combined political cartoonist, drama and music critic, and newsgatherer of club activities for various New York papers, he turned to the advertising field and during the early 1920s worked as an illustrator, copywriter, free-lance artist, and professional photographer. He thus acquired a knowledge of selling, advertising, and merchandising that was to be useful throughout his life.

In 1927 Rohde was one of a small group, including Walter Dorwin Teague, Donald Deskey, and Raymond Loewy, who established the profession of industrial design in this country (though Rohde generally created furniture rather than industrial objects). At a client's request, Rohde could prepare advertising literature and direct the publicity in addition to designing. In 1929 he established his own industrial design office, introducing new merchandise and acting as a consultant to manufacturers of consumer goods. During his short fifteen-year career he designed for General Electric, Rohm and Haas, Hudson Motor Car, Kroehler Manufacturing, Herman Miller Furniture, Heywood-Wakefield, Troy Sunshade, and Simmons.

An important figure in the development of modern furniture, Rohde was influential in promoting European avant-garde design in this country. His furniture and interior designs aimed for efficient use of space, convenience, flexibility, and adaptability, important concerns in the twentieth century. Like Frank Lloyd Wright, he abandoned traditional craft methods of constructing furniture and applied engineering principles to make it lighter and stronger.

He was involved in the great world's fairs of the 1930s, designing the interiors of a house called "Design for Living" at the Century of Progress Exhibition in Chicago in 1933,[12] and serving on the committee of architects and designers who suggested the general plan for the New York World's Fair of 1939. Interiors, showrooms, department stores, and other designs by Rohde appeared regularly in publications such as *Architectural Forum.* His work was shown in the 1934 exhibition of contemporary American art sponsored by The Metropolitan Museum of Art and in other major industrial arts exhibits throughout the country. From 1936 to 1938 he was a director of the Design Laboratory, a free industrial art school in New York established by the Federal Arts Project of the Work Projects Administration; from 1939 to 1943 he headed the Industrial Design Department of the School of Architecture at New York University. A founder and member of the Society of Industrial Engineers, he also belonged to the American Designers Institute.[13]

One of Rohde's important clients was D. J. De Pree, president of the Herman Miller Furniture Company, for whom Rohde began designing in 1931, having convinced De Pree to expand into modern lines. Although a radical view in financially troubled times, it directed the company into the pursuit of innovative technology and design for which it became famous. By 1934, the modern designs had become so important that Herman Miller decided to phase out the more traditional furniture. De Pree shared Rohde's vision of modern design as a means of improving the quality of contemporary life. The functional new designs were instrumental in alleviating the problems of limited space and inefficient working areas in apartment living. "We came to believe," says De Pree, "that faddish styles and early obsolescence are forms of design immorality, and that good design improves quality and reduces cost because it achieves long life, which makes for repeatable manufacturing. . . ."[14]

Gilbert Rohde's death in New York at the age of fifty brought to an abrupt end his innovative, productive career.

HEYWOOD-WAKEFIELD COMPANY (1897–   )

Heywood Brothers and Company and the closely affiliated Heywood and Morrill Rattan Company were consolidated in 1897 with the Wakefield Rattan Company. For several decades afterward the new firm drew its leadership from among men with long prior experience in the constituent companies. The business continued to expand, warranting the issue of an additional million dollars of common stock in 1913 to permit enlargement of the firm's Chicago plant and the purchase in 1916 of the outstanding stock of the Washburn and Heywood Chair Company.

Like its nineteenth-century predecessors, Heywood-Wakefield was known for innovative furniture, including the designs of Gilbert Rohde. The firm continues in business today, employing around five hundred people in the manufacture of school and auditorium seating.

Side Chair, circa 1930

Inspired by the work of Finnish architect Alvar Aalto, Gilbert Rohde was among the American industrial designers in the 1930s who created laminated and bentwood furniture for mass production. This example of his work (Fig. 49) was manufactured by a firm known for its innovative designs since the nineteenth century (Figs. 69 and 70). Originally one of a pair—its mate is owned by The Metropolitan Museum of Art—the chair represents a form new to the American market and economical to produce. It thus reflects Rohde's belief that modern furniture should be both of excellent design and available to the average homeowner or apartment dweller.

The undulating seat and back are created from a single piece of wood, a separate element from the bent, laminated wood supports. The rose vinyl upholstery, vinyl gimp, and brass tacks around the side are probably original. By using a contoured wooden form in place of heavy springs and upholstery, Rohde was able to provide comfort and lightness. Like other furniture he designed (e.g., modular sectional sofas and bookcases), it was multifunctional and could be used in almost any room in the house.

49. Side chair, Gilbert Rohde, New York, c. 1930. Walnut, vinyl upholstery, brass tacks. 31½ x 16¼ x 21½ (80 x 41.3 x 54.6 cm). The undulating seat and back of this chair are of one piece of wood, a separate element from the bent laminated wood supports. The contoured wooden form replaces the more traditional springs and upholstery. Manufactured by Heywood-Wakefield Company. "Fine Furniture/ by/Heywood-Wakefield/ Est. 1826 Gardner, Mass." and "Style 2794/Finish Walnut/Upholstery 4222/ Heywood-Wakefield Gardner, Mass." on separate paper labels attached to bottom of chair. Lent anonymously.

49

CHARLES EAMES (1907–1978)

One of the most important furniture designers in the twentieth century, Charles Eames was born in St. Louis, Missouri, where he spent most of his first thirty years. He was the son of Celine (Lambert) and Charles O. Eames, a photographer and painter. At the age of ten Charles Eames began to support himself by delivering groceries and folding envelopes. At fourteen he became a laborer in a steel mill, and later, as a draftsman there, began to learn about architecture. Although he won a scholarship in 1924 to study architecture at Washington University in St. Louis, the following year he began educating himself and working for Trueblood and Grat, one of the city's large architectural firms.

Early in 1929 Eames went to Europe, where he became familiar with the work of Le Corbusier, Walter Gropius, and Ludwig Mies van der Rohe. Returning to St. Louis at the start of the Depression, he opened his own architectural office (Gray and Eames) in 1930. Eames soon closed up shop and went to live in Mexico, returning to St. Louis in 1935 to open another office (Eames and Walsh).

In 1936 Eliel Saarinen, the director of Cranbrook Academy of Art in Bloomfield Hills, Michigan, offered Eames a fellowship, which he accepted; the next year he became head of the school's Department of Experimental Design. Others at Cranbrook at the same time were Florence Schust Knoll, Ed Bacon, Harry Weese, Marianne Strengel, Ben Baldwin, Jack Spaeth, Ralph Rapson, and Harry Bertoia. With the director's son, Eero Saarinen, and the assistance of Ray Kaiser, Eames collaborated on designs for the molded plywood chair entered in the 1940 Organic Design in Home Furnishings competition organized by The Museum of Modern Art in New York (Fig. 50). They won first prize in each of the two main categories. According to Eliot Noyes, then director of the Museum's Department of Industrial Design, "A design may be called organic when there is an harmonious organization of the parts within the whole, according to structure, material, and purpose."[15] Their unique design proposed the use of plywood shaped in two directions to fit the contours of the human body.

Seeking to solve the problem of producing this chair, Eames moved to Southern California with his wife, the painter and sculptor Ray Kaiser Eames, whom he had married in 1941. He supported himself by working in the Art Department of Metro-Goldwyn-Mayer and devoted all his spare time to developing an inexpensive method of shaping plywood. Using a bicycle pump as a compressor to mold the wood, Eames and his wife experimented in their apartment. In 1942 they started their own development laboratory in association with John Entenza, Gregory Avon, Margaret Harris, and Griswold Raetze. The group received a U. S. Navy commission to produce molded plywood splints and stretchers, which the Eameses had already developed. In 1943 Eames served as director of research and development for the West Coast operations of the Evans Products Company, and after World War II returned to furniture design, having perfected his molding process.

In 1946 he was invited by The Museum of Modern Art to exhibit his designs in its first one-man furniture show. Eliot Noyes described Eames's achievement in *Arts and Architecture*, September 1946: "He has not only produced the finest chairs of modern design, but through borrowing, improvising, and inventing techniques, he has for the first time exploited the possibilities of mass production methods for the manufacture of furniture. With one stroke he has underlined the design decadence and the technical obsolescence of Grand Rapids" (p. 6). In the same year, George Nelson, the new director of design for Herman Miller Inc., recommended that the firm manufacture Eames chairs, which they did.

After the success of his Museum of Modern Art show, Eames returned to the West Coast, where he created designs for architecture, furniture, graphics, film production, fabrics, and exhibits. His partner in all these enterprises was his wife Ray, a former student of the painter

Hans Hofmann. Referring to the work done in his California studio, Eames noted: "She is equally responsible with me for everything that goes on here."

Another Eames achievement is the house they built for themselves in 1948 in Pacific Palisades, Santa Monica, California. Designed as part of a research program for the magazine *Arts and Architecture*, the house contains factory-produced windows, structural beams, and sliding doors—all of which could be ordered from a catalog. Although the materials are traditionally considered appropriate only for commercial buildings, the house is extraordinary in its use of bright panels of color, expanses of glass, and open-truss construction, a prototype for High Tech in the 1980s. It was also in 1948 that Eames began experiments with reinforced plastic.

Eames's other major furniture designs include chairs of molded polyester in 1950 (Fig. 85)—one of the earliest experiments with plastic—which were put into production; the classic lounge chair and ottoman, 1951 (Fig. 1); and the polished die-cast aluminum chairs, 1958.

50. Competition drawing, Charles Eames and Eero Saarinen, assisted by Ray Kaiser. In colored pencil and collage on 30- by 20-inch (76.2 x 51.8 cm) white posterboard, this is one of ten drawings submitted by Eames and Saarinen for The Museum of Modern Art's Organic Design in Home Furnishings competition, 1940. This prize-winning design was the prototype for both Eames's and Saarinen's subsequent chair designs. Its plywood shell was to be molded in two directions and joined to metal legs. The Museum of Modern Art.

A3501

CONVERSATION

FABRIC

PLYWOOD

ALUMINUM

THICKNESS OF PLYWOOD VARIES
WITH STRUCTURAL DEMANDS

FABRIC

RUBBER

PLYWOOD

RUBBER SEAL

ALUMINUM

ONE QUARTER FULL SIZE

Side Chair (DCM Chair), 1946

Among the most famous and innovative designs of this century is the DCM chair (Fig. 51), in continuous production since it was introduced in 1946. First manufactured by Evans Products, Venice, California, it was initially only distributed by Herman Miller, which purchased the rights to make the chair in 1946. The design was innovative because the panels of the back and seat were molded in two directions to create a three-dimensional sculptural form contoured to the human body, eliminating the need for upholstery. (Alvar Aalto's and Marcel Breuer's laminated wood chairs of circa 1934 were bent in only one direction.) Two-directional bending had been achieved by John Henry Belter in the nineteenth century (Fig. 36), though the only surviving evidence so far discovered is a patent drawing, a patent model, and five known examples.

Another innovative feature of the DCM chair was the use of rubber shock mounts to give the chair resiliency. By employing newly developed glues and an electric charge—a technique developed in the aircraft industry in World War II—it was possible to attach the rubber mounts to the plywood shells without using screws, which would have produced a visible, aesthetically unpleasing joint on the seat and back.

Made in both dining and lounge heights, this chair uses steel rods five-eighths of an inch (1.6 cm) in diameter for the front and rear legs and seven-sixteenths (1.1 cm) in diameter for the connecting spine which carries the backrest. The molded five-ply wood panels are five-sixths of an inch (2.1 cm) thick. Early versions of the chair were made of ash, walnut, and

51

51. Side chair (DCM chair), Charles Eames, Venice, Calif., design introduced 1946. Chromium-plated steel rods, plywood seat and back, rubber shock mounts. 29¾ x 19⅞ x 20⅞ (75.6 x 50.5 x 53 cm). Popularly known as the "Eames chair," this is one of the most famous furniture innovations of the twentieth century. It has been in continuous production since the mid-1940s. The innovation was the molded panels of the back and seat, which were bent in two directions to create a three-dimensional form that fits the human body, thus eliminating the need for upholstery. Manufactured by Herman Miller Inc. Lent by the Herman Miller Inc. Resource Center.

birch (the birch could be stained red or black). A wooden rather than metal frame was also available. The rubber tips on the original chair are today replaced by self-leveling nylon glides.

Folding Screen, 1946

According to the 1952 Herman Miller catalog, the Eames screen (Fig. 52) "offers an excellent solution for problems involving division of areas, screening off objects or activities, or providing backgrounds for furniture groupings. The molded elements fold into each other to form a compact unit when not in use. Their shape enables the screen to stand free open or closed. . . ." The wood finishes were birch, calico ash, or oak.

This ingenious design, similar to one by Alvar Aalto, is another example of Eames's success in working with molded plywood. Each curved section is made by a pressing process similar to that used for both Belter's and Eames's chairs. Each vertical section (made of either thirty-four-inch, or as in this instance, sixty-eight-inch lengths of plywood) is joined by means of a canvas hinge sandwiched into the lamination. The result is aesthetically impressive since it is related to sculptural forms. It represents an important break with traditional screens, which through the 1920s and 1930s retained their three- or four-part forms with decoration applied to each section. The decoration of the Eames screen is integral to the form itself. Unfortunately, the demand was not great enough to sustain production by Herman Miller, and today these screens are considered rare.

52. Folding screen, Charles Eames, Venice, Calif., design introduced 1946. Molded ash plywood, canvas joints. 68 x 10 (172.7 x 25.4 cm) closed. Another example of Eames's experimentation with molded plywood, this ingenious folding screen represents a break with the traditional three- or four-part form. Eames's design used integral decoration rather than the traditional applied type. Manufactured by Herman Miller Inc. Lent by the Herman Miller Inc. Resource Center.

52

PETER J. DANKO (b. 1949)

One of the most successful and innovative of the younger generation of American craftsmen, Peter Danko graduated from the University of Maryland in 1971 with a major in fine arts. Later in the same year he began to work with a cabinetmaker in the creation of commercial fixtures in the Washington, D.C., area. In 1976, Danko moved his studio to Alexandria, Virginia, and began to develop a line of limited-edition pieces in addition to his one-of-a-kind commissions, while experimenting with functional wood sculpture and furniture. In 1976, at the age of twenty-seven, he designed and patented the piece which has made him famous—the "Danko chair" (Fig. 53).

Like Eames, Danko has designed furniture which is both functional and sculptural. His early experimental work, which began in 1971, included seed-pod lamps, handlebar-gearshift-bowtie lamps, and a trestled table that opens like a drawbridge. He sketches constantly and feels that "bizarre" experimentation is essential to the creative design process.

53

Danko has continued to make furniture in his Alexandria studio, creating innovative designs for tables with synergetic glass-crystal pedestal bases, a wood and upholstered rocking chair, a dining table that expands from five to ten and a half feet, in addition to other chairs, desks, lamps, and tables employing steam-bent, laminate-bent, and other wood-working techniques. He has been awarded a National Endowment for the Arts grant in the Design Arts program to continue his development of new production techniques. His aim is to design furniture that integrates a warm and beautiful design with an efficient and economical means of production.

Armchair ("Danko Chair"), 1976

The "Danko chair" (Fig. 53) is the first plywood chair made from a single sheet of laminated wood to be put into production. The chair is made of ten plies (only fifteen-sixteenths of an inch [2.4 cm] altogether) which are precut so that the grain of one runs at right angles to the next. The core ply is poplar and the face veneers may be of oak, walnut, or cherry. The chair is formed by placing the wood plies in a mold, then gluing and bending them to shape. The seat is made from the piece of wood between the front legs, thus avoiding any waste of material.

Danko uses a press machine which exerts 150 tons of force for the armchair and 130 for the side chair. After the molding and cutting, the wood is sanded and finished. Until recently, a few hours of hand labor were required and the chairs were produced individually in his shop in Alexandria, but Danko, with representatives of Thonet in York, Pennsylvania, has developed the technology to manufacture the chair quickly and inexpensively. With the same concerns that characterized the work of innovative American designers of the 1940s and 1950s (and of Aalto and Breuer in the 1930s), Danko has designed a chair for the 1980s. "At first glance the chair is so obviously made from a single piece of plywood and yet it's a mystery as to how it was accomplished. It's only later that one discovers that it's comfortable, superstrong, stackable, lightweight, economical and its own chair rail."[16]

The form exemplifies the effort of designers such as Gerrit Thomas Rietveld, Marcel Breuer, and Verner Panton to make a chair from a single piece of the same material. It is the first one-piece plywood chair since the 1930 design by Gerald Summers (Fig. 54). In 1978 Danko's chair was acquired by The Museum of Modern Art for its Design Study Collection. Thonet has now put the chair into production, introducing it at the 12th National Exposition of Interior Contract Furniture (Neocon) at the Merchandise Mart in Chicago in June 1980.[17]

53. Armchair ("Danko chair"), Peter J. Danko, Alexandria, Va., designed 1976. Red oak, poplar, upholstery. 31 x 22 x 23 (78.7 x 55.9 x 58.4 cm). Danko's is one of the first plywood chairs made out of a single sheet of laminated wood. According to the designer, it is "comfortable, superstrong, stackable, light-weight, economical . . . ." Lent by Thonet Industries Inc.

54. Armchair, Gerald Summers, c. 1930. A further step in the bending of laminated wood is seen in this plywood chair, pressed out complete from a single board, requiring little assembly. Photograph from *Architectural Review Supplement*, September 1939.

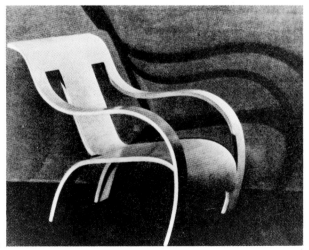

54

MATERIALS

Designers seeking to be innovative are frequently foiled because so many apparently new devices and forms are, in fact, not new at all. As John F. Pile, himself a furniture designer, pointed out in 1979: ". . . almost every proposal turns out to have been discovered and exploited in the past. Thus the urge toward originality and innovation that every designer feels is frustrated repeatedly. The route to an escape from this trap is, reasonably enough, the realization that some new material or technique will make new forms possible and may even require new forms to make it useable."[1]

Designers and craftsmen have from earliest history experimented with the use of a wide variety of materials in the construction of furniture. While wood has generally been viewed as the most obvious material for making tables and chairs, both paper and metal have a long tradition in furniture making.

Just as the nineteenth century brought tremendous changes in the building and transportation industries, so too did the furniture industry reflect the rapid and remarkable achievements of the Industrial Revolution which enabled materials to be bent, stretched, poured, and molded into hitherto impossible shapes and ornamentation. The availability of bent and molded plywood, for example, permitted the design of chairs with shapes not previously feasible. Likewise, the invention of machinery which facilitated the separation of rattan, reed, and cane was the impetus for the expanded use of rattan in chair seats, then for whole chairs and other forms. The accessibility of cast iron put into the designer's hand a material with which to create endless varieties of chairs, tables, and benches using pipes, flat bars, and rods. Later, tubular steel came into use, resulting in pieces that were "light and springy, not easily damaged," and that could "ultimately [be] produced very inexpensively."[2]

More recently, technical advances in the fabrication of plastics have opened up seemingly endless possibilities for furniture craftsmen. "More complex . . . than the traditional materials," plastics "can be formulated in an infinite variety of chemical compositions and processed in many ways."[3] Hence it is difficult to make generalizations about plastic furniture, and even more difficult to keep up with innovations in this field.

The range of new materials available to furniture makers in the nineteenth and twentieth centuries makes this area one of primary concern in a discussion of innovative furniture. The availability of new materials has stretched the imagination of designers and convinced many observers that there are no limits to innovation. (P.T.)

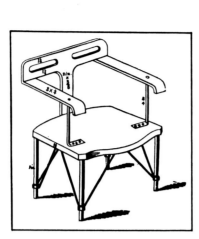

55. Two cast-iron chairs, early nineteenth century. The one on the left is an "elbow kitchen chair, made by a Mr. Mallet." These striking innovative designs anticipate functional furniture of the twentieth century. From J. C. Loudon, *Encyclopedia of Cottage, Farm, and Villa Architecture and Furniture* (London, 1833).

55

GASPER GODONE (working 1830–1870)

The shop of piano and musical instrument maker Gasper Godone was located on Broadway in New York City for most of his career. Since the cast-iron music stand or canterbury (Fig. 56) bears the mark GODONE'S STANDS N.Y. on the front and back of the base, it was probably manufactured as well as sold by the firm.

From 1830 to 1834, Godone was listed as a piano maker, and from 1835 until 1852 as a musical instrument maker, first at 412½ and later at 403½ Broadway. In 1853 Godone moved to 773 Broadway, where he was joined the next year by a relative, Napoleon Godone. In succeeding years Gasper's name generally bore the designation "music," while Napoleon was described as "keeper" or "importer," both now at 599 Broadway, suggesting that the two carried on different functions within the firm, one as the overseer of the manufactory, perhaps, and the other as the entrepreneur. During the 1860s, the company moved to 279 West 24 Street, where it remained until 1868.

That year a first-time listing, for "Godone and Dietz, importers," at 50 Harvard, refers to the new partnership between Napoleon Godone and Carl Theodore Dietz. Whether Gasper Godone remained in the firm is unclear. The fact that he was still listed with the title "music" but only at his home address suggests that his business address was the same as that of Godone and Dietz. Gasper Godone was last included in the New York directories in 1870, along with several others of the same surname: Angelo, "broker"; John, "music"; and Napoleon, "importer." Although Gasper Godone's firm made a variety of products, only one piece of cast iron bearing his stamp is known. (P.T.)

Music Rack (Canterbury), 1835–1850

Cast iron, made of carbon with varying amounts of silicon, manganese, sulfur, and phosphorus, was produced by the Chinese as early as the sixth century A.D. In Europe foundries were producing cast iron by the twelfth century; because it could be poured in the desired forms, it was cheaper to make than wrought iron, which had to be worked with hammers.

Cast iron was first used to make small domestic objects, such as firebacks, stove plates, kettles, guns, firedogs, bake pans, pots, and hardware items. By the late eighteenth century, it had found its way into architectural use, particularly for columns and panels in nonresidential buildings.

By the early nineteenth century, cast iron was also considered a possible material for furniture. In his *Encyclopedia of Cottage, Farm, and Villa Architecture and Furniture*, published in London in 1833, J. C. Loudon illustrated two chairs (Fig. 55), both of cast iron. The smaller of the two, an iron elbow kitchen chair, is ascribed to a Mr. Mallet. The back and elbows were cast in one piece, while the elbow supports were of gas tubing. The second chair was of cast and wrought iron with a wooden seat, "the whole forming an exceedingly light and yet stable chair, weighing less than most oak ones."

In the United States the use of iron was limited to small-scale production until the 1840s, when anthracite and bituminous coal became available to replace the charcoal which had formerly been the major source of the carbon. The discovery of these coal deposits, primarily in Pennsylvania's Lehigh Valley, revolutionized the iron industry and "enabled manufacturers to supply the material needed for railroads, street railways, bridges, commercial structures and for decorative purposes."[4]

By the 1840s cast iron had replaced wrought iron for the making of ornamental objects. Because it was less expensive, these items were widely distributed throughout the country, often through catalogs (Figs. 57 and 58). An early American use of cast iron in a decorative form, this music rack (Fig. 56), although basically classical in form, with sides in the shape of lyres, also incorporates elements of the rococo style, seen in the naturalistic C-scrolls on the body and the graceful curves of the bracketed legs.

While most cast-iron furniture was to be found outdoors, in gardens, parks, and cemeteries (Fig. 59), many examples have survived of cast-iron household furniture, including beds, stands, and tables. The use of the metal for a canterbury, however, is unusual and reflects the maker's inventiveness in his search for cheaper and more durable materials. (P. T.)

56

56. Music rack (canterbury), Gasper Gadone, New York, 1835–1850. Cast iron, tulip poplar. 18½ x 19¾ x 18½ (47 x 50.2 x 47 cm). This high-style music rack represents an early use of an innovative material—cast iron—in a decorative form. Basically classical in design, with lyre-shaped sides, it also includes rococo elements: the naturalistic C-scrolls on the body and curves of the bracketed legs. To make the rack more functional, casters have been applied for movability. "GODONE'S STAND N. Y." on front and back of base. Lent by The Metropolitan Museum of Art, gift of Wunsch Foundation Inc.

CHAPTER XXV.
CAST IRON FURNITURE.

STYLES of Cast Iron Chairs, Settees, &c., are made expressly for Gardens, Lawns, Piazzas, Summer Houses, and house purposes. Some of these are shown in the following illustrations :

Fig. 300.

Rustic Settee—Price $10.

Fig. 301.

Grape Settee—Prices $9 to $15.

Fig. 317.

UMBRELLA STAND.
Prices—From $1 50 to $6. (Eight styles are made.)

Fig. 302.

Gothic Settee—Price $17 and $20.

Fig. 303.

Hall Chair—Price $4 50.

Fig. 304.

Hall Chair—Price $4 50.

Fig. 318.

STORE STOOL.
Prices.—From $2 75 to $4 75. (Various patterns, covered with plush and hair cloth.)

Fig. 305.

Grape Chair— Price $5.

Fig. 306.

Morning Glory Chair—Price $6.

Fig. 316.

IRON TABLE.——**Prices.**—With Marble top, from $5 to $25.

57

57. A plate from Hutchinson and Wickersham's 1857 *Descriptive Catalogue* indicates the variety of forms made in cast iron, including revivals of rococo, Gothic, and Renaissance styles. Inspired by English cast-iron work, many of these designs were popular patterns freely pirated by American companies, so that identical pieces may appear in catalogs by competing firms.

58. Interior, warehouse of the New York Wire Railing Company, 312 Broadway, New York. Owned by Hutchinson and Wickersham, New York Wire Railing displayed its products in the parent firm's 1857 catalog with this description: "A New Phase in the Iron Manufacture; Important Inventions and Improvements; Historical Sketch of Iron; Descriptive Catalogue of the Manufactures of the New York Wire Railing Company, Hutchinson & Wickersham." Their decorative iron work took a variety of forms, including two upholstered chairs that may have been inspired by Thomas E. Warren's 1849 patented revolving armchairs (Fig. 101).

59. A rustic cast-iron garden bench, late nineteenth century. The young lady, pausing in her game of croquet, appears perched on the bench's edge—the cold hard metal would hardly encourage her to linger. Nevertheless, benches were the most popular forms of cast-iron furniture. The rustic pattern seen here also appears as Fig. 300 in the Janes, Kirtland and Company catalog, where it is noted that the "rustic settee" was among the styles made expressly for gardens and lawns. Photograph courtesy of The Society for the Preservation of New England Antiquities.

58

59

LALANCE AND GROSJEAN (working 1852–post-1900)

The firm of Lalance and Grosjean is listed in the standard business directories for New York City in the second half of the nineteenth century. First mentioned in 1852, Alfred Lalance was described as an "importer of French hardware" at 120 Pearl Street. The following year he appears with a partner, Florian Grosjean. The resulting company, Lalance and Grosjean, remained in business for over fifty years, until after the turn of the century.

Their line of goods varied from French hardware to cutlery to tinware, and after 1871 they described themselves as manufacturers of tinware, hardware, metals, hollow ware, iron-ware, house furnishings, and agateware. From 1853 to 1855 Lalance and Grosjean were located at 120 Pearl, followed by ten years at 70 Beekman, four at 273 Pearl, and ten at 89 Beekman. For their remaining years in business, they were at 19 Cliff.

Because Lalance's home address was listed as France, one can surmise that perhaps the firm was primarily an import house, managed by local agents, at least until the 1870s, when the firm expanded its New York City retail operation and began manufacturing. Proof of Lalance and Grosjean's manufacturing role is supplied by references to the company in the *Official Catalogue of the International Exhibition* of 1876. At the Centennial Exhibition they displayed "granite ware, . . . a category of metal hollow ware" used for kitchen pots and pans, and an assortment of "iron culinary ware," stamped "Lalance and Grosjean Manufacturing Co., New York, N.Y."[5]

The foreign background of Lalance and Grosjean explains their connection with François Carré, also French, who took out a U.S. patent for his bent steel chair, considered one of the earliest of its kind (Fig. 60). It is possible that these chairs were made mainly in France, were imported by Lalance and Grosjean for sale at their "hardware" store, and were marked with their impressed button stamp (Fig. 61). (P. T.)

Garden Chair, 1866

The U.S. patent for this chair (Fig. 60) was filed by François A. Carré, "of Paris, France," who claimed in his specifications to have invented a "new and useful Improvement in the Manufacture of Seats and Backs of Chairs, Stools, Settees, etc."—namely, the use of "curved strips of sheet steel" to form chair backs and seats "materially different from metal seats and backs as heretofore made."

The innovative steel strips replaced other metals, like iron, that had been used for garden furniture. According to Carré, iron seats were "hard, clumsy and inconvenient." Likewise, chair seats made of "wire braided in imitation [of] caned seats" were generally uncomfortable; metal seats made of spiral springs were perhaps more comfortable, but they tended rather quickly to sag, rendering them "inconvenient and useless."

Carré's new chair combined "strength and durability with neatness and convenience," all desirable characteristics in seating furniture. The patent for this chair must have been purchased by Lalance and Grosjean, whose mark is on the brass button on the center of the seat (Fig. 61). While the presence of this label strongly suggests that the chair was manufactured in the United States, similar examples were also made in France, as seen in a catalog of the Société Anonyme des Hauts-Fourneaux & Fonderies du Val d'Osne, circa 1870, whose No. 12 (third row) shows an apparently identical chair, said to be made of iron (Fig. 63).

The continued demand for bent-steel chairs is substantiated by a *Catalogue of Bent Steel Furniture*, published in 1892 by Schlesinger, Wiessner and Company, New York City, formerly of Vienna. This firm sold its products widely in the United States, claiming to have operated "one of the largest factories of this kind for about thirty years." The catalog shows a "Boulevard Arm Chair" similar to the Lalance and Grosjean example and its introduction notes: "Indestructible Bent Steel Furniture is particularly adapted for use at the seashore, in parks and gardens, public resorts, hotels, on steamers and in hospitals and other places where furniture is subject to damage from elements and other destructive influence, and also positively vermin proof, being without joints or openings of any kind."

Because bent steel was strong and durable as well as elastic—and thus comfortable—chairs of this variety continued to be popular in the twentieth century, enjoying particular success in the 1920s and still manufactured in the 1940s. Although not of American origin, the form influenced American innovative designs. (P. T.)

60. Garden chair, Lalance and Grosjean, New York. Bent steel strips and rods. 35 x 18½ x 27 (88.9 x 47 x 68.6 cm); seat diameter 18½ (47 cm). Steel strips have replaced cast iron in this chair based on an innovative French design. The designer and patentee, François A. Carré, stated that iron had "little if any elasticity." His light, comfortable, and flexible steel seats continued to be popular well into the twentieth century. Patent 54,828, May 15, 1866. Lent anonymously.

60

61

F. Carre,

Chair Bottom,

N.º 54,828.   Patented May 15, 1866.

62

61. Mark on garden chair shown in Fig. 60: "LA-LANCE & GROSJEAN/273/ PEARL ST./N. Y./ PATENTED/MAY 15/1866" impressed on a brass button in the center of the seat. Examples of American garden chairs marked in this fashion are rare.

62. Patent drawing of Carré's "Chair Bottom" (elevation and plan). The National Archives.

63. A French garden chair identical to the Carré patented chair appears as Fig. 12 (third row) under the heading "Iron Tables & Chairs." From the catalog of the Société Anonyme des Hauts-Fourneaux & Fonderies du Val d'Osne, Paris, c. 1870.

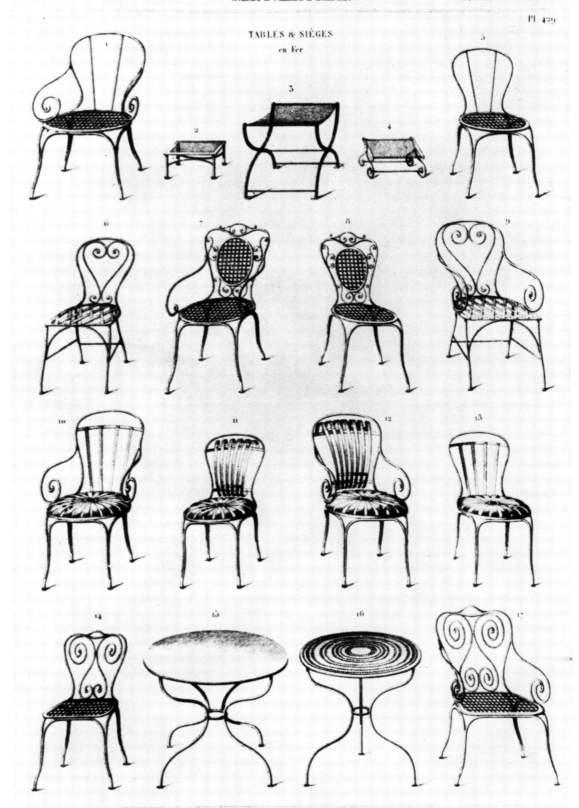

SOCIÉTÉ ANONYME DES HAUTS-FOURNEAUX & FONDERIES DU VAL-D'OSNE.

ANCIENNES MAISONS J.P.V. ANDRÉ ET J.J. DUCEL ET FILS.

Ornements en Fonte de Fer.   Créateurs de l'Industrie de la fonte d'Art   58, Boulevart Voltaire Paris.

Pl. 429

TABLES & SIÉGES

en fer.

GEORGE J. HUNZINGER (1835–1898)

George Hunzinger came to the United States in the 1850s from Tuttlingen, Germany, where his ancestors had been involved in the cabinetmaking trade since the seventeenth century. His father and brother were, in fact, both cabinetmakers, and descendants today carry on the family furniture making business in this same small town near the Swiss border.

Hunzinger joined a large population of German furniture makers in New York City, numbering over 3,000 in 1850. Beginning in 1861, Hunzinger became best known for his patent furniture. His first patent was for a reclining chair, the footboard of which could be transformed into a table; the whole chair could be folded for easy carrying.

In 1866 Hunzinger opened his own business at 192 Laurens Street in New York City. Here he regularly employed four or five men. Within two years he had built up a stock worth $10,000. From this propitious beginning, Hunzinger's financial reputation steadily improved; R. G. Dun and Company (now Dun and Bradstreet) regularly reported him to be "well spoken of as industrious and hardworking," with a reputation for "fair dealing and promptitude in his business affairs."

So fast did his firm grow that by 1872 Hunzinger employed fifty men, and the next year he broke a five-year lease on his store at 402 Bleecker Street, where he had been since 1870, to move into new quarters at 143 Seventh Avenue. This building was destroyed by fire in 1877, along with two other well-known furniture factories, those of Pierre J. Hardy and Roux and Company. Despite the devastation (his insurance covered only half his loss), Hunzinger was able to rebuild his company, moving into a newly constructed factory at 323–27 West 16 Street in 1879. Late in the 1880s, his two sons, George Jr. and Alfred, joined the firm. By the 1890s Hunzinger's interests seem to have shifted from chairs to tables; several patents for this form were taken out by the company in that decade. After Hunzinger's unexpected death in 1898, the business continued under the leadership of George Jr., with his brother Alfred acting as salesman and several of his six sisters working in the office.

By this time, Hunzinger's furniture had a wide market, including the East Coast and the Midwest. Less innovative than the company's earlier products, "chairs and rockers, library suites, Morris chairs, card tables, three position chairs, and sun parlor furniture" were regularly available from the firm.

George Hunzinger and Sons stopped making furniture in the 1920s and became a real estate and stockholding company.[6] (P. T.)

Armchair, 1876

George J. Hunzinger is today known for his many unusual and intriguing chair designs which combined innovative technical elements with new decorative motifs. His distinctive roundels and turnings, resembling machine parts, are particularly noteworthy. Two of the numerous patents he received for mechanical and structural inventions can be seen in this chair (Fig. 64).

The earlier of the two patents, granted in 1869 (Fig. 128), was for the diagonal side braces that connected the front feet of the chair with the upper back, a device seen on a number of other Hunzinger chairs. In his patent application, he explained the benefits of such braces: "The back legs of chairs are very liable to become loosened at the point of connection with the seat. . . . This looseness arises from pressure against the back of the chair, and from tipping the chair backward upon the hind legs."

Hunzinger continued to be concerned about durability. In 1876 he applied for a patent for a woven-wire chair seat and back, consisting of a series of peripheral grooves and pins that held a wire band to the chair frame (Fig. 65). Of this "Improvement in Chair Seats and Backs," Hunzinger claimed: "The chair seat or back is made with reference to the use of wire in place of cane, to form an open-work seat, and to insure great strength and beauty, and to facilitate the interweaving of the wires."

The chair was clearly designed with beauty in mind. The wire was to be "covered with threads wound or braided upon the same, and the said wires might be painted or varnished." The original red fabric and red paint survive on this example.

Noteworthy, too, is Hunzinger's use of a cantilevered chair seat, supported by diagonal turned members—an early application of a design element which became very important in twentieth-century furniture.

All of these ingredients—the use of steel mesh in the seat, the emphasis on durability, the cantilevered seat, and overall spareness in decoration—distinguish this chair from the heavy, upholstered, elaborately carved furniture more typical of the Victorian era. (P. T.)

64. Armchair, George J. Hunzinger, New York. Walnut, steel mesh upholstery covered with red fabric, red paint. 30¼ x 20¼ x 23¾ (76.8 x 51.4 x 60.3 cm). This chair's woven-wire seat and back anticipated the wire garden furniture of the late nineteenth century and the chairs of Harry Bertoia in the twentieth century (Fig. 91). In addition to innovative material, this chair seat employs the cantilever principle. Patent 176,314, April 18, 1876. "HUNZINGER/N. Y./PAT. MARCH 30/1869" and "PAT. APRIL 18, 1876" stamped on back of right rear stile. Lent anonymously.

64

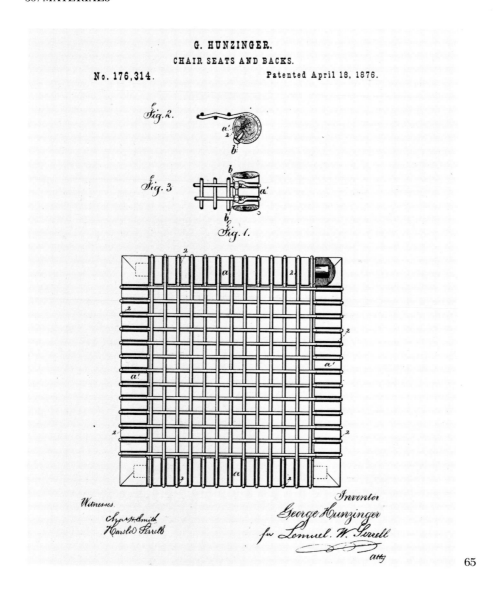

65. Patent drawing of Hunzinger's "Improvement in Chair Seats and Backs." Hunzinger noted that the substitution of wire for cane in the openwork seat and back insured "great strength and beauty." The lines of the seat are continued in the wooden members of the chair, another example of the designer's inventive genius. U. S. Patent Office.

66. Garden settee, designer unknown, 1875–1900. Woven and twisted steel wire. 36⅝ x 50 x 24 (93 x 127 x 61 cm). Some of the most imaginative nineteenth-century furniture was made of wire, an innovative material, light and graceful but extremely fragile. Because wire garden furniture was rarely marked, it is difficult to pinpoint the date or place of manufacture. Lent anonymously.

Garden Settee, 1875–1900 (designer unknown)

By the mid-nineteenth century, furniture makers took advantage of technological advances in the manufacture of metal by employing reinforced steel wire to make chairs and benches that could withstand all climatic conditions and were thus ideal for outdoor use.

This unmarked garden settee (Fig. 66) is a good example of its type, incorporating an overall curvilinear form and individual gracefully curved ornaments. Suggesting in its outline contemporary rococo-revival sofas, it is nonetheless much freer in execution and considerably lighter in feel, in part because of the nature of the material.

Catalogs of ironwork manufacturers from the second half of the nineteenth century featured wire tables, chairs, plant stands, and other items in their general line of garden furniture. One such firm was M. Walker and Sons, Philadelphia (1849–1881), whose inventory included such diverse items as wrought-iron and wire railing, wrought-iron farm fence, iron bedsteads, and ornamental wirework for greenhouses, gardens, etc. (Fig. 67).

While wire furniture enjoyed considerable popularity, it was never as widely used as cast-iron designs, perhaps because it was rather flimsy compared to the sturdy iron pieces. Relatively few nineteenth-century examples have survived. (P. T.)

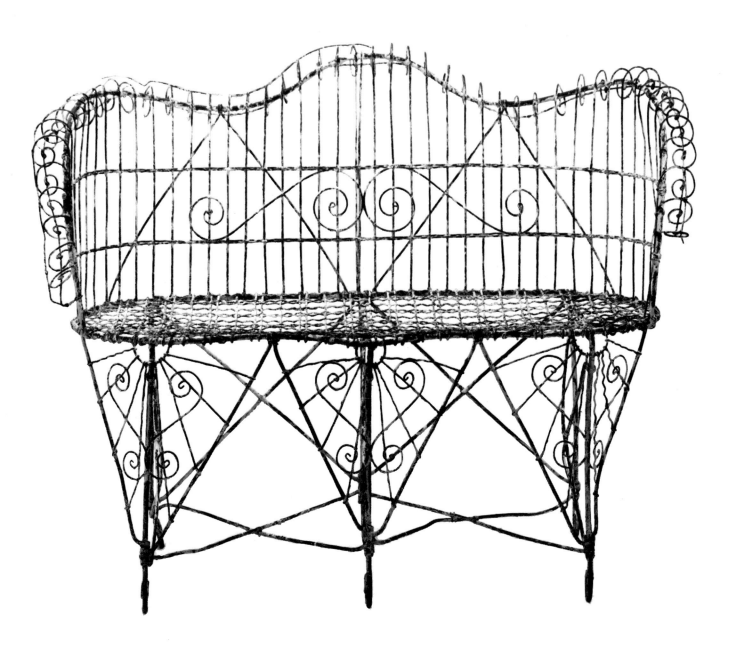

66

67

M. WALKER & SONS, PHILADELPHIA, PA.

ROYAL METAL MANUFACTURING COMPANY (1900–1962)

The Royal Metal Company, which in 1901 became the Royal Metal Manufacturing Company, was first listed in the Chicago city directory in 1900 as a maker of "art metal specialties" at 106 and 108 Oakley; its manager was Joseph Salomon. The company was included in Chicago directories annually until 1962, described in 1901–2 as "manufacturers of metal base folding tables" and from 1903 to 1923 as manufacturers of metal furniture.

The location of the firm changed frequently: 34 and 36 West Washington in 1901; 42 and 44 South Clinton in 1905; 1817–19 Dearborn in 1906; 2318 South Western in 1912; 1138 South Michigan in 1923; 100 South Michigan in 1929; 175 North Michigan in 1940; and finally Merchandise Mart Plaza in 1958.

After 1912, Joseph Salomon was described as the president of the firm, having in 1896 been vice-president of the Chicago Architectural Iron Works at 112 North Oakley, apparently the predecessor of the Royal Metal Manufacturing Company. Another Salomon, Irving, was president of the company from 1928 to 1959. (P. T.)

68

68. Child's chair, Royal Metal Manufacturing Company, Chicago, Ill. Twisted steel rods, plywood seat with steel band. 20 x 10 x 12½ (50.8 x 25.4 x 31.8 cm). A more durable version of the lighter, more fanciful wire furniture, this child's chair is made of twisted steel rods, an innovative material in its day. Associated with cafés and soda fountains at the turn of the century, these functional designs are still popular. Although manufactured in great numbers, apparently few labeled examples have survived. Patented February 2, 1909. "ROYAL M.M. CO./CHICAGO/PAT FEB 2 1909" marked on circular disk joining stretchers. Lent anonymously.

Child's Chair, 1909

Small, lightweight, and durable, metal chairs of this type (Fig. 68) have enjoyed wide popularity since the nineteenth century. With a strong similarity to the cast- and wrought-iron design by "Mr. Mallet" (Fig. 55), these chairs frequently have slender legs and rounded wooden seats.

Other versions, illustrated in two American ironwork catalogs of the 1850s, show chairs with square wire-mesh seats, slender X-shaped legs, and heart-shaped backs terminating in tight scrolls. The introduction of steel into furniture making resulted in a slightly different form: twisted steel rods riveted to a steel band enclosing a wooden seat, with curved steel rods conforming to the back. These inexpensive chairs were in plentiful supply in the early twentieth century.

Perhaps because of its durability and small size, the steel rod chair was early associated with heavily frequented cafés or soda fountains. In the Buffalo Brand Metal Manufacturing Company catalog of the first decade of this century, for example, a steel rod chair is described as "our high-grade Soda or Cafe Chair, the strongest and best constructed chair on the market."

Even today this chair is known as an "ice cream parlor chair," proof of the strong tradition of usage for nearly a century. The combination of a new material with an innovative form resulted in a chair which has withstood the changes of fashion. Today, of course, such chairs could also be said to be nostalgia items reminiscent of quieter times when one could linger in the neighborhood soda fountain. (P. T.)

WAKEFIELD RATTAN COMPANY (1844–1897)

Cyrus Wakefield was born in Roxbury, New Hampshire, in 1811, and left there at the age of fifteen for Boston, where he found a job in a grocery store. In 1836 he opened his own grocery business with his brother Enoch, using the name Wakefield and Company. With an eye for adventure and an enviable business sense, Cyrus Wakefield began to conceive of a new moneymaking scheme: a way of using the rattan which he saw piled upon the nearby wharves, a material employed to protect the cargo brought by sea from the Orient.

Initially Cyrus sold the rattan to basket makers, who took off the outside covering and used only the reed. The outer cover was then sold to chairmakers, who used it for seats. This enterprise proved successful for the Wakefield brothers and in 1844 they sold the grocery business and began a jobbing trade in rattan. Recognizing that the major drawback to continued success was the high degree of handwork involved in stripping off the outer layer of cane, Cyrus Wakefield wrote his brother-in-law, an associate of Messr. Russell and Company of Canton, China, to send samples of Chinese cane which was stripped before being shipped. The use of imported rattan could significantly reduce the cost.

Imports from China stopped with the outbreak of the Opium War (1840–1842), but by this point Cyrus Wakefield had developed his own methods of manufacturing rattan, using the reed as well as the cane. With two machines in a plant on Canal Street in Boston, the Wakefield Rattan Company soon became known throughout the world for the variety of baskets and hoopskirts it produced. But as steel began to replace reed in hoopskirts, Wakefield focused his attention on the manufacture of cane for chair seats. Realizing the importance of modernization, Wakefield introduced the newest machines into his factory, and further increased his profits by making use of every part of rattan, inventing and patenting a process of spinning the larger shavings into yarn for mats, floor coverings, and baling cloth.

During the 1860s and 1870s Wakefield's business included the sale of rattan, cane, reed, rattan furniture, matting, cane seating, and reed baskets. The company's success was not interrupted by the death of its founder because his nephew, Cyrus Wakefield II, ably continued in his uncle's footsteps as president. After the younger Wakefield took charge, in fact, the company enjoyed brisk growth, including the addition of warehouses in Chicago and San Francisco and, in 1887, of a factory in Chicago.

When Cyrus Wakefield II died in 1888, Charles H. Lang Jr. became manager. In 1897 the company was consolidated with its longstanding rivals, Heywood Brothers and Company and the Heywood and Morrill Rattan Company. Discussion of an association between these three firms had actually begun a decade earlier with a plan to establish a joint manufacturing enterprise in Chicago. Instead, however, Wakefield Rattan decided to buy its own building, an episode that perpetuated the rivalry between these three firms until they were consolidated ten years later.[7] (P. T.)

Center Table, 1877

Rattan furniture became so commonplace in the American home by the 1880s that, as a commentator observed in 1886, one or two pieces were considered "indispensable in modern apartments."[8] Thanks in part to the inventions of Cyrus Wakefield, this material enjoyed great popularity until supplanted by the lighter wicker used to make the more open forms of the 1880s and 1890s.

The closely woven appearance of this table (Fig. 69) is typical of rattan furniture. The close weave is also apparent in the items shown in the Wakefield Rattan Company's 1878 price list, issued shortly after the table was patented (Fig. 70). Not fitting into any particular style

69

69. Center table, Wakefield Rattan Company, Boston, Mass. Rattan. 30½ x 28 x 23½ (77.5 x 71.1 x 59.7 cm). In contrast to the elaborate and fanciful designs of much wicker furniture, the chaste, simple lines of this table appeal to modern sensibilities. Although the piece bears a patent date, the patent grant has not been found. "PATENTED APRIL 17, 1877/photo. No. 321/ Manufactured by the Wakefield Rattan Co., Boston & New York" on paper label underneath table top. Lent by Margot Johnson.

category, Wakefield's rattan designs express a complete understanding of the nature of the material. Because it could be bent, decorative features such as scrolls and other cursive designs were frequently found. Unfortunately, rattan and wicker pieces are fragile and have thus not survived in the great numbers in which they were produced.

Wicker was made as early as 1851 in this country, as evidenced by the display of a New York firm in the London Crystal Palace Exhibition (Fig. 71). Used both outdoors and in the parlor through the nineteenth and early twentieth centuries (Figs. 72 and 73), it remains a popular material today. (P. T.)

1st May, 1878.

PRICE LIST
OF
Rattan Furniture, &c.

MANUFACTURED BY THE

WAKEFIELD RATTAN COMPANY.

COMPLIMENTS OF

JOSEPH PAGE,

HOUSE FURNISHER,

China, Glass and Silver Plated Ware,

1002 & 1004 ARCH STREET,

PHILADELPHIA.

70. Like cast iron and wire, wicker and rattan furniture was produced in a variety of forms, often intricate, such as those pictured on the front page of the Wakefield Rattan Company's 1878 price list. That the list was distributed "compliments of" a Philadelphia house furnisher suggests that Wakefield items could be purchased in similar establishments throughout the country. Photograph courtesy of the Smithsonian Institution.

71

71. A wicker garden chair displayed at the Crystal Palace Exhibition, London, 1851, from the *Illustrated Catalogue.* The simplicity and practicality of American innovative furniture were admired at the exhibition, where large and elaborate pieces were more typical. According to the catalog, "A Wicker Garden-Chair, contributed by Mr. Topf, of New York, possesses much novelty, and no little taste, in its ornamental design." Early examples of American wicker are rare because of the material's fragility.

72. A parlor, late nineteenth century. Associated today with informal outdoor use, wicker furniture in the nineteenth century was found in the most elegant houses. The parlor shown, typical of a family of modest means, contains the essential furnishings of the day, including wall-to-wall carpeting and wicker chairs. Photograph courtesy of The Society for the Preservation of New England Antiquities.

72

73

73. Wicker plant stand, c. 1920. The material evokes an era when there was time and leisure to care for gardens and pets. This imaginative plant stand combines four functions in one form. Photograph courtesy of Greenfield Village and the Henry Ford Museum.

74. Horn armchair, designer unknown, 1880–1890. Horn, metal claw foot enclosing glass balls, brass tacks, red naugahyde (not original). 33 x 30¾ x 22½ (83.8 x 78.1 x 57.2 cm). Horn furniture, an innovative use of an organic material, often took on extraordinary sculptural forms which evoked the pioneering power of the American West. Lent by the Smithsonian Institution Furnishings Collection.

74

Horn Armchair,1880–1890 (designer unknown)

Used selectively in later nineteenth-century furniture, horn was a natural material, usually from steers, but occasionally from other animals such as elk and deer. Pieces such as this armchair (Fig. 74) were made to be used in libraries, trophy rooms, and hunting lodges. Evoking the powerful thrust of the American West, horn was particularly popular in the last two decades of the century when equally ponderous stuffed furniture was also in vogue.

While horn furniture is thought to have been designed by one of Louis Comfort Tiffany's fashionable decorating firms, it is also known to have been made in Europe and, as Fig. 75 illustrates, was sold commercially by Texas furniture firms. One of these was Wenzel Friedrich's. Winner of several awards for his designs, Friedrich sold a complete line of horn furniture, including tables, settees, hat racks, and benches. The seating furniture is shown

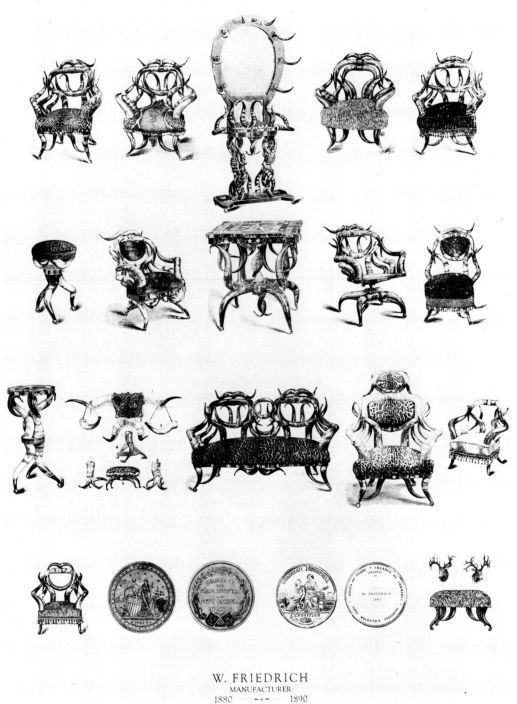

W. FRIEDRICH
MANUFACTURER
1880 ———·—— 1890

75. Lithograph of horn chairs, tables, and other items manufactured by Wenzel Friedrich. Limited to a small variety of forms, surviving examples of horn furniture are primarily chairs. The nineteenth century's regard for the style and material is demonstrated by the awards Friedrich received at the New Orleans World's Industrial and Cotton Centennial Exhibition, 1884–1885. Photograph courtesy of the San Antonio Museum Association.

with a variety of upholstery materials, including animal skin, leather, and fabric with attached fringe. Perhaps the best known of the horn chairs in public collections today is the one given to Theodore Roosevelt, now at his family's homestead, Sagamore Hill, on Long Island.[9]

While to the twentieth-century eye horn furniture may seem awkward and uncomfortable, it did represent an innovative use of material. Sitting in a horn chair, one could recall a hunting venture or imagine a ride through vast herds of cattle—romantic evocations of the days when the West was won. (P. T.)

Rustic Plant Stand, 1850–1900 (designer unknown)

In contrast to technically innovative furniture made of bentwood and plywood, this plant stand, with its highly finished top and rough base (Fig. 76), represents an entirely different approach to design and construction. While most cabinetwork in the late nineteenth century carefully disguised joints and seams, "joints in rustic furniture are butted and nailed, and the blemishes of the wood are left unaltered by plane, sandpaper, or varnish."[10] Such methods were in keeping with the philosophy of the transcendentalists and naturalists, whose teachings were widely known during this period.

Rustic architecture, specifically for use in landscaped gardens, had a wide following in England by the mid-eighteenth century, although tree trunks and branches had been used in Italian and German architecture as early as the sixteenth century.[11] The first examples of rustic art in the United States date from the 1830s, when "log and root" architecture was used in cemeteries and later in city and private parks. By the following decade, examples of "rustic" seating were illustrated in American periodicals, including *The Horticulturalist and Journal of Rural Art and Rural Taste*, which featured a whole series of articles on this subject. In 1857, *Godey's Lady's Book* included an article on willow-and-branch garden decorations, with instructions for making them. In order not to waste the winter months, the author recommended using "That season of the year in which there is but little to do in the way of absolute work in the garden, [for] the formation of rustic seats. Trees which are not wanted for their bark are generally cut down in winter, or in very early spring; so that their branches are now generally quite ready to be sawn into the shapes required for making rustic chairs and tables."[12]

While much of the rustic furniture found in camps in the Adirondacks and the Poconos was "homemade," great quantities of it were produced commercially by such firms as O'Brien Brothers of Yonkers, New York, and Laurelton Rustic Manufacturing Company, New Rochelle, New York. Perhaps this plant stand, with its molded top reminiscent of many factory-produced walnut stands of the 1870s, was made in one such rustic furniture manufactory. Rustic furniture in use is shown in the extraordinary gazebo in Fig. 78. (P. T.)

76

76. Rustic plant stand, designer unknown, 1850–1900. Wooden top with molded edge, tree branches, knots, and roots. 28 x 17 x 17 (71.1 x 43.2 x 43.2 cm). In its innovative use of natural materials, this plant stand "may be viewed as a reaction against sophistication and the refinements of the cabinet-maker's art," according to Craig Gilborn (*Antiques*, June 1976, p. 1213). Lent by the Smithsonian Institution Furnishings Collection.

77. A nineteenth-century price list illustrating the variety of rustic furniture forms—the object of revived interest in the early 1980s. Photograph courtesy of the Smithsonian Institution.

78. Rustic gazebo, with rustic furniture behind its trellislike façade. The opportunity for play must have delighted the children. Photograph courtesy of The Society for the Preservation of New England Antiquities.

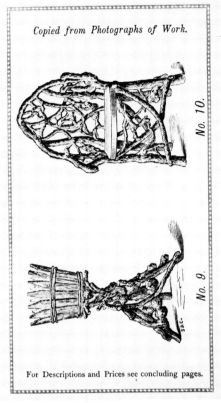

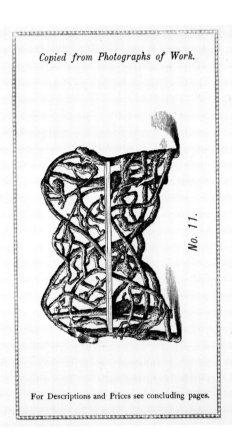

Copied from Photographs of Work.

No. 10.

No. 9.

For Descriptions and Prices see concluding pages.

Copied from Photographs of Work.

No. 11.

For Descriptions and Prices see concluding pages.

PRICE LIST.

No. 1, HANGING BASKETS.

Size,	9 inch	10 inch	11 inch	12 inch.
Price,	$1.25	1.50	1.75	2.00

These Baskets are finished with grape-vine handles, topped with black walnut Knobs holding the Screw eyes.

Baskets finished with looped top handles at same prices.

No. 2, STANDING OR TABLE BASKET.

12 inch Bowls, . . . price, $2.50

No. 3, PORCH OR BAY-WINDOW STAND.

Extreme height, 3 feet 10 inches,
Length of Vase *inside*, 2 feet,
Width   "   "   9½ inches,   price, $8.00
Depth   "   "   7   "

No. 4, PORCH OR LAWN BASKET.

ONE OF OUR RICHEST AND MOST ELABORATE ARTICLES.

Price, $9.00

77

78

FRANK LLOYD WRIGHT (1867–1959)

Frank Lloyd Wright was born in 1867 in Richland Center, Wisconsin. From the age of eleven he lived and attended school in Madison and spent springs and summers working on the large farm of his mother's industrious family in the nearby valley.

Early in 1887, after studying engineering at the University of Wisconsin for about a year, Wright left for Chicago to begin his architectural career. His first job was in the office of J. Lyman Silsbee, whose work was primarily domestic and in the Queen Anne and romanesque revival styles. Wright's talent enabled him to secure work a year later as a draftsman for Adler and Sullivan, then Chicago's most innovative architectural firm. He soon became chief draftsman and a close associate of Louis Sullivan. While working on commercial commissions, including those for the Chicago Auditorium and the Schiller Building, Wright designed dwellings after office hours. Among these were the first designs for the Hillside Home School for the Misses Lloyd Jones in 1887, his own residence in the Chicago suburb of Oak Park, which he built in 1889, and the Charnley house in Chicago, erected in 1891, which he later called "the first modern building."

In 1893 Wright left the firm of Adler and Sullivan to establish his own practice in the Schiller Building (an Adler and Sullivan opus) in downtown Chicago. Initially he designed apartment buildings and scores of houses, some of them inspired by the ornament of Louis Sullivan. In 1897 he moved his practice to Steinway Hall in Chicago and later to his Oak Park house, adding a wing which he had designed in 1895 to serve as an architectural workshop, later known as the "Studio." By 1900, after ten years of experimentation, Wright's artistic principles and ideas were synthesized in the organic unity of his "Prairie houses," where dynamic and dazzling spatial interiors were unified with the external forms, of which the first exemplar was the Willitts house in 1901. He designed both built-in and movable furniture to complement the architecture. The Prairie style—which was of outstanding prophetic distinction—culminated in Wright's plans for the Avery Coonley house, designed in 1907, and the Frederick G. Robie house, designed in 1908.

After twenty-two years of successful architectural practice, Wright left in 1909 to go to Italy, where he prepared a retrospective publication of his work. On his return to the United States in 1911, he built a new home in Spring Green, Wisconsin, which he named Taliesin, the Welsh word for "shining brow." It was destroyed by fire in 1914 but rebuilt the same year. During the next decade, two of Wright's most important commissions were the Midway Gardens in Chicago (1914) and the Imperial Hotel (1914–1922) in Tokyo.

In 1928 Wright married Olgivanna Lazovich, with whom in 1932 he founded the Taliesin Fellowship, the now renowned work-study school, a pioneering venture that promulgated his architectural principles. She had also encouraged him to write his autobiography, of which the first version was published in the same year.

In his late sixties Wright began a new career. With the Edgar Kaufmann house, known as "Fallingwater," designed in 1935, and the S. C. Johnson Administration Building in 1936, and the introduction of the easily and inexpensively constructed "Usonian houses," Wright made bold new advances in architecture and decorative design. Commissions mounted, the Taliesin Fellowship grew, and in 1938 his winter home, Taliesin West, was built in Scottsdale, Arizona. In 1955, when Wright was eighty-eight, his first lines of commercial furniture for Heritage-Henredon and fabrics and wallpapers for Schumacher and Company were introduced for sale to the public. At the time of his death in 1959, his Solomon R.

Guggenheim Museum in New York City was being completed. Wright had become universally recognized as one of the greatest architects. Although an innovator in furniture design as well as architecture, he never patented any of his inventions. The Larkin Building, designed in 1903, contained many "firsts" in the designs for the interior, including some of the earliest metal office furniture in the United States. His metal furniture designs were developed further in the S. C. Johnson Administration Building.

Armchair, 1936

Metal furniture, though common in the nineteenth century, was rarely found in offices until the turn of the twentieth.[13] Moreover, nineteenth-century designers of metal office furniture were indifferent to the capacity of the material, misusing it merely as a substitute for wood. It was Frank Lloyd Wright's furniture for the Larkin Building in 1903 that was the first to express the nature of metal, as well as the nature of the structure.

More than three decades later, Wright's furniture for the S. C. Johnson Administration Building (see Fig. 79) again expresses the character of the material, designed as a natural consequence of his concept for the architecture. The curved and rounded forms of chairs and desks are in harmonious relation to each other, to the rounded, tapered columns which terminate at the ceiling in a delicate sequence of round, widening slabs, to the massive curvilinear wall-corners, and to the rounded glass tubing—where walls meet ceiling in a continuous crown of curved light enveloping the entire building.

The harmony embraces the color as well: the color of floors and walls integral with the russet paint and upholstery of the chairs, still in their original condition and functional in their original setting, a permanent emblem of the principle of organic architecture.

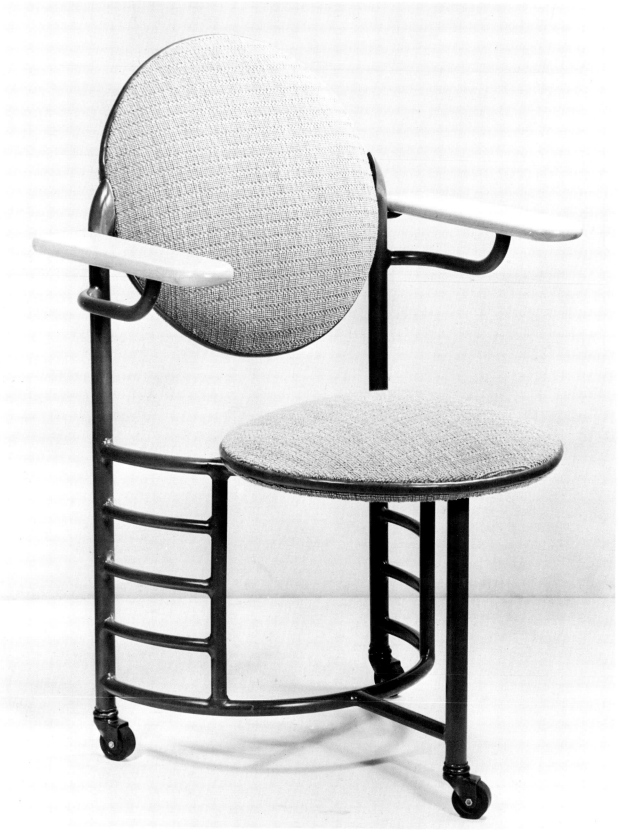

GILBERT ROHDE: see biographical note in Technique section.

Desk, circa 1934

Avant-garde American designers in the 1920s and 1930s experimented with many of the new materials and techniques available, such as chromium-plated tubular steel and plastics. According to a 1934 catalog of the Troy Sunshade Company, titled "Troy Streamline Metal" and featuring designs by Gilbert Rohde, steel "is so strong that long slender members can be formed with sweeping curves which could *not* be produced in wood." Furthermore, the chromium-plated steel "will never tarnish, needs no care, and gives a surface so hard that it is not scratched or marred with ordinary use." Although much chromium-plated tubular steel furniture was intended for office or other commercial uses, it could be adapted equally well to residences. According to the catalog, table and desk tops were available in a number of innovative materials—including linoleum, cork, and lacquered metal—as well as ebony.

This desk (Fig. 80) exemplifies the modern design ideas which Rohde and others pioneered in this country: simple, clean lines and geometric forms that expressed the function of the piece.

The square tubular metal frame—made of a single unbroken piece—provides the basic structure from which the drawer unit is suspended, an idea derived from a Marcel Breuer design for Thonet. The thick black bakelite and lacquered surfaces rest on top of the structure. Each section, of different materials, expresses its function. The combination of black surfaces with the silver-colored chromium and nickel-plated steel was a popular *moderne* color scheme. The asymmetrical composition was also part of the *moderne* aesthetic. Although Rohde's radically simple designs were successful, more traditional styles of furniture continued to be popular with the majority of American consumers.

EDGAR BARTOLUCCI (b. 1918)

Born in Philadelphia, Edgar Bartolucci grew up in Union City, New Jersey. He studied at Parsons School of Design and the Commercial Illustration Studios in New York, New York University, and the Institute of Design in Chicago.

In 1944 he formed a partnership with Jack Waldheim in Chicago. Among the numerous pieces of furniture they designed and manufactured was the "Barwa" chair (Fig. 81). They also created the first Design and Color Laboratory for the Container Corporation of America, with special equipment to test the visual impact on consumers of the corporation's new graphics. During this period their commissions included factories, department store interiors, cafeterias, offices, and exhibits, culminating in the design of the Layton School of Art in Milwaukee, after which their partnership ended.

In the early 1950s Bartolucci moved to New York, where he designed houses, motels, and small factories. He was also copublisher and art director of *Furniture Forum*, a trade magazine. Later in the decade he became involved in designing exhibits and point-of-sale displays for CBS, eventually forming his own company to design and produce such displays for major national firms. In the 1970s he began to manufacture them in Great Britain for use by American firms throughout the European Common Market. Since 1977, when he sold his interest in the company, Bartolucci has been a consultant to major corporations on their point-of-sale problems.

79. Armchair, Frank Lloyd Wright, Spring Green, Wis., designed for the S. C. Johnson Administration Building, 1936. Painted steel, walnut, upholstered seat and back. 36 x 17¾ x 20 (19.4 x 45.1 x 50.8 cm). Lent by S. C. Johnson and Sons Inc.

JACK WALDHEIM (b. 1920)

Although Jack Waldheim spent much of his career in Chicago, he was born and attended public schools in Milwaukee and moved back there in 1951 to teach art classes at the Layton School of Art. He has been a full professor in the Fine Arts Department at the University of Wisconsin at Milwaukee since 1969.

Waldheim studied journalism at the University of Wisconsin in Madison, and graduated from the Institute of Design in Chicago with an M.A. in 1945. For many years he had his own design office at 49 East Ontario Street, Chicago, in partnership with Edgar Bartolucci. The "Barwa" chair, which the partners designed and initially manufactured, was patented by Waldheim; it was later produced by Finkel Outdoor Products in Los Angeles.

"Barwa" Chair, 1947

Based on Le Corbusier's famous lounge chair, this design (Fig. 81)—whose name combines the first three letters of Bartolucci's name and the first two letters of Waldheim's—allows several comfortable postures between sitting and reclining. A logical development of the Marks adjustable chair (Fig. 111), it again shows that concern for physical well-being has been a spur to innovative design. The tubular aluminum frame is light, and therefore quite portable, as well as efficient and clean. Unlike costly upholstery, the canvas slipcover is inexpensive and easily replaced.

The position of the chair can be quickly and simply changed by moving the body forward or backward. Considered in this section because of its innovative use of tubular aluminum, the Barwa chair might also have been included under "comfort" or "portability." Although not intended as a toy, the form has amused and fascinated children, who delight in its many positions.[14]

Mrs. Robert Augustus Leighey recalls purchasing this chair at Modern Design in Washington, D.C., about 1949 for use in her home, which had been designed by Frank Lloyd Wright in 1940 for Mr. and Mrs. Loren Pope. Acquired by the Leigheys in 1946, the building now belongs to the National Trust for Historic Preservation and is known as the Pope-Leighey house.

80. Desk, Gilbert Rohde, New York, c. 1934. Bakelite top, lacquered wood drawer section, chromium-plated tubular steel legs and frame. 29 x 42 x 22 (73.7 x 106.7 x 55.9 cm). Like other industrial designers of the 1930s, Rohde was fascinated by new materials—in this instance bakelite and chromium-plated tubular steel. His experimentation helped create a new aesthetic for the modern period. Manufactured by the Troy Sunshade Company, Troy, Ohio. Lent anonymously.

81. "Barwa" chair, Edgar Bartolucci, Tuxedo, N.Y., and Jack Waldheim, Milwaukee, Wis., design introduced 1947. Tubular aluminum frame, spring-held canvas. 38 x 20¼ x 52 (96.5 x 51.4 x 132.1 cm). Among several comfortable positions of the Barwa chair, reclining with the feet higher than the head was recommended by physicians in the 1930s and 1940s as conducive to good health. Movability and portability were attained by the use of tubular aluminum, a new lightweight material for furniture in the twentieth century, and stretched canvas in place of the traditional heavy upholstery. Patent 2,482,306, September 20, 1949, and 2,659,419, November 17, 1953. "Barwa [in banner]/LOS ANGELES 63, CALIFORNIA/Designed by Bartolucci Waldheim" on paper label on back support. Lent by Mrs. Robert Augustus Leighey.

80

81

DAVIS J. PRATT (b. 1917)

Born in Marion, Indiana, Davis Pratt attended the University of Chicago from 1936 to 1939 and was a member of the charter class of the School of Design in Chicago (later known as the Institute of Design). Before graduating in 1945, he spent four years with the Presentation Branch of the Office of Strategic Services in Washington, D.C., and then in Ceylon. After a short period of free-lance designing in New York, he returned to Chicago in 1946 to teach the foundation course and product design at the Institute of Design, while also doing free-lance architectural and display work. In 1952, after a brief stint designing school equipment for the Welch Manufacturing Company in Chicago, he started his own firm to design and manufacture household furnishings. Since 1957 he has been a lecturer in design at Southern Illinois University, Carbondale, Illinois.

Pratt's entry in The Museum of Modern Art's 1940 Organic Design in Home Furnishings competition became part of the MOMA Art in Progress exhibition in 1944. Pratt's wife, Elsa Kula, and his brother John assisted in the design of his prize-winning chair (Figs. 82–84). Subsequent Pratt projects include the development of an adaptable house (a system of building components enabling the homeowner to expand, modify, or contract his dwelling in response to the changing size and makeup of his family), a demountable camper unit (a build-it-yourself system to mount on standard station wagons), a portable pontoon barge, and low-cost dining furniture.

Chair, circa 1948

Davis Pratt's use of the inflatable tube—a technical achievement developed by the tire industry—was an innovative response to the need for light, portable, and comfortable seating (Fig. 82). By placing an inflated ring in an outer skin of heavy pile fabric, Pratt distributed the resilience over a larger surface. The ring, which was separated into two parts to form the back and seat, was placed on a metal frame that could be folded flat for shipping. "I was led to the inflatable cushioning idea," Pratt says, "by a general dissatisfaction with the complexity of spring and pad cushioning. As far as I know, I was the first to attempt this, especially in terms of utilizing an automobile inner tube for the purpose."[15] The chair was not patented. Attempts to have it put into commercial production were unsuccessful, despite its low estimated cost. As a co-winner with Charles Eames's metal shell chair of the second prize for seating units in The Museum of Modern Art's International Competition for Low-Cost Furniture Design, 1948, it was chosen for the MOMA design collection.[16] Pratt produced about two hundred of a prototype closely related to his prize-winning design; other inflatable chairs were developed from the prototype.

The form pioneered by Pratt has continued to be popular. Its successors include Laurence Koch's inflatable chair, a 1964 version in plastic by the Danish designer Verner Panton, and the numerous Italian versions produced today.

82. Chair, Davis J. Pratt, Chicago, Ill., designed c. 1948. Inflated rubber tube, fabric cover, rubber-tipped metal legs. 26 x 25⅛ x 29½ (66 x 63.8 x 74.9 cm). Pratt's use of an inflatable rubber tube, an important innovative application of new technology and materials to achieve portability and comfort, has inspired many successors. Lent by Davis J. Pratt.

83. Pratt's inflatable chair shown disassembled with inflated inner tube, skin, and frame.

84. The Pratt chair with the inflatable tube placed inside the skin, constructed to shape it into a back and seat.

82

83

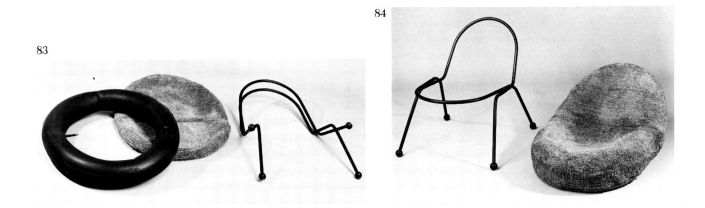

84

CHARLES EAMES: see biographical note in Technique section.

Low Armchair (LAR Chair), 1949

This Eames chair is important in the history of innovative furniture because it is the first to have a seat of molded polyester (popularly known as fiberglass)—the original commercial use of this material for a consumer product. It was, according to Edgar Kaufmann Jr., "the first one-piece plastic chair to feature the natural surface of its material."[17] The chair appears in several variations: with metal rod legs, or wire with wood rockers, or, as in this instance (Fig. 85), with a metal-wire central supporting pedestal (hence the chair is sometimes referred to as the "Eiffel Tower"). There were several color and upholstery options.

The chair was developed from an award-winning design (joint second prize) in the 1948 International Competition for Low-Cost Furniture Design, directed by Edgar Kaufmann Jr. and sponsored by The Museum of Modern Art. Intended to meet both residential and commercial needs, it was put into production by the Herman Miller Furniture Company in 1949. According to a contemporary Herman Miller catalog, the "plastic shells of these armchairs are molded of a thermosetting resin reinforced with glass fibers,"[18] a combination of materials used in aircraft production for high resistance to impact and weather. The original competition entry, made of metal, was created in collaboration with Ray Eames, Don Albinson, Francis Bishop, James Connor, Robert Jacobsen, Charles Kratka, Frederick Usher Jr., and members of the Engineering Department at the University of California, Los Angeles.

The LAR chair is a further extension of the ideas developed by Charles Eames and Eero Saarinen nearly a decade earlier when their joint entry won first prize in the Museum of Modern Art's Organic Design in Home Furnishings competition. The relation between the two versions is confirmed in Eames's comment on Mies van der Rohe's 1946 sketch for a "conchoidal" chair (Fig. 87), designed to be produced in plastic: "The plastic shell forms of the 1950 fiberglass chairs were essentially refinements and adaptations of resin-bonded-wood chairs that Eero Saarinen and I designed in 1940."[19] The 1940 design was limited by the nature of the material; the attachment of wooden or metal legs was always a problem. It was overcome with the use of fiberglass, which was flexible yet had great strength and endurance, as well as being easy to maintain.

One of the entries in the 1948 low-cost furniture exhibition was an experimental lounge chair (Fig. 88), the result of research on the use of resin-impregnated wood fiber by James Prestini, Robert Lewis, James Speyer, and Daniel Brenner of the Armour Research Foundation. Their report on the material won an award. The team's entry, with seat back, arms, and legs devised for production in a single unit, was inspired by the abovementioned Mies chair.

Eames's chair was also developed as a stacking side chair (Fig. 86). Another variation made use of bent wire rather than plastic, with an upholstered pad in fabric or leather. So many imitations of the basic Eames plastic chair have been made that it is extremely familiar throughout the country. Production of the simple form continues with Herman Miller, but elaborate versions such as the "Eiffel Tower" are no longer manufactured.

85. Low armchair (LAR chair), Charles Eames, Venice, Calif., design introduced 1949. Molded polyester shell, metal wire, rubber shock mounts. 31 x 24⅞ x 24 (78.7 x 63.2 x 61 cm). Plastic offered great potential for new sculptural forms. This chair is a development of the 1940 prize-winning design in wood by Eames and Eero Saarinen. Manufactured by Herman Miller Inc. Lent by the Herman Miller Inc. Resource Center.

86

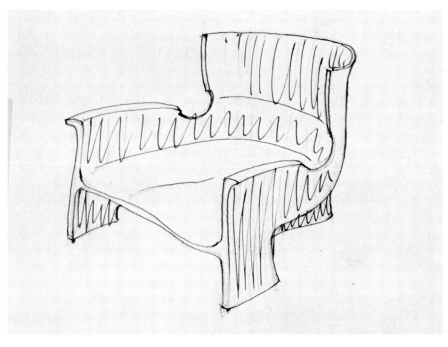

87

86. Manufacturing the LAR plastic chair, one of several variants of the basic design. In the 1940 wood version, attaching the legs to the body was difficult. The use of durable and flexible molded polyester for the body solved the problem. Photograph courtesy of Herman Miller Inc.

87. Drawing of a "conchoidal" chair, Mies van der Rohe, 1946, designed for manufacture in plastic but never produced. Eames saw a relation between Mies's design and his own and Eero Saarinen's 1940 resin-bonded wood chairs. Photograph courtesy of The Museum of Modern Art.

88. Lounge chair, Robert E. Lewis, James L. Prestini, and Armour Research Foundation (which included James Speyer and Daniel Brenner), designed in 1948 for The Museum of Modern Art's International Competition for Low-Cost Furniture Design. Inspired by Mies's "conchoidal" form, this prototype-only chair experiments in the use of resin-impregnated wood fiber. The design team won a special $2,500 prize for research on the material. Speyer and Brenner were students and associates of Mies. Photograph courtesy of The Museum of Modern Art.

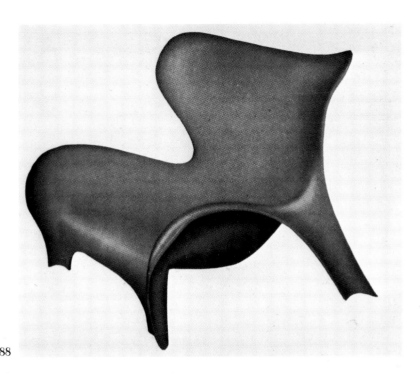

88

EERO SAARINEN (1910–1961)

The son of Finnish-American architect Eliel Saarinen, Eero Saarinen was raised in an environment that encouraged experimentation and fostered his innate talent for drafting and designing. From the age of five, Saarinen demonstrated his considerable artistic abilities, sitting on the floor of his father's large studio to draw his own versions of architectural details.

In 1923, the Saarinen family came to the United States, Eliel having won second prize in 1922 in the international Chicago Tribune Tower contest. Three years later Eliel received the commission for what was to become his major American architectural monument, the buildings for the Cranbrook school complex in Bloomfield Hills, Michigan (1925–1940s).

At nineteen Eero began designing the furniture for the adjacent Kingswood School for Girls (1929–1933). His formal education in this period included studying sculpture in Paris for a year and attending the Yale School of Architecture, where he received so many prizes that when he graduated with honors in 1934, he was given a medal for winning the most awards. Granted a traveling fellowship to Europe as well, he took the opportunity to return to Finland, carrying out several commissions there, among them the design of a Swedish theater in Helsinki in conjunction with his father and Jarl Ecklund.

Returning to Michigan in 1937, Saarinen became associated with his father in some of the most important architectural achievements during the second quarter of the twentieth century. He is perhaps best known as the architect of the General Motors Technical Center near Detroit, the chapel and auditorium at the Massachusetts Institute of Technology, Dulles Airport, the John Deere Building, and the TWA terminal at Kennedy International Airport.

His furniture has also been important, beginning with his and Charles Eames's famous entry in The Museum of Modern Art's Organic Design in Home Furnishings competition in 1940 (Fig. 50).

Saarinen's major furniture designs have been manufactured by Knoll. Florence Schust Knoll (now Bassett), wife of Hans Knoll, the founder of his own furniture company in 1939, was a close family friend of the Saarinens while a young student at Kingswood School. In 1946 she suggested that Saarinen "concentrate first on a big comfortable chair that [she] could curl up in," an idea which reached fruition in the molded plastic "womb chair."[20]

Saarinen's interest in furniture continued in the 1950s, when he designed chairs and tables with only three parts: top, stem, and bolt (Fig. 90). Attempting to replace "the ugly clutter of cases and legs going in different directions," he was able to achieve the stability of four legs with a single porcelain-enameled aluminum pedestal that did not need to be weighted at the bottom.

It was Saarinen's understanding of materials and his architect's sense of balance and good design that allowed him to achieve an exceptional level of proficiency in furniture design. From his father, Eero had learned a lesson which was critical for his success: "Always design a thing by considering it in its next larger context—a chair in a room, a room in a house, a house in an environment, an environment in a city plan." Saarinen's womb chair clearly embodies this principle, as do his extraordinary architectural creations for General Motors and TWA. (P. T.)

Easy Chair ("Womb Chair"), 1948

Eero Saarinen took advantage of the latest developments in plastics technology, specifically fiberglass, in the design for his easy chair (Fig. 89), on which he began working in 1946. Anxious to produce molded plastic furniture, Saarinen and Knoll were able to convince a boat manufacturer to fabricate a chair shell of molded fiberglass and resin. While the basic trend toward the reduction of parts through molding had been started by Saarinen and Charles Eames with their 1940 design for a molded plywood multicurved shell, the availability of plastics following World War II brought the idea of minimizing parts to a new level.

Although the search for innovative materials was obviously of consequence to Saarinen and his sponsors, even more important was Saarinen's response to the "need for a large and really comfortable chair." Saarinen wrote at length about his "womb chair" in 1957, explaining how he arrived at the design:

"People sit differently today than in the Victorian era. They want to sit lower and they like to slouch. In my first post-war chair, I attempted to shape the slouch in an organized way by giving support for the back as well as the seat, shoulders and head. The 'womb' chair also has three planes of support. Then, there is the fact that a comfortable position, even if it were the most comfortable in the world, would not be so for very long. The necessity of changing one's position is an important factor often forgotten in chair design. So, too, is the fact that an equal distribution of weight over a large surface of the body is important. The womb chair attempts to achieve a psychological comfort by providing a great big cup-like shell into which you can curl and pull up your legs (something which women seem especially to like to do). A chair . . . should not only look well as a piece of sculpture in a room when no one is in it, it should also be a flattering background when someone is in it—especially the female occupant."[21]

Anyone who has sat in Saarinen's womb chair, which remains popular today, would attest to his success in realizing his aims. Another feature of the design was that it could be mass-produced, since it employed simple parts—shell, tubular steel legs, and fabric-covered latex foam upholstery which could be tacked directly to the shell.

Saarinen's womb chair follows in a direct line from nineteenth-century bentwood furniture and the experiments with molded plywood in the early decades of the twentieth century. It also anticipates his later efforts to eliminate even more parts, which resulted in his pedestal chair and table (Fig. 90), "a startling and elegant shape composed of a shell of plastic and fiberglass mounted on a single aluminum pedestal."[22] While the use of molded plastic is today unremarkable, it was in 1948 an exciting innovation for the entire furniture industry. (P. T.)

89. Easy chair ("womb chair"), Eero Saarinen, Bloomfield Hills, Mich., design introduced 1948. Tubular steel legs, latex foam rubber over molded reinforced plastic shell. 35½ x 20½ x 40 (90.2 x 52.1 x 101.6 cm). Like Charles Eames, Eero Saarinen developed the technology they had jointly begun c. 1940 for reducing the number of chair parts by a molding process. Saarinen was able to convince a boat manufacturer to produce a shell of molded plastic, which led to his famous womb chair. Manufactured by Knoll International. Lent by the manufacturer.

90

HARRY BERTOIA (1915–1978)

Born in Italy, Harry Bertoia is nonetheless claimed as an American designer because he received all his artistic training in this country. Starting with his years at Cass Technical High School in Detroit, where he studied drafting and metalworking, Bertoia acquired the skills of a multitalented craftsman whose work included sculpture, jewelry, graphics, and furniture. In 1937–1943, he studied at Cranbrook Academy, where he met such leading figures in furniture design as Eliel and Eero Saarinen and Charles Eames. It was also at Cranbrook that he met the artist Brigitta Valentiner, whom he married in 1943.

Since metalworking was pre-eminent in his artistic training, it is not surprising that when Bertoia went to work for Knoll International in 1950, he began exploring the potential of metal in furniture design. Given free reign to experiment at Knoll's studios in East Greenville, Pennsylvania, he produced his well-known diamond chair in 1952. After that, Bertoia turned his attention to various forms of sculpture, from multiplane construction to welded bronzes to spill casting, using a variety of innovative techniques that reflected his persistent interest in the potential of metal. (P. T.)

Armchair ("Diamond Chair"), 1952

Incorporating materials which modern technology made practical for mass production, Harry Bertoia's design for Knoll International has become a modern classic (Fig. 91). Frequently referred to as the "diamond chair," it consists of 1) a steel cradle made of welded wires which crisscross in diamond-shaped sections; 2) side braces which serve as legs and also support the cradle; 3) a foam rubber cushion which is upholstered in a variety of materials and which can be detached for cleaning.

Because of the tremendous popularity of the diamond chair, it is difficult to comprehend that only thirty years ago such a form was merely an idea in the mind of one man and required the cooperation of an entire Knoll team in order to prepare it for production.

As a sculptor, Bertoia was as concerned with the chair's aesthetic success as with its function and marketability. Taking his inspiration from a plastic-coated wire dish rack, Bertoia began work on this self-directed project in 1950 at the Knoll experimental studios in East Greenville, Pennsylvania. In two years he had developed a full range of related chairs using welded steel rods. Of these chairs, Bertoia wrote: "In the sculpture I am concerned

90. Pedestal chairs and tables, Eero Saarinen. The shells are plastic and fiberglass; the pedestals, aluminum. These elegant designs are the result of Saarinen's experimentation with materials and his effort to eliminate parts. Photograph courtesy of Knoll International.

primarily with space, form and the characteristics of metal. In the chairs many functional problems have to be satisfied first . . . but when you get right down to it, the chairs are studies in space, form and metal too. If you will look at them, you will find that they are mostly made of air, just like sculpture. Space passes right through them "[23]

Here Bertoia was expressing the strong relationship between design and function, and the appropriateness of the sculptor's role in the manufacture of seating furniture. As was observed in 1952, "furniture is becoming either an integral part of the architectural shell or else sculpture, and . . . the chairs in particular . . . now claim the eye from every angle."[24]

Innovative uses of material are also of interest to the sculptor. Bertoia's employment of a strong wire mesh framework was made possible by advances in metallurgy and metalworking techniques derived from the production of new military hardware in World War II.

The tradition of using wire mesh in furniture construction had begun a hundred years earlier, with George Hunzinger's armchair (Fig. 64) and, later, the development of wire mesh bed springs. These forms, however, depended on a wooden or metal frame to support the mesh elements. Bertoia revolutionized the concept by incorporating the support in the mesh itself: the diamond-shaped grids bend outward to form armrests and the chair back arches concavely to cradle the human spine and shoulders. Building upon the innovation of the nineteenth century and upon Eames's wire techniques, Bertoia carried the potential of the material one step further. (P. T.)

91. Armchair ("diamond chair"), Harry Bertoia, East Greenville, Pa., design introduced 1952. Welded wires. 30½ x 33¾ x 28 (77.5 x 85.7 x 71.1 cm): Constructed of materials that can be mass-produced, the "diamond chair" has become a classic twentieth-century furniture form. Like Isamu Noguchi, Bertoia brought his aesthetic and technical training as a sculptor to furniture design. Manufactured by Knoll International. Lent by the manufacturer.

91

FRANK O. GEHRY (b. 1929)

Born in Toronto, Canada, Frank O. Gehry, FAIA, went to California as a truck driver, but in 1949 began studying fine arts and architecture at the University of Southern California. During these early years Gehry was primarily influenced by the California modernist school of post and beam architecture with Japanese overtones.

After a brief period as an architect with Victor Gruen Associates in California, Gehry headed east, where he served in the U.S. Army, attended the Harvard Graduate School of Design, and worked with landscape architect Hideo Sasaki as an architectural designer and planner in Boston. Returning to California in 1957, Gehry has been in private practice as an architect and furniture designer since 1962. Frank O. Gehry and Associates Inc., located in Santa Monica, has from its inception attracted a steady contingent of young architects who have been impressed with Gehry's forward-looking ideas.

One such innovative area has been Gehry's interest in furniture made of laminated cardboard. These sturdy, economical, and aesthetically appealing pieces, marketed under the name "Easy Edges," have attracted wide notice among design critics. Gehry's architectural commissions also reflect his experimental approach, suggested by such buildings as the Ron Davis Studio/Residence, work for the Rouse Company, and his own controversial residence. Gehry's practice is marked by the constant give and take between art and architecture, a mutuality clearly apparent in his cardboard furniture. (P. T.)

Contour Rocker, 1970

The use of paper in furniture construction has been documented as early as the second century A.D., when the Chinese began to use papier-mâché for useful and decorative objects. Made of molded and decorated pulp, lacquered for durability, these objects were never as popular in the United States as in Europe or the Orient, although there were several small papier-mâché factories located in Connecticut in the nineteenth century. An important reason for the success of such furniture was its economy, since papier-mâché is composed of waste that is normally discarded.

The paper furniture of Frank Gehry was likewise conceived with economy in mind. Commissioned to design the interiors for the Joseph Magnin stores in Costa Mesa and Almaden, California, Gehry was disturbed by the costliness of store fixtures which quickly became obsolete. His persistent interest in new products and their application to total building design led him to think of using cardboard in place of more conventional fixture materials.

While it was not possible, because of the construction schedule, to put these ideas into production for the Magnin stores, shortly thereafter Gehry and Associates did begin to manufacture "Easy Edges," a line of commercial and residential furnishings made of laminated layers of corrugated cardboard. The designs were durable, structurally sound, economical, and disposable (Figs. 92 and 93).

Gehry's innovation attracted quick and positive notice. In 1970, when his furniture had only just been put in circulation, the authors of *New Furniture* singled out his designs as the only truly experimental work produced that year.[25] His new uses of material warranted Gehry's application for patent rights, originally filed in 1971. This first application was abandoned, owing to "certain economic disadvantages because of the waste material which may occur in some cases. Moreover, it is impractical to partially assemble such furniture for subsequent reassemble in order to reduce shipping expenses."[26]

The problems with the 1971 application were overcome by the following year when Gehry again filed for a patent. The solution, which resulted in furniture which looked essentially the same as the earlier model, incorporated the following changes: "Each of the individual pieces

92. Contour rocker, Frank O. Gehry, Santa Monica, Calif., design introduced 1970. Cardboard. 26 x 42 x 23 (66 x 106.7 x 58.4 cm). While the use of paper in furniture construction was not new, Gehry's handling of it was. Instead of molding pulped paper, as in the earlier papier mâché, he laminated layers of cardboard with the corrugations running in opposite directions, making it possible to produce sturdy, durable, inexpensive furniture with strong curves and angles. Patent 4,067,615, January 10, 1978. Lent by Eleanor K. Johnson.

93

is separately cut to the desired shape so that the amount of waste material is substantially reduced. Moreover, the construction is such that the individual parts may be manufactured at one location and shipped to a second location for subsequent assembly. Hence, primarily, the present invention provides economic advantages over the method and article [of the earlier model]."[27]

The patent was issued in 1978. In the intervening years, while the patent was still pending, Gehry received constant recognition for his corrugated cardboard designs. In 1972, for example, his experimental furniture received one of the top ten awards of the Resources Council's Second Annual Product Design Awards Program, given to designers and manufacturers "for excellence of adaptation or reproduction, innovative design, imaginative use of materials and color and craftsmanship."

Gehry's cardboard forms are truly innovative because, unlike earlier paper furniture, they depend neither on molding nor on assembling paper bent like a box. His method of laminating cardboard, with the corrugations running in opposite directions, made it possible to achieve strong curves and angles, just as John Henry Belter's method of bending wood allowed him to push wood to its limits. While Gehry's designs are ultimately aesthetically pleasing, by and large the most significant breakthrough was his ability to produce usable furniture at low cost. (P. T.)

93. Cardboard chair and ottoman, Frank O. Gehry, Santa Monica, Calif., design introduced 1970. The makers describe the material as scuff-resistant, with a "suede-like surface . . . a velvet touch." Photograph courtesy of Frank O. Gehry.

PAUL TUTTLE (b. 1918)

Although born in St. Louis, Missouri, Paul Tuttle has spent most of his thirty-year design career in California. After four years in the U. S. Army during World War II, Tuttle went to Los Angeles, where he studied briefly at the Arts Center School and then began a part-time working arrangement with Alvin Lustig, the influential designer and teacher. Because of Tuttle's lack of traditional design training, his approach was very original and analytical. During this period, his neighbor was a retired cabinetmaker who gave advice on Tuttle's first furniture—a chair, a table, and a bench. In 1951 the chair received an award in the Designer-Craftsman exhibition at the Saint Louis Art Museum as a counterstatement to the industrialization of the World War II period. Charles Eames selected the table as an example of the successful adaptation of traditional craftsmanship to contemporary design, and it was shown in 1951 in The Museum of Modern Art's Good Design exhibition organized by Edgar Kaufmann for Chicago's Merchandise Mart.

Tuttle was for a time a member of the Frank Lloyd Wright Fellowship at Taliesin West, Scottsdale, Arizona; Wright admired his originality and exploration. When he eventually

94. High stool from the "Leonardo Collection," Paul Tuttle, Santa Barbara, Calif., design introduced 1979. Steel or ashwood legs, steel-reinforced self-skin polyurethane foam seat and back, steel stretcher. 42 x 20 x 19⅝ (106.7 x 50.8 x 49.9 cm). Tuttle has used new materials here for the seat and crest rail of a traditional furniture form. Manufactured by Strässle International, Switzerland. Lent by Atelier International Ltd.

94

returned to Los Angeles after traveling in Europe, Tuttle began work for the Welton Beckett office, designing merchandising spaces, most notably for the Joseph Magnin stores. Subsequently he designed furniture and residential interiors for the architectural office of Thornton Ladd. One of his total concepts for a residence was given the 1956 Progressive Architecture Award for interiors.

In 1956 Tuttle moved to Santa Barbara, where he received several architectural commissions and designed a number of pieces of furniture which were fabricated. Later the Swiss industrialist Hans Grether commissioned him to design the spaces and furnishings of his corporate offices in Basel. Tuttle continues as design consultant to this firm. He has also been associated with Strässle International, a Swiss furniture manufacturer known for fine craftsmanship and experimental design.

Until the early 1960s Tuttle had worked exclusively in wood, but he designed some plastic furniture for the Strässle factory, and then began to work in metal. One result was a 1975 design for a metal chair which employed strap steel in a wide radius intersected by rigid arrow-straight tubing, indicative of his engineering ability.

Although Tuttle has generally designed furniture for expensive custom manufacture, he has also accepted commissions aimed at a broader distribution and price range, such as some pieces for the Landes Manufacturing Company using easily fabricated, interchangeable, brightly painted tubular forms. In all of his designs and experimentation, Tuttle is known for his inventive exploration of materials.[28]

High Stool, 1979

Commissioned by Strässle International of Switzerland to create a line of commercial seating, Paul Tuttle has adapted innovative materials to a strongly traditional form. This design (Fig. 94), part of his "Leonardo Collection," is very much in the manner of Hans Wegner. It is based on the nineteenth-century Windsor clerk's stool, itself a longlegged adaptation of the low-back Windsor. Interestingly, Tuttle maintains the crested rail and saddle seat, originally shaped and carved for comfort. However, unlike its ascetic wooden predecessors, this chair's seat and back are molded of polyurethane foam, virtually turning them into cushions.

The molds for the chair parts were initially carved in wood by Tuttle. Each contoured seat and back comes out of the mold with a tough outer skin and a soft, pliable core. Washable, replaceable, and comfortable, the foam components of the chair enhance its desirability for commercial use. Tuttle has reaffirmed a nineteenth-century form in twentieth-century terms.

The "Leonardo Collection" was first introduced by Atelier International at the 12th National Exposition of Interior Contract Furnishings (Neocon) at the Merchandise Mart in Chicago, June 1980.

COMFORT

The desire for comfort influenced English and American furniture design in the eighteenth century, although there were many exceptions, especially among the elegant neoclassical styles. It was in the nineteenth century, however, that comfort became a key constituent of furniture forms, and it has remained a concern in the twentieth as well.

In seating, the concept of comfort is best illustrated by the easy chair—a form which, as Nikolaus Pevsner has pointed out, hardly existed before the Victorian period.[1] The wing chair, an English invention of the seventeenth century, and the *bergère*, a French invention in the eighteenth, are types of the easy chair still popular today.

Nineteenth-century furniture forms designed for comfort were derived from seventeenth- and eighteenth-century prototypes. The sofa from the Long Gallery at Knole, circa 1620, was admired by Charles L. Eastlake and illustrated in his *Hints on Household Taste* (1868) (Fig. 96). Its rectangular shape complied with his reform precepts, disclosing the wooden framework construction, whose joints were tenoned and pinned together in a manner Eastlake esteemed; an iron rack at each end, by which the sides could be raised or lowered, permitted the feather-stuffed sofa to be used as a "day bed." Although designed without a single curve, wrote Eastlake approvingly in *Hints on Household Taste,* "After two hundred and fifty years of use, this sofa is still *comfortable. . . .*"

One of the most important inventions relating to comfort appeared in 1828, when Samuel Pratt patented his spiral or coiled inner spring. Loudon illustrates the device only in connection with mattresses, but it made possible what is now understood as deep traditional upholstery for chairs and other forms of seating. Discussing the development of the upholstered chair in the twentieth century, Dennis Young has observed:

"The traditional approach to the manufacture of upholstered chairs was the production of a skeleton of solid wood members jointed together in such a way that voids occurred in the parts of the chair where the concentrations of a sitting body weight were greatest. These voids were then spanned and filled with combinations of webbing, hessian, steel springs, hair and cotton linters to produce controlled resilient supporting areas. It was through the combination of rigid skeleton and resilient 'flesh and muscle' that this traditional structure gave flexible support and cushioning to various body weights and sizes in a wide range of changeable sitting positions."[2]

As new means of providing "resilient 'flesh and muscle' " were discovered—rubber webbing, latex, and other synthetic materials, and the tension spring—innovative forms of furniture emerged. The 1928 invention of latex foam, in particular, gave rise to new upholstery techniques, seen for example in Saarinen's "womb chair" (Fig. 89). Complete upholstered units, like Gilbert Rohde's modular designs, could be molded in one operation (Fig. 119). The 1920s also produced other solutions to the need for resilience, as in Marcel Breuer's and Mies van der Rohe's pioneering use of tubular steel to give resilience through the cantilever principle, an innovation also developed by American designers, including

Rohde. The traditional deep easy chair that survived alongside these nonupholstery solutions to the problem of comfort sometimes took on a "blocky" form in the 1920s, as seen in Rohde's drawing (Fig. 119), becoming lower, more massive, with wider arms.

Despite the fact that comfort has been a primary concern for twentieth-century designers, some of their innovative forms have failed to fulfill this function; one example is the "Hardoy" version of the sling chair, which does not permit graceful sitting or effortless rising. And although Charles Eames's famous plywood chairs were designed with the contour of the human body in mind, they were not entirely comfortable either. As George Nelson has pointed out, comfort in seating design is related to time as well as form. His own slat bench was comfortable for brief periods, but for longer use the body requires a form that "provides for a maximum of shifting around."[3]

A type of innovative furniture which has fulfilled the desire for comfort especially well is that designed for invalids, which had an enormous influence on residential furniture in the eighteenth and nineteenth centuries. According to its patent specifications, the Marks folding chair was originally designed as an "Invalid's Chair" (Fig. 111), but because of its great comfort it became popular for the healthy in many American parlors. At the London Crystal Palace Exhibition in 1851, Pevsner comments, "there was quite a range of intelligently devised furniture for invalids . . . numerous chairs designed on the principle re-invented for the able-bodies of a more informal age by Marcel Breuer and Le Corbusier. . . ."[4]

A twentieth-century parallel to these forms is the "Warren chair" by Roger Kenneth Leib (Fig. 122) which can be tipped back without lifting the feet off the floor or markedly increasing the angle between the back and femurs, as do airplane seats. It also enables the sitter to "move" occasionally—for circulation and exercise—yet it has no rockers, spring mechanisms, or platform base. The same spring-steel construction that allows a rocking motion also helps the sitter to rise from the chair, assisted if necessary by the forward extension of the armrests. Originally intended for invalids, Leib's chair has proved so comfortable that interior designers have adopted it for residential use.

95

95. Illustration by Tenniel from *Through the Looking Glass*, 1870, showing Alice curled up in an easy chair. Comfort has been achieved here in an upholstered and tufted armchair whose wooden frame is still a visible and important part of the construction. Photograph courtesy of the Macmillan Company Ltd.

96

96. Multipurpose up-
holstered sofa from the
Long Gallery at Knole, as
depicted in Charles L.
Eastlake's *Hints on Household Taste*, 1876 edition.
"By means of an iron rack
attached to each end,"
Eastlake explained, "the
sides can be raised or lowered to any angle, thus
enabling the sofa to be used
as a couch or a settee, at
pleasure." The movable
sides, back, and seat cushions were stuffed with
feathers.

97. Invalid furniture was
enormously important in
the development of furni-
ture forms for comfort, as
exemplified by this reclining wheelchair shown
alongside an ordinary
rocking chair. Photograph
courtesy of The Society for
the Preservation of New
England Antiquities.

97

Armchair, circa 1880 (designer unknown)

The development of the overall upholstered chair in the nineteenth century is one of the most important but overlooked aspects of Victorian furniture. Later depictions of Edwardians relaxing in comfortable overstuffed chairs are numerous (Figs. 99 and 100). The chief innovation (discussed by Giedion in *Mechanization Takes Command* and by others) was hidden beneath the high-style upholstered surface: the spring and cast-iron frame construction which replaced the wooden frame and stuffing of eighteenth-century designs. The completely upholstered chair was innovative aesthetically as well, exhibiting a strongly sculptural form instead of the traditional rail and stile construction.

This chair (Fig. 98) has a Baltimore history, and is upholstered in a so-called Turkey carpet said to have been given by Czar Nicholas I to Thomas Winans of that city in 1851. Although this type upholstery was fairly common, few of these chairs have survived with their original covering. The short, turned legs (with casters for movability) are covered by fringe—another aesthetic consideration—which gives continuity to the upholstered form. The formation of arms and back in separate planes is unusual.

98. Armchair, designer unknown, c. 1880. Wood, metal frame, "Turkish carpet" upholstery, fringe. 30⅛ x 30¾ x 24½ (76.6 x 78 x 62 cm). This chair illustrates the development of the spring and cast-iron frame, which replaced the earlier wooden frame and stuffing seen in Fig. 96. The upholstery was typical of the period and may be original. Lent by the National Museum of History and Technology, Smithsonian Institution, 67.6.

98

99

99. Although intended to depict a mantel design, this engraving shows equally well the upholstered easy chair, a variation on the "Turkish chair." The ottoman, a typical Victorian form, enhanced the sitter's comfort. From Henry Hudson Holly, *Modern Dwelling in Town and County.* (New York, 1878).

100. The use of the spring and iron frame achieved both comfort and a sculptural form. Because of widespread neglect and lack of appreciation, few of these nineteenth-century upholstered chairs have survived. Photograph courtesy of The Society for the Preservation of New England Antiquities.

100

THOMAS E. WARREN (working 1849–1852)

In the patent specifications for his armchair, Thomas E. Warren identified himself as from Troy, New York, a great ironmaking center. He is listed in *Prescott & Wilson's Troy Directory* between 1849 and 1852 as a broker, at 175 River Street, with his residence at 185 Third. The 1849–50 directory lists John R. Warren, carpenter, and the 1855–56 edition lists Greenman and Warren, cabinet furniture, 312 River Street. According to John H. White, Warren's 1851 invention of a sheet-iron car was one of the earliest designs for a railroad passenger car of this material. White surmised that Warren's design was inspired by architectural ironwork manufactured in Troy, since the classical and Venetian-style mountings have a strong architectural flavor. Patent No. 10,142 was granted on October 18, 1853, but it has not been ascertained whether any cars were actually constructed.[5]

The American Chair Company, manufacturer of Warren's chair, was known for its reclining seats for railroad cars. From 1829 through 1858 there is only one listing for the company in the Troy directories; that was at 117 and 119 River Street. At the Franklin Institute's Twentieth Annual Exhibition in 1850, the firm received a "second premium" for "Spring Iron Chairs," making it one of the few non-Philadelphia companies that exhibited and/or received recognition during the thirty-year history of these annual trade fairs. Their 1850 entry was listed in the catalog as "Cabinet Furniture—upholstery #2305 6 Centripetal Spring Chairs, made by American Chair Co., Troy, New York, deposited by Stafford & Cookman, Philadelphia."[6] Stafford and Cookman, the cabinetmaking firm which "deposited" the chairs, may have been the local representative for the American Chair Company. According to Pevsner, "The exhibitions of the American Chair Co. [at the London Crystal Palace Exhibition, 1851] are a specially enlightening case of how the technically adventurous was expressed in artistic terms. . . ."[7]

Centripetal Spring Armchair, 1849

A remarkable invention of its day, this revolving spring-based armchair (Fig. 101) was represented in several variations at the 1851 London Crystal Palace Exhibition (Fig. 103). *The Illustrated Exhibitor* praised the virtues of this "very handsome" piece: "The framework . . . is made wholly of cast iron, the base consisting of four ornamental bracket feet, mounted on castors, and secured to a center piece, to which eight elliptical springs are attached. The springs are connected to another center piece, which sustains the seat of the chair on a vertical pin; on this, the chair-seat revolves, while at the same time the springs sustaining the seat from the under-frame give to it an agreeable elasticity in every direction. The freedom with which the chair may be turned on its center, renders it very convenient to a person who may want to turn to his library-shelf or side table, as he can do so without leaving his seat. The castings are good, and the design neat and pretty; the whole reflecting much credit on the inventor and on American art."

Warren's patent was for a new method of constructing springs (Fig. 104), which he detailed in the specifications: "the employment of two or more sets of bow shaped or other regular curved leaves, substantially such as herein described, being made of metal of the same thickness and breadth throughout, or nearly so, and firmly attached by their ends or bearings to the boxes or other fixture by which they are held in place, each leaf composing said springs working separate from the others, as above specified, and firmly fastened at their ends or bearings, as applied to chairs and other similar purposes, as described and represented."

In 1850 Warren used similar springs in his patented "Improvement in Car Seat Backs" (Fig. 105) for railroad-car chairs. In 1853 he patented a design for manufacturing "Iron Carriage Bodies for Railroads and Other Purposes."

Warren's chair is important because its spring devices, invented to increase the comfort of railroad travel, were also incorporated in parlor furniture. It is also one of the earliest known American designs using a cast-iron frame for seating which, when combined with upholstery, was both comfortable and multifunctional.

Several versions of the chair have survived; examples can be seen in The Metropolitan Museum of Art, The Saint Louis Art Museum, the Smithsonian Institution, and The Hermitage.

101. Centripetal spring armchair, Thomas E. Warren, Troy, N.Y. Cast iron, steel spring, painted wood, sheet-metal back, twentieth-century velvet upholstery. 39¾ x 24½ x 30½ (101 x 62.2 x 77.5 cm). Spring-based construction, seen in railway car seats of the period, is here successfully adapted for use in parlor furniture. Manufactured by the American Chair Company. Patent 6,740, September 25, 1849. "17" painted in black ink, in script, on bottom of chair. Lent by Elinor Merrell.

101

102

103

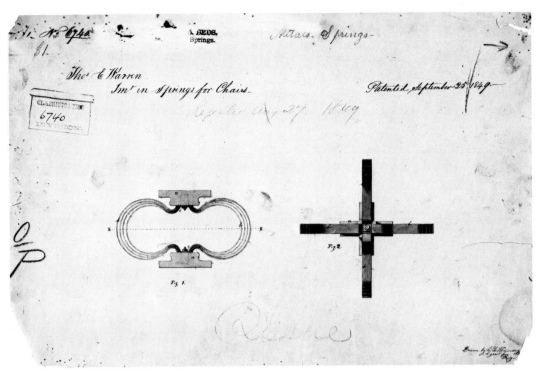

102. A number of variations on Warren's chair were manufactured—with or without arms, fringe, and headrest. This example, covered in green brocade, has an elaborate version of the cast-iron base (as does the chair in Fig. 103). All the Warren chairs include the patented spring support. Photograph courtesy of The Saint Louis Art Museum.

103. Variations of Warren's chair, shown at the London Crystal Palace Exhibition of 1851. According to the exhibition catalog, "America has long been noted for the luxurious easiness of its chairs . . . instead of the ordinary legs conjoined to each angle of the seat, they combine to support a stem . . . between which and the seat the spring is inserted. . . . It will allow of the greatest weight and freest motion on all sides. . . ." From the *Art Journal's* catalog for the Crystal Palace Exhibition (London, 1851).

104. Patent drawing of Warren's "New and Improved Mode of Constructing Springs" (elevation and plan). The specifications detail the use of two or more sets of bow-shaped metal "leaves" attached to fixtures at each end. Photograph courtesy of The National Archives.

105. Warren's patent drawing of "Car seat backs." The invention, which employed a spring device similar to that in Fig. 104, made bumpy train rides more comfortable. Patent No. 7,539, July 30, 1850. Photograph courtesy of The National Archives.

104

105

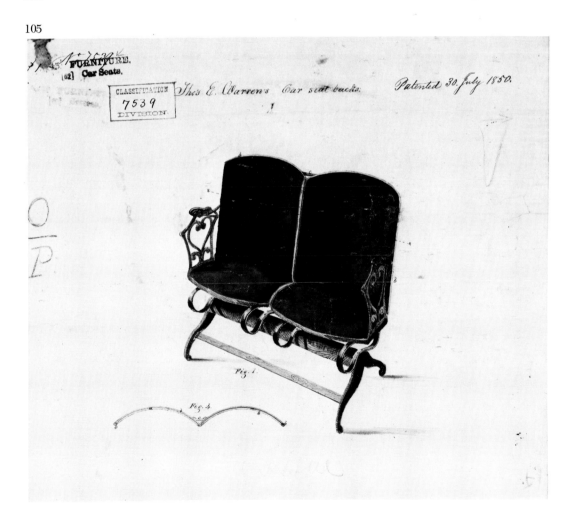

106. Rocking chair, c. 1855. Originating in a design manufactured by R. W. Winfield and Company, Birmingham, England, this chair was owned by the famous New York manufacturer, inventor, and philanthropist Peter Cooper. It combines an innovative material—cast iron—with an innovative form which provided comfort. Similar American versions were patented by Herman Berg and Richard Hoffman in 1867. Photograph courtesy of The Cooper Union.

107. Platform rocker, Heywood Brothers and Company, Gardner, Mass., 1886. Oak, caning, upholstered headrest, iron supports. 42½ x 23⅜ x 32½ (108 x 59.4 x 82.6 cm). An improvement on the rocking chair, this platform rocker is innovative in its use of a continuous bentwood construction for the arms, stiles, and crest, its cast-iron spring device, and its adjustable upholstered headrest, all contributing to a comfortable, functional design. "HEYWOOD BROS. & CO. GARDNER MASS. PAT JAN. 7, 1873" impressed in metal medallions on each side of scrolled arm at seat level. "PATENTED MAY 13, 1873" impressed on each side of cast-iron clamps at base support. Lent anonymously.

107

HEYWOOD BROTHERS AND COMPANY (1826–1897)

In 1826 Walter Heywood started a chairmaking shop, assisted by two of his brothers, Levi and Benjamin, who owned a country store. In 1829, with Walter and Benjamin remaining in Gardner, Massachusetts, to oversee the manufacturing, Levi moved to Boston to open a retail outlet. When the factory was destroyed by fire in 1834, it was rebuilt in Crystal Lake, where there was adequate water power to drive the new wood-turning equipment, such as lathes and a circular saw. The partnership of B. F. Heywood and Company was formed in 1835, consisting of Walter and Benjamin Heywood and a younger brother, William, as well as Moses Wood, also of Gardner, and James W. Gates and Levi Heywood of Boston.

As president, Levi Heywood exhibited not only managerial sense but mechanical ability. Responsible for introducing important new machinery into the factory, he apparently played such a prominent role that his partners withdrew from the firm, leaving him sole owner. He brought in machines for making chairs with wooden seats and for wood-bending, inspiring Michael Thonet to write after a visit to the Heywood factory: "I must tell you candidly that you have the best machinery for bending wood that I ever saw. . . ." Heywood also invented machines for splitting and shaving rattan. Hand-caning of chair-seat frames ceased when he introduced power looms to weave cane into a continuous web. Other inventions used in the Heywood factory included a cane-splicing process, power machines for bending wood, and a machine for making special springs. He also substituted wetted reed—the rattan's pith, whose porous surface permitted staining—for rattan itself in chairmaking.

With the death of Levi Heywood and his son, Charles, in 1882, the surviving partners of what was now called Heywood Brothers and Company were Henry and George Heywood, Alvin M. Greenwood, and Amos Morrill. A few years later, members of the third generation of Heywoods came into the business. The name Heywood Brothers and Company ended in 1897 when the firm was consolidated with the Wakefield Rattan Company.[8] (See Heywood-Wakefield Company in the Technique section, above.)

Platform Rocker, 1886

Several remarkable innovations make this rocker (Fig. 107) noteworthy: the use of a continuous bentwood construction to form the crest, rear stiles, and elaborate S-scroll arms; the cast-iron spring device of the supports to allow movement; and the adjustable up-holstered headrest attached to the wooden rod in back of the chair. Startling in 1886, these innovations are here combined in a unique, aesthetically pleasing, and functional design which anticipates furniture of the twentieth century. The curves of the back, arms, and seat are echoed in those of the cast-iron spring support. Ornament is used discreetly under the front seat rail and at the bottom of the spring support. A certificate and letter, dated June 28, 1973, from the Heywood-Wakefield Company, ascertains that, according to their catalog, the chair was made in 1886. The catalog shows the chair in a number of variations, including a stationary and a swivel model.

GEORGE J. HUNZINGER: see biographical note in Materials section.

Platform Rocker, 1882

According to George Hunzinger, "rocking chairs having stationary bases for resting upon the floor have long been regular articles of manufacture." Known as "platform rockers," they were widely produced in the United States after the late 1860s, replacing the standard eighteenth-century form with curved rockers which tended to creep forward with vigorous movement.

In the 1870s, when the platform rocker reached prominence, J. Wayland Kimball commented in *Kimball's Book of Designs* on the popularity of these chairs: "Foreigners call the rocking chair a peculiarly American luxury, yet the necessary length of the rockers on the floor cause[s] this favorite chair to be occasionally in the way, and not infrequently too noisy

108. Platform rocker ("spring rocking chair"), George J. Hunzinger, New York. Mahogany, metal spring device, late nineteenth-century up-holstery (probably not original). 41½ x 26½ x 32 (105.4 x 67.3 x 81.3 cm). Platform rockers were widely used in this country after around 1870, replacing the traditional rocking chair, which was noisier and tended to inch along the floor. Aesthetically satisfying design elements, such as the repeated use of adjoined circles and the vigorous corkscrew turn-ings, are here combined with Hunzinger's "im-provements." Patent 264,880, September 26, 1882. Lent anonymously.

108

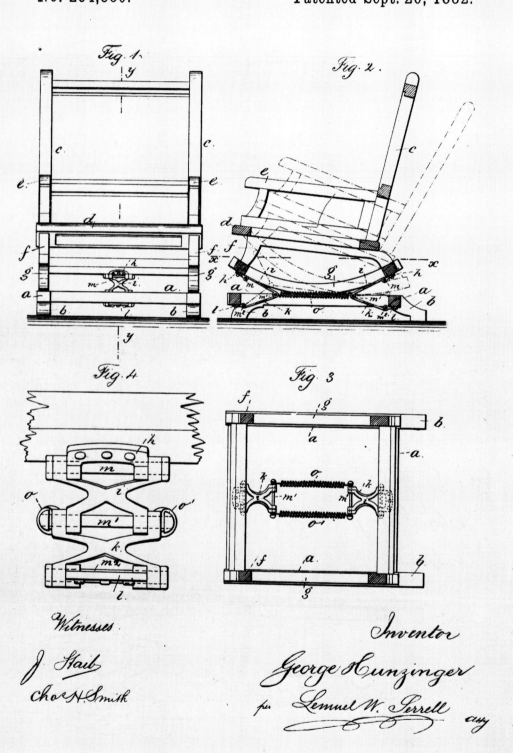

109. Hunzinger's patent drawing of "Spring Rocking Chair." U.S. Patent Office.

for comfort. These disadvantages have been very ingeniously overcome in the chairs of certain makers who, in different ways, build them so that there is no rocker on the floor and the movements are always noiseless."[9]

In this, Hunzinger's most successful patent (Fig. 108), imaginative design elements, such as the reiterated adjacent circles under the arms and back and the incisive corkscrew turnings, are combined with innovations which Hunzinger claimed allowed the chair to "rock with the greatest ease [with] no tendency for one part to slip upon the other." An added attraction was the fact that "there will be little or no noise in the spring and hinges as they move." The sitter could thus be assured of a comfortable chair that rocked smoothly, without creaking, by means of a "combination hinge and spring mechanism which insures a stable connection of the parts, and at the same time a positive and easy spring movement."

A large number of Hunzinger's platform rockers have recently been discovered—some privately owned and quite a few in the collection of the Margaret Woodbury Strong Museum. The Brooklyn Museum owns a similarly inventive example. All attest to the imagination and industry of the Hunzinger firm.

Patents for platform rockers continued to be filed throughout the final decades of the nineteenth century, constantly claiming improvements on existing models. So great was the concern for comfort and so lively the imagination of some inventors that patents were sought (and granted) for such contraptions as a platform rocker equipped with an "air compressing and discharging apparatus . . . to aid in keeping the person who sits in the chair cool" (1901). These inventions were extensions of the more plausible ones popularized by George Hunzinger and others. (P. T.)

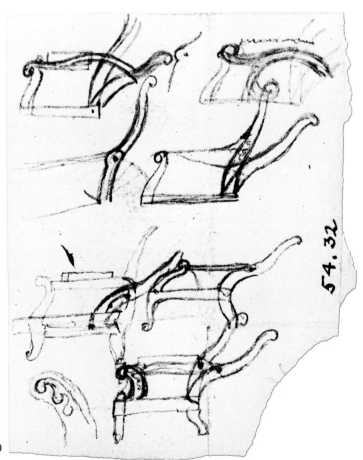

110. Pencil sketches of a reclining armchair, John Jeliff, Newark, N. J., 1870–1880. These rough drawings by a prominent Newark cabinetmaker in the second half of the nineteenth century indicate the designer's effort to visualize the form from several viewpoints. Photograph courtesy of the Newark Museum.

110

MARKS ADJUSTABLE FOLDING CHAIR COMPANY (1877–1897)
CEVEDRA B. SHELDON (working 1873–1877)

Frank R. Marks, apparently a native of Pennsylvania, is first listed as a maker of chairs at 717 Broadway in New York in 1876, and soon established the firm of F. R. Marks and Company at 816 Broadway. The following year it became the Marks Adjustable Folding Chair Company. In its subsequent twenty years, the firm moved to 850 Broadway, 930 Broadway, 23 Union Square West, and finally 1144 Broadway, where it was liquidated in 1897. No longer managed by Marks, a new firm called Marks Adjustable Chair Company opened on the same premises. Interestingly, Marks is also listed as a maker of bicycles in 1895.

Cevedra B. Sheldon was first listed in *Trow's New York City Directory* for 1873–74 as a grain merchant, at 6 State, a business address shared with a relative, Edgar W. Sheldon, "inspector." He is next listed in the 1877–78 directory as a builder, at 109 West 49 Street, and also at his residence in Brooklyn. Evidently he was a talented entrepreneur with many interests. It is not known whether Sheldon was employed by the Marks Adjustable Folding Chair Company, which manufactured the chair he designed and patented in 1876.

Invalid Chair, 1876

This iron-framed invalid chair was immensely popular in the United States and Europe in the last quarter of the nineteenth century. Sold in England as well as America, it was painstakingly described in a contemporary English periodical, *The Cabinet Maker & Art Furnisher*, June 2, 1889: "The Marks Folding Chair is constructed to fulfill the requirements of lounge chair, smoking chair, library chair, invalid chair, deck chair and bed, and it plays these many parts in a thoroughly satisfactory manner. . . . The framework is of wrought iron throughout, enamelled and thoroughly protected from rust. As back, seat, and leg-rest are caned with Wakefield cane, closely woven, the chair may, if preferred be used . . . without the addition of cushions. Both the back and leg-rest permit of being adjusted to any angle without the occupant of the chair rising from the seat. . . . The leg-rest can be raised . . . to such an angle that the feet are higher than the seat, and can be lowered again to any desired angle at will. When the article is to be used as an arm chair, the leg-rest folds back upon the seat, and is practically unnoticeable . . . it is possible to obtain all sorts of positions . . . without any undue exertion, as the various parts work with the greatest ease. When fitted out with cushions the new chair is luxuriously comfortable, and the body must be weary indeed which would not yield to its seductive influences. To convert the chair into a bed the back is lowered, and additional legs, hitherto concealed, are let down to form a support [Fig. 113]."

The interest in comfort for invalids resulted in a design of great utility and flexibility. The chair was innovative in combining several purposes in one form, as well as in its use of a new material for furniture—the very durable iron. The design may have been included among the folding designs exhibited by the Marks Adjustable Folding Chair Company in the Chicago World's Columbian Exhibition, 1893 (Group 90, "Furniture of Interiors, Upholstery and Artistic Decorations," in Department H—Manufacturer, United States). A number of these chairs are now in museum collections, including The Metropolitan Museum of Art, attesting to their aesthetic importance.

111. Invalid chair, Cevedra B. Sheldon, New York. Iron frame, cane seat, walnut, upholstered cushions and arms, painted decoration, casters. 46 x 29⅞ x 25½ (116.8 x 75.9 x 64.8 cm). Immensely popular in the United States, this invalid's reclining chair was made in the year of the Philadelphia Centennial Exhibition, and may have been exhibited at the Chicago World's Columbian Exhibition in 1893. It illustrates not only comfort but innovative materials and multipurpose use. Patent 173,071, February 1, 1876. Manufactured by the Marks Adjustable Folding Chair Company. "Solæ M'frs. / Marks A. F. Chair Co. Limited 930 B'way/ Pat' Feb 1, 1876" impressed on side of metal frame. Lent anonymously.

112. The Marks/Sheldon chair with the footrest extended for casual relaxation.

111

112

113

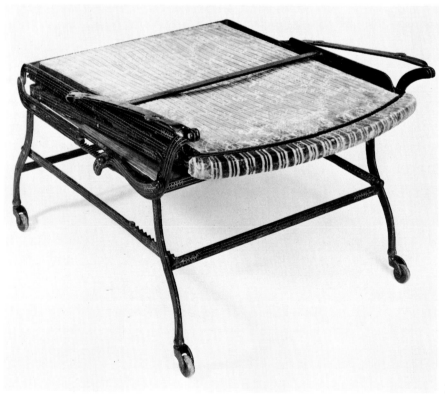

114

115

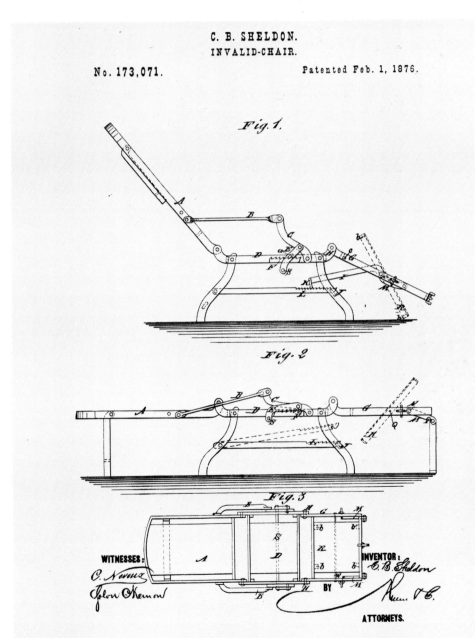

113. In full recumbent position for naps and dozing.

114. The compactness of the design is evident in this view of the chair in folded position without its cushions.

115. Embossed stamp on the iron side railing of the Marks chair.

116. Patent drawing of Sheldon's invalid chair (side elevations and plan). Ink on paper. 18½ x 14 (47 x 35.6 cm). The designer's "new and useful Improvement" was a "contrivance of the adjusting back-support; and also, of the cane bottom of the foot support. . . ." Lent by the U.S. Department of Commerce, Patent and Trademark Office.

116

ALLEN AND BROTHERS (1847–1902)

One of Philadelphia's best-known furniture firms in the second half of the nineteenth century, Allen and Brothers consisted of William and Joseph, who commenced business on their own in 1847. Previously they had served apprenticeships with their father, William Allen Sr., at his shop in the Northern Liberties section of Philadelphia, established in 1835.

The sons' firm, known first as W. and J. Allen, had several different locations, the longest period (1860–1896) being spent in a six-story building constructed to their specifications at 1209 Chestnut Street. It was here that the reclining armchair (Fig. 117) was sold. The three lower floors were salesrooms, while the upper stories were used for upholstering and finishing the furniture which was made at their factory at Twelfth and Pleasant Streets. William Jr. was in charge of the store and Joseph managed the factory; in 1864 they were joined by their younger brother, James, who took over supervision of the finishing department.

When William Jr. died, his two brothers continued the business, which was described by Charles Robson in 1875 as follows: "The most skilled workmen to be obtained in Europe or America are employed, and they are of various nationalities. A thoroughly competent workman has charge of the veneering department, under the supervision of the senior partner. . . . The greatest care is exercised with regard to temperature in all the departments of the building. In fact, strict regard for what would seem to be matters of trifling moment with most manufacturers is a characteristic of the establishment."[10]

The reputation of the firm was enhanced by its highly acclaimed contributions to the 1876 Centennial Exhibition, including a walnut sideboard ornamented with marble columns and decorative metal bases and capitals, and an elaborately carved and paneled door inlaid with slabs of marble. Noted for its first-class furniture, Allen and Brothers remained in business until 1902, when the surviving brother, James, closed the business after sixty-seven years of continuous family ownership. (P. T.)

Reclining Armchair, 1894

One of the earliest designs for a reclining chair appeared in Ackermann's *Repository of Arts,* an English periodical, in 1813. Conceived by the architect William Pocock, the "Reclining Patent Chair" was the prototype for hundreds which were made in the following decades. In America, for example, the firm of Browne and Ash, upholsterers and cabinetmakers at 421 Broadway, New York, advertised "Improved Patent Self Acting Reclining, Elevating and Revolving, Recumbent Chairs and Sofas" in 1855. Likewise, the well-known Philadelphia cabinetmaker George J. Henkels featured a reclining chair which "graduates its position to the will of the person, and enjoys the merit of utility, without complication of machinery" in his essay on furniture in Samuel Sloan's *Homestead Architecture.*[11]

The Allen and Brothers chair (Fig. 117) was taken more specifically from the well-known one designed in 1883 by William Watt and manufactured in England by Morris and Company. Known today as the "Morris chair," the form was produced widely in Europe and in America. One of the earliest American-made examples (1887) is in The Metropolitan Museum of Art. Some versions were extremely simple, consisting of only the most basic elements. While Allen and Brothers did make a plain model, the one shown here was embellished with lions' heads, a popular decorative motif in the late nineteenth century.

"Seekers after comfort," according to an article in the *Decorator and Furnisher* of March 1883, "can find it exemplified in the Morris chair." Although not unique to this country, the Philadelphia example is significant for its comfort-enhancing mechanical innovation. The patent specifications claim as unique the combination of the following: (1) a seat frame provided with rearwardly extending arms, the back ends of which have "approximately

117. Reclining armchair, Allen and Brothers, Philadelphia, Pa. Mahogany; brass hinges, ratchets, and casters; original upholstery. 41½ x 25½ x 32 (105.4 x 64.8 x 81.3 cm). This reclining chair was derived from a well-known English design of 1883 by William Watt, executed by Morris and Company. Known today as the "Morris chair," the form was very popular in both Europe and America. Patent 514,403, February 6, 1894. "ALLEN AND BRO. PHILADELPHIA PA./ PAT. FEB 6, 94" impressed on inside of each brass ratchet. Lent by John H. Nally.

vertical notches" or slots; (2) "a tilting back pivoted to the main frame"; (3) "a vertically movable rod extending transversely through said slots to the rear of the back," with "keepers for the rod formed in or applied to the back. . . ."

This patent provided a more workable reclining mechanism than that in the English prototype. The Allen and Brothers chair, therefore, is innovative in its application of technology to an existing "modern" form. (P. T.)

118

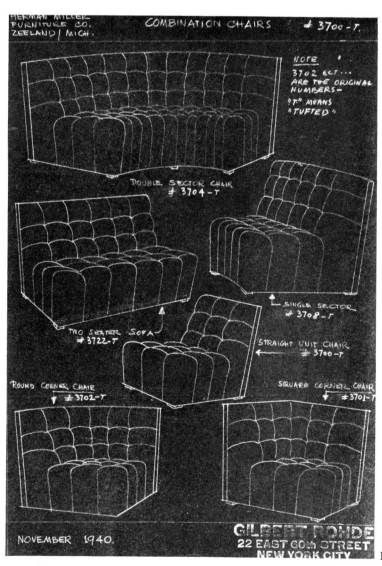

119

118. A "Morris chair" in a nineteenth-century interior. A simpler type than the example in Fig. 117, this version is upholstered in Morris fabric, which is known to have been imported and sold in this country. Photograph courtesy of The Society for the Preservation of New England Antiquities.

119. Perspective drawing of "Combination Chairs," Gilbert Rohde, 1940. Blueprint. 10⅞ x 8¾ (27.6 x 22.2 cm). Originally conceived in 1937, this design was revised in 1940, probably with the addition of the tufting seen here, resulting in an Art Deco version of the overall upholstered Victorian chair. Its modular sections could be arranged in numerous combinations, much like the Don Chadwick design (Fig. 123) also produced by Herman Miller. "HERMAN MILLER/FURNITURE CO./ZEELAND/MICH./ COMBINATION CHAIRS #3700-T" inscribed at top;"NOVEMBER 1940" at lower left; GILBERT ROHDE/22 EAST 60TH STREET/NEW YORK CITY." at lower right. Lent by the Herman Miller Inc. Resource Center.

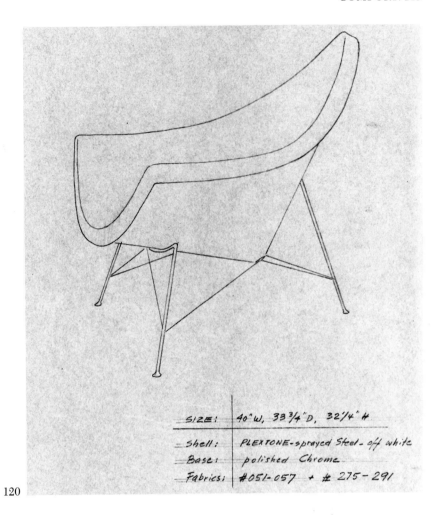

SIZE: 40"W, 33¾"D, 32¼"H

Shell: PLEXTONE-sprayed Steel-off white
Base: polished Chrome
Fabrics: #051-057 + # 275-291

120

120. Perspective drawing of "Coconut Chair #5569," George Nelson, 1955. Pencil on tracing paper. 11 x 8½ (27.9 x 21.6 cm). Designed to be made of polished chrome with a steel shell, 40 x 33¾ x 32¼ (101.6 x 85.7 x 82 cm), Nelson's chair was extremely comfortable and aesthetically pleasing. Lent by the Herman Miller Inc. Resource Center.

121. Perspective drawing of a "Sling Sofa," George Nelson, designed 1962. Ink and pencil on tracing paper. 8⅝ x 11 (21.9 x 27.9 cm). Introduced by Herman Miller in 1964, this leather-cushioned sling design features a chromium steel tube frame bonded with epoxy resins. Its seat is supported by a molded rubber sheet stretched inside the frame, and its back by rubber straps. Lent by the Herman Miller Inc. Resource Center.

121

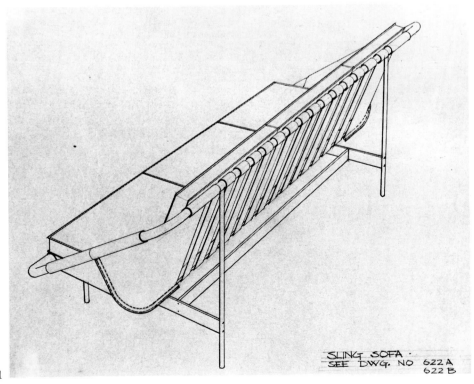

SLING SOFA.
SEE DWG. NO 622A
622B

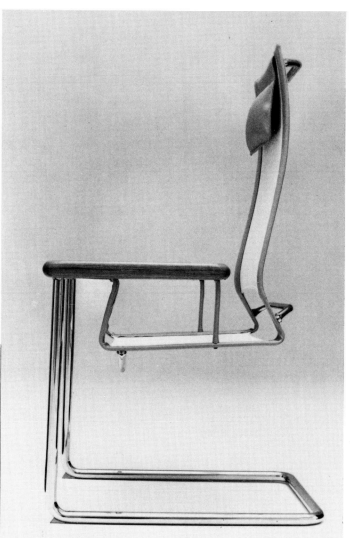

122

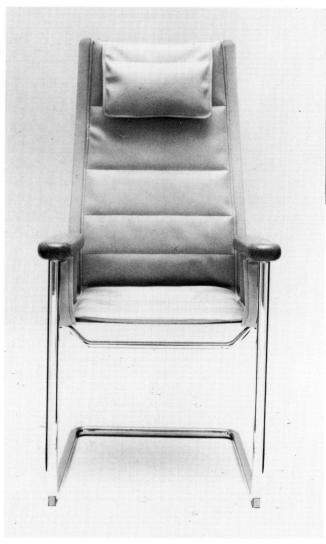

122. Armchair ("Warren chair"), Roger Kenneth Leib, Chicago, 1980. Designed for orthopedic purposes, the "Warren chair" has proved so comfortable that it is now found in ordinary residential use. The precedent was set in the nineteenth century, when invalid furniture also became popular for the healthy. Photograph courtesy of Roger Kenneth Leib.

DON CHADWICK (b. 1936)

Born in Los Angeles, Don Chadwick received a degree in industrial design from the University of California at Los Angeles in 1959. In the same year he began to work for Victor Gruen and Associates, architects and planners involved with graphic and interior design projects, primarily for shopping centers.

He started his own design practice in 1964, and in 1975 joined the design faculty of the Department of Art at UCLA, teaching courses in industrial design. In 1979 he formed a design partnership with Bill Stumpf—Chadwick, Stumpf and Associates—and they are now involved with Herman Miller on major design projects currently in prototyping.

Chadwick's first furniture designs as a student show Scandinavian influence, especially of Hans Wegner. Later he was influenced by the Bauhaus and then "became intrigued with the reinforced plastic technology and developed ideas and prototypes of shell-type chairs, studying the work of Eames and Saarinen."[12] In the late 1960s, Chadwick became interested in the plastic processes Italian designers were experimenting with, which led to his involvement in the technology of molded, flexible, and rigid urethane foam.

The influence of the technology and precision required in his early work on aerial photography and in the aerospace industry is apparent in his modular seating design for Herman Miller Inc., introduced in June 1979.

Modular Seating Unit, 1974

Highly sophisticated technological innovations in materials have enabled Chadwick to design an interchangeable modular seating arrangement which achieves maximum comfort (Fig. 123). As in the Victorian overall upholstered chair (Fig. 98) and French and Italian designs of the mid-1960s, Chadwick here abandons the traditional rail and stile arrangement in favor of a new sculptural form. An earlier prototype by Gilbert Rohde is seen in Fig. 119; the Chadwick design differs in several respects, including its use of molded polyurethane.

The upholstered units are molded with high resiliency foam. The modular system is composed of five simple sections: a rectangular upholstered shape and four wedge shapes, two with narrow backs and wide fronts, two with the proportions reversed. Each module is neatly tailored and fully upholstered for use either as an end or as the inside seat of an arrangement. The modules can be linked by slot-in connectors to form an almost limitless variety of custom layouts, from straight lines to small arcs, full circles, and wandering serpentines. A single straight module functions as a complete chair.

123. Modular seating unit, Don Chadwick, Los Angeles, Calif., designed 1974, produced 1979. Urethane foam cushioning molded over plywood, steel, and molded styrene bead structure; molded black polystyrene base; molded polystyrene connector riveted to steel bar. 27 x 28 x 30 (68.6 x 71.1 x 76.1 cm) per small wedge. Although designed for commercial purposes, Chadwick's modular seating is also used in the home. By moving the wedge-shaped modular units, one can create many alternatives to the serpentine arrangement pictured here. Manufactured by Herman Miller Inc. Lent by the Herman Miller Inc. Resource Center.

123

PORTABILITY

The need for furniture that can be easily transported has existed since ancient times when the folding chair was first invented. Such forms were early developed for use in military camps (Fig. 124) as well as aboard ship. With the increased mobility of life in the nineteenth and twentieth centuries, the need for light, inexpensive, yet durable and sturdy portable forms also grew.

Camp furniture (both military and civilian) and other closely related outdoor forms comprise one of the major categories of portable furniture considered here, exemplified by the folding chair so popular in the nineteenth century as well as our own. An enduring favorite is the type now known as the "director's chair" (Fig. 125) with its simple wooden scissor-legs and slip-on canvas seat and back. Though without cushions or pads, it is extremely comfortable for long periods of time, can be used for a variety of purposes, and folds compactly for easy shipping and storage. Another perennial indoor/outdoor design is the sling chair (Fig. 137), originally produced in wood and now also available in metal.

The need for portable and low-cost furniture continued to be an important concern in the twentieth century. Reviewing the 15th Exhibition of Contemporary American Industrial Art at The Metropolitan Museum of Art in 1940, Talbot F. Hamlin pointed out that "one thing is sadly lacking . . . good, simple, stock furniture at low cost."[1] The International Competition for Low-Cost Furniture Design at The Museum of Modern Art in 1948, organized by Edgar Kaufmann Jr., addressed this problem, with special attention to the new postwar conditions:

"At the end of World War II American families found themselves faced with a tremendous housing problem. In part they had to make the best of existing accommodations by crowding them with far greater numbers than had been intended originally, or else they had to try to secure one of the new dwellings which were erected, though too slowly to satisfy the need. In either case families found themselves in smaller homes than had been usual. If these homes were to be in any sense livable or comfortable, their furnishings had to be efficiently planned and trimly scaled. Deeper than this lay the important question of cost. The market supplied furniture at many price levels, but . . . it was hard to find desirable furniture at low cost. American ingenuity and American technology had provided this country with an admirable standard of living, but seemingly in regard to the home and its furnishings these forces were not yet fully mobilized. In the hope that new ideas and better results could be found, a Competition was launched under the auspices of The Museum of Modern Art and an enterprising group of American retailers and manufacturers. . . ."[2]

Two other categories of portable furniture surveyed here speak to the situation described by Kaufmann. One includes the forms designed for stacking, represented by Florence Knoll's stool (Fig. 142) and the Eames side chair (Fig. 143), two among the many modern designs which have responded to the need for seating that not only is light, durable, and portable but that can be tightly "nested" for storage. The second includes low-cost "knock-down" furniture, constructed of parts which can be dismantled for shipping and reassembled with ease. The Johnson storage unit (Figs. 150 and 151) exemplifies the type. Prior versions of the concept include the American Hitchcock chair of the early nineteenth century and the bentwood furniture of Thonet. Packaged furniture is particularly popular in the United States, where mail-order buying has a long history.

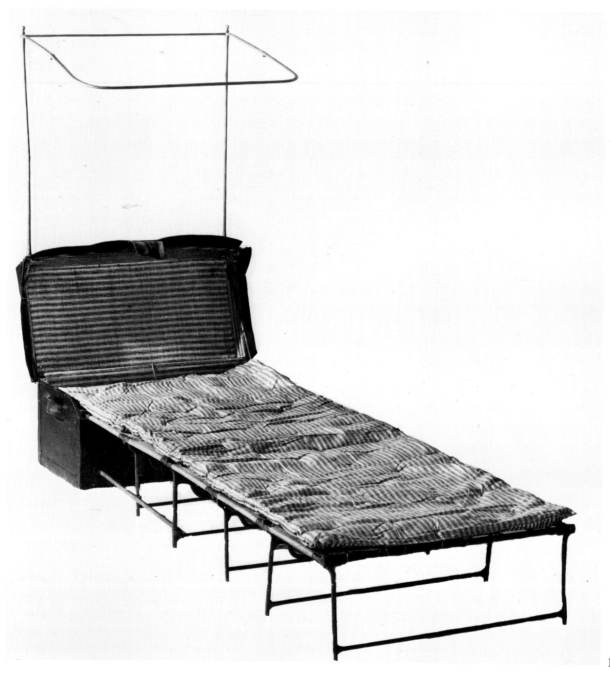

124

125

124. Chest-bed, c. 1780, owned by General George Washington—an example of the folding furniture forms used in military camps and aboard ship. Made of leatherbound metal and lined with feather ticking, it was presented to Washington by General Peter Gansevoort, Schuylerville, N.Y. Greenfield Village and the Henry Ford Museum.

125. Folding armchair, designer unknown, probably Baltimore, c. 1860. Mahogany, canvas back and seat (not original). 38 x 24 x 19½ (96.5 x 61 x 49.5 cm). The classic portable "director's chair" is as ubiquitous today as in the nineteenth century. The popularity of the form goes back to ancient Greece and Rome. Lent anonymously.

Folding Armchair, circa 1860 (designer unknown)

This classic innovative chair form goes back to ancient Greece and Rome and has been revived periodically. It is seen here in an early American version (Fig. 125), from the Victorian period, which became increasingly popular throughout the century. The turnings of the stiles, arms, legs, and stretchers are particularly crisp and fine. The wood stiles and X-shaped base originally supported an upholstered back and seat, here replaced with canvas. Versions of this form, known today as "directors' chairs," are currently produced by many manufacturers, including Gold Medal, whose role in innovative furniture design is discussed below in connection with the sling chair. The form remains in wide demand today because it is cheap, easy to store, and available in a number of bright colors. Early versions differ from contemporary examples in their use of elaborate turnings and fine brass hardware.

126

GEORGE J. HUNZINGER: see biographical note in Materials section.

Folding Chair, 1866

Among George Hunzinger's earliest and most successful patents was one taken out in 1866 for a "reclining chair" (Fig. 127). Its back tilted for comfort and the legs folded for portability. The X-shaped supports used by Hunzinger and his contemporaries—seen in ancient furniture—were a staple feature of cots, stools, chairs, and other forms of camp furniture, which reached its height of popularity in America in the late nineteenth century (Fig. 140).

Hunzinger's design, employing a campstool-type base, served as a reference point for many of his own later chairs as well as those produced by other furniture makers, such as J. S. Stansbury, whose adjustable reclining chair was patented in 1869. In Hunzinger's thoroughly workable design, as he noted in an advertisement, when the chair is "folded by closing up the X-legs the front ends of the arms rise with the upper ends of the legs . . . so that the chair will occupy less space than when spread for use, and these arms, connecting the upper ends of the X-legs, with the frame for the back, might be employed if the cross-bar were fixed rigidly between the legs, or movable, as shown."

Once again in this folding chair, Hunzinger demonstrated his continuing effort to combine functionality, aesthetic quality, and comfort in a single piece of furniture. Hunzinger also made versions of this chair which would appear to fold but which in fact were stationary. The chair's relatively low cost made it accessible to a broad section of the American public. The simplicity of the design makes it appear nearly as "modern" today as it did over one hundred years ago. (P. T.)

126. Patent model of folding chair, Pierre J. Hardy, New York. Hardy's invention was a hinge mechanism to facilitate the folding process. The new hinges were "formed as caps for the tops of the legs . . . and introduced between the folding X-legs and the side rails of the arms." The upholstery on the model has obviously shredded. Patent 67,759, August 13, 1867. U.S. Patent Office.

127. Folding chair, George J. Hunzinger, New York. Ebonized walnut, period carpet tapestry upholstery. 33 x 24¾ x 25 (83.8 x 62.9 x 63.5 cm). The campstool form of the base is incorporated into a sturdier and more comfortable overall design. Patent 52,416, February 6, 1866. "HUNZINGER/Feb/6/. 1866. PATENT/FEB 6, 1866" stamped on left rear stile. Lent anonymously.

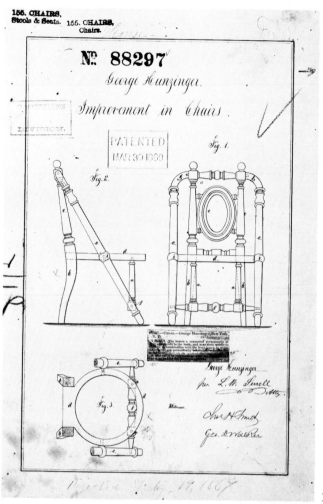

128

129

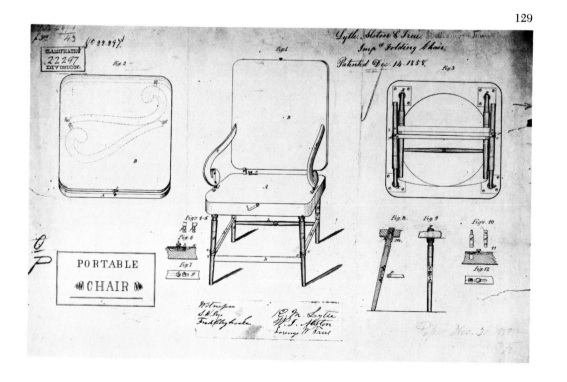

128. Patent drawing of "Improvement in Chairs," George J. Hunzinger, New York. Ink and pencil on paper. 14½ x 10 (36.8 x 25.4 cm). Hunzinger's improvement was "to strengthen the chair" at the point of connection with the seat by means of "a brace running on each side diagonally from the upper part of the chair-back to the lower part of the front legs, and connected near the middle with the side of the seat or seat-frame." Patent 88,297, March 30, 1869. Lent by The National Archives.

129. Patent drawing of "Imp[rove]d Folding Chair," Lytle, Alston and True, Williamson County, Tenn. The patentees claimed to have invented "certain new and useful Improvements" to "form a strong, light, compact and portable chair or stool: one that is not easily broken; not liable to get out of order, is quickly set up, and easily packed. . . ." Patent 22,297, December 14, 1858. The National Archives.

130

130. Folding chair, B. J. Harrison, c. 1866. Extremely popular in the second half of the nineteenth century, this chair is admired today for its simplicity and functional form. While Hunzinger's more expensive chairs were often covered with elaborate upholstery and fringe, the only ornament here is the turnings of the cross legs and stiles. The Metropolitan Museum of Art, Robert C. Goelet Fund, 1973.

131. A folding chair in the Chess Room at the Junior Century Club, New York, 1880s, similar to the B. J. Harrison design (Fig. 130). This type was produced by many manufacturers and used everywhere from funeral parlors to clubs. From *Harper's Weekly*, November 24, 1883. Photograph courtesy of the Smithsonian Institution.

131

SAMUEL G. MCCULLOUGH (1843–1927)

An obituary in the *Sidney* (Ohio) *Daily News,* December 5, 1927, notes that Samuel G. McCullough was the son of William G. McCullough, a prominent member of the town who lived at 429 North Ohio Avenue. When Samuel McCullough married Kate Smith in 1876, their elaborate wedding received extensive coverage in the town paper. Although McCullough is identified as from Sidney on his patent specifications, he is not listed in the city directory or the census in 1880, the date of his folding chair patent. That may have been the year he moved to Pittsburgh, where he is first listed in 1882 as a "car inspector" at 68 Decatur. According to his obituary, McCullough worked for over forty years for the Baltimore and Ohio Railroad. He died in Pittsburgh at the age of eighty-four.

Patent Model of Folding Chair, 1880

The preoccupation with folding chairs in the nineteenth century is reflected in the numerous patents taken out for various devices, as well as in a number of extant examples. McCullough's patent model (Fig. 132) falls under the general category of camp furniture, although folding chairs were also used in parlors.

McCullough explained his invention in the patent specifications which accompanied the drawing (Fig. 135) as follows. The hinges permit compact folding; when the chair is in use, "lateral movement" is prevented by the iron braces (G) between the legs and the front stretcher. The back is doubly braced: first, by a stretcher (I) with tenoned ends "which are inserted in holes in the side arms, whereby said stretcher may be turned" either to prevent, or to permit, folding on the hinge; second, by iron braces (L) extending "from the back to stretcher E," which keep the stretcher from sagging at the hinge when the chair is in use.

133

134

132. Patent model of folding chair, Samuel G. McCullough, Sidney, Ohio. Wood, canvas. 15⅜ x 9⅜ x 10¹³/₁₆ (39.1 x 23.8 x 27.5 cm). Compactness and portability were especially required in camp furniture. McCullough's invention was for the hinges and braces of the chair. Patent 226,092, March 30, 1880. Lent by the National Museum of History and Technology, Smithsonian Institution.
133. The iron braces on the back of McCullough's folding chair.
134. McCullough's patent model in folded position.

135

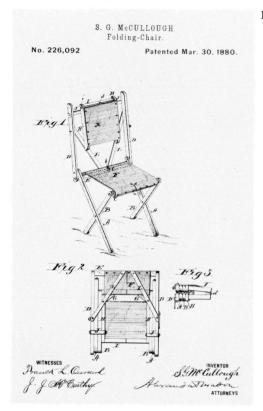

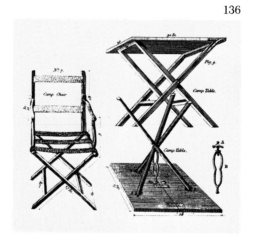

136

135. Patent drawing of McCullough's folding chair. The patent specifications explain McCullough's invention in detail, but basically his claim was for an improved bracing. Photograph courtesy of the Smithsonian Institution.

136. Camp chair and camp table, British, late eighteenth/early nineteenth century. The back and bottom of the foldable chair were "formed of girth webbing." The table, consisting of two hinged "flaps" supported by triangular legs "fixed in the centre . . . by means of an iron triangle," was simple, durable, easily folded, and thus portable. From Sheraton's *The Cabinet Dictionary* (London, 1803).

GOLD MEDAL INC. (1892–)

Organized as the Racine Camp Furniture and Novelty Manufacturing Company, Gold Medal has continued to produce innovative camp furniture throughout this century. The Wisconsin firm was founded by R. B. Hand, W. G. Gittings, and J. G. Teall. In 1894, it moved to its present location at 1700 Packard Avenue. Its early line included sleeping bags, cots, tents, stools, and folding chairs. Subsequent original or novelty products included folding and roll-up tables and portable homes, garages, and bathtubs. When the company won a gold medal at the World's Columbian Exhibition in Chicago in 1893, it changed its name to Gold Medal Camp Furniture Manufacturing Company. In 1930 it became the Gold Medal Folding Furniture Company, and in 1974 Gold Medal Inc.

With camp furniture its specialty, Gold Medal published a camper's guidebook called *Complete Sportsman Library.* Around the time of the Spanish-American War the firm became one of the primary suppliers of folding camp cots for the U. S. Army.

One of the most famous of the company's designs was the "director's chair," a form which, although not unique to Gold Medal, the company has kept in continuous production in the United States. Today the firm occupies a large plant in Racine and a plant in Baxter, Tennessee, which supplies wood parts for assembly in Racine.

Sling Chair, early twentieth century

The prototype of this famous chair (Fig. 137) goes back at least to 1877 in England when Joseph Beverley Fenby of Yardley was granted a patent for "Improvements in Camp or

Folding Stools, Chairs, Tables, and Beds." It is not known whether the chair was put into production in England; in America it was first brought out around 1895 by the Gold Medal Camp Furniture Manufacturing Company. According to Gold Medal, Fenby sold the rights in various countries, the U.S. rights going to Jason Marvin Bowers of New York. Gold Medal started manufacturing the chair with a natural wood frame and khaki-colored canvas covers. Popular among campers and hunters, it received unusual publicity because of its use by such famous men as Thomas Edison and Theodore Roosevelt.

The design of the Gold Medal chair has changed very little: a 1980 catalog shows it in natural wood and white canvas, much as it appeared in Fenby's patent drawing over a hundred years earlier. Its virtues continue to be extolled: it "folds compactly for easy storage and portability" and offers "hours of comfort" for indoor or outdoor use. Packed in a single carton, the current version weighs only eleven pounds.

Various names have been given to this popular form. Gold Medal refers to it as their "circus chair," designed by R. Standish Gittings. Among architects and designers, a nonportable metal version, made of a seemingly continuous iron rod, is known as the "Hardoy" chair, after one of its three designers, Argentine architect Jorge Ferrari-Hardoy. The basic design, in both wooden and metal versions, has been pirated by numerous manufacturers.[3]

137. Sling chair, Gold Medal Inc., design introduced early twentieth century. Canvas, wooden frame. 39 x 30½ x 30 (99.1 x 77.5 x 76.2 cm). This popular folding camp chair, an earlier version of which was patented in England by Joseph Beverley Fenby in 1877, remains in production today by its first American makers. Patent 4,014,591 (issued to R. Standish Gittings), March 27, 1977. Lent by Gold Medal Inc.

137

138

139

138. A Gold Medal camp chair in use, late nineteenth century. The convenience of light, portable camp furniture for domestic purposes is seen here. Photograph courtesy of Gold Medal Inc.

139. Gold Medal's folding camp table and chair "at home" in Mukden (now Shenyang), China, c. 1900. The booted man is F. J. Schmidt, war correspondent for *Collier's Weekly* during the Boxer Rebellion, shown here receiving a Chinese viceroy. Schmidt sent this remarkable photograph to Gold Medal's president. Photograph courtesy of Gold Medal Inc.

140. A page from the catalog of the Gold Medal Camp Furniture Manufacturing Company, late nineteenth century. These line-cut illustrations, supplied by the manufacturer to retail outlets, indicate the variety of forms available, all sturdy yet light and foldable. Photograph courtesy of Gold Medal Inc.

Electrotypes of "Gold Medal" Folding Furniture and Camp Equipment—Cont.

FURNISHED TO DEALERS WITHOUT CHARGE.

All illustrations on this page are "line cuts"—from either woodcuts or zinc etchings. *Order by "electro" number.*

Electro No. 555
(Chair No. 6)

Electro No. 558
(Stool No. 5)

Electro No. 554
(Chair No. 6)

Electro No. 605
(Stool No. 5)

Electro No. 557
(Stool No. 5)

Electro No. 562
(Chair No. 149)

Electro No. 606
(Chair No. 6)

Electro No. 566
(Table No. 7 Without Shelf)

Electro No. 565
(Table No. 7 with Shelf No. 8)

Electro No. 593
(Chair No. 107)

Electro No. 561
(Chair No. 149)

Electro No. 563
(Chair No. 10)

Electro No. 677
(Table No. 7)

Electro No. 592
(Railroad Stools Nos. 115 and 115B)

Electro No. 570
(Water Pail No. 46, Open and Closed)

Electro No. 678
(Table No. 7 with Shelf No. 8)

Electro No. 567
(Table No. 38)

("Duplex" Folding Basket No. 116—Open and Closed)

Electro No. 596

Electro No. 569
(Water Pail No. 45—Open and Closed)

Electro No. 631
(Cot Mattress No. 132)

Electro No. 549
(Cot Mattress No. 132)

Electro No. 643
(Camp Chest No. 143)

Electro No. 621
(Infant's Folding Bath Tub No. 21-0)

Electro No. 599
(Folding Bathtub No. 20)

Electro No. 589
(No. 12 Carrying Sack for Cots)

Electro No. 573
(Camp Combination No. 43E)

Electro No. 574
(Camp Combination No. 43E)

Electro No. 571
(Camp Combination No. 43E)

Electro No. 572
(Camp Combination No. 43E)

DEALERS' SERVICE DEPARTMENT   **GOLD MEDAL CAMP FURNITURE MFG. CO., Racine, Wis.**

141

141. A Model-T Ford
equipped for camping. In-
creased use of the auto-
mobile in the early twen-
tieth century encouraged
the use of camp furniture.
Outfitted with Gold Medal
products, this Model-T presents an intriguing image of
American life during a
period of growth and
technological innovation.
Photograph courtesy of
Gold Medal Inc.

142. Stacking stool,
Florence Schust Knoll, design introduced 1948. Steel
rod legs, plywood-filled top
covered with plastic lami-
nate. 18 x 13 x 13 (45.7 x 33
x 33 cm). Manufactured by
Knoll International. Dis-
continued in 1966, the design was reproduced by
Knoll International in 1980
especially for the Innovative Furniture in America
exhibition. Lent by the
manufacturer.

143. Side chair, Charles
Eames, Venice, Calif., design introduced 1955.
Eames's molded polyester
side chair, seen here in its
compact stacking form, is
an obvious spacesaver.
Photograph courtesy of The
Museum of Modern Art.

FLORENCE SCHUST KNOLL (b. 1917)

Born in Michigan, Florence Schust attended Kingswood School and later the Cranbrook
Academy of Art. Her contact there with Eliel Saarinen and his work led her to begin to study
architecture. She attended the Architectural Association of London, returning to America at
the outbreak of World War II to complete her degree at the Illinois Institute of Technology in
Chicago under Mies van der Rohe.

In 1943, after working for several architectural firms in New York City, Schust joined the
staff of the Knoll Furniture Company. A year later she married the firm's founder, Hans
Knoll, who had emigrated from Germany and established his company in New York in 1939.
Florence Knoll became a full partner in the business and set up the Knoll Planning Unit to
handle its interior design operations. While both Knolls were deeply committed to the cause
of modern design, it was through Florence Knoll's efforts that the firm was able to attract
outstanding architects and designers to create furniture.

After her husband's death in 1955, Florence Knoll took over the presidency of the
company. In 1958 she married Harry Hood Bassett, a Florida banker, and the following year
retired from company office. She continued as a design consultant with Knoll until 1965.

Stacking Stool, 1948

Many distinguished designers, including Charles Eames (Fig. 143), have turned their
attention to stacking chairs in an effort to provide light, portable seating which can be
compactly stored when not in use. Florence Knoll's stool resulted from the same concern.
The design is based on an earlier one in wood by Alvar Aalto.

142

143

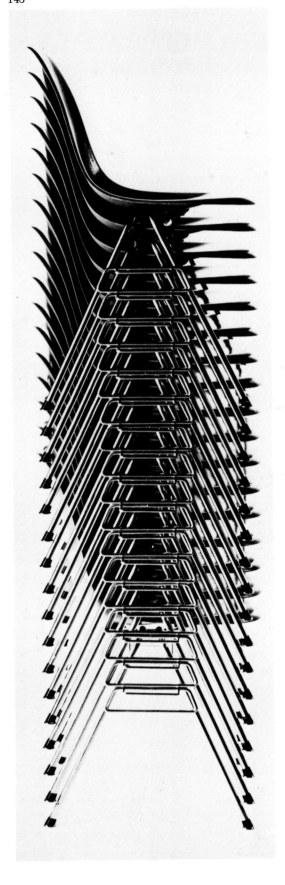

RALPH W. HENNINGER (b. 1935)

Ralph Henninger was born in Chicago and attended public schools in Glendale, California. Sculpture was his earliest interest, but at the age of seventeen he began to turn his attention to painting and the expressive possibilities of color. His first painting won the national "Art Inspired by Music" competition sponsored by Steinway and Sons.

After graduating from high school in 1956, he received scholarships to the Dayton Art Institute (1957) and the California School of Fine Arts in San Francisco (1958–1959). In the years since, Henninger's interests have been extremely broad—violin making, carpentry, mechanics, mind expansion, and astral projections, as well as a wide range of design work, including toys, sporting equipment, and tools.

From 1973 to 1977 he lived in Scottsdale, Arizona, accepting commissions to design and build furniture for several interior designers, including George Wiseman. While doing some furniture restoration for Scottsdale antique dealers, Henninger was told there was nothing new left to do in furniture design. That was the challenge which led to his oak folding chair (Figs. 144–147). "Rather than argue the point," he recalls, "I went home and designed the chair. It took about three hours to design and about ten to build. I was awarded a patent on the design. There are some flaws in the design and engineering of this chair. However, I feel I have solved them. . . ."[4]

Folding Chair, 1975

This portable oak chair was a finalist in the International Chair Design Competition sponsored by the San Diego chapter of the American Institute of Architects in 1977—one of the few competitions since the Museum of Modern Art's International Competition for Low-Cost Furniture Design in 1948. According to the jury, Henninger's chair "has versatility in that it is useful in several different versions, it folds flat, it folds to make a backrest, it folds out legs to make a chair, one can fold the backrest down and make a table out of it. It is a very beautifully detailed and constructed object. Anyone could make one of those chairs with a knowledge of craftsmanship, and in this day when there is such an interest in handcrafted things, this is a very sophisticated example of what one can do with handcraft to produce a really useful object."[5]

Although patented, as of 1980 the design had not been put into production.

144. Folding chair, Ralph W. Henninger, Fortuna, Calif., designed 1975. Oak. Closed: 21¾ x 15¼ x 2¼ thick (55.2 x 38.7 x 5.7 cm); open: 34½ x 15¼ x 16¼ deep (87.6 x 38.7 x 41.3 cm). The beauty and fine craftsmanship of this portable chair are visible even in its closed form. Patent D249,305, September 12, 1978. Lent by Ralph W. Henninger.

145

146

147

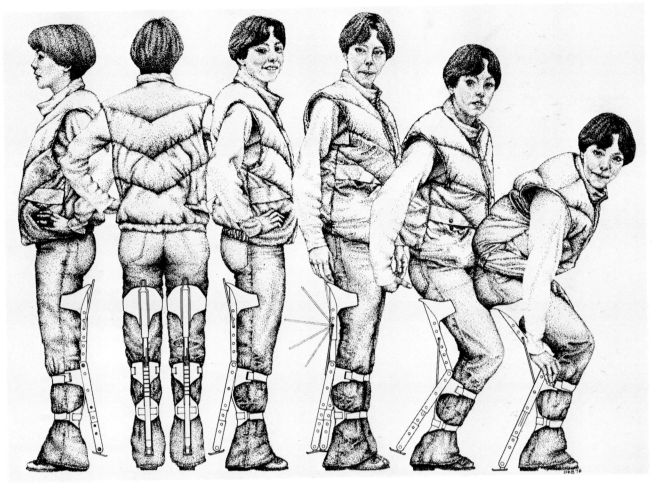

148

DARCY ROBERT BONNER JR. (b. 1952)

Darcy Robert Bonner Jr. was born in Dallas, Texas. He entered Tulane University's School of Architecture in New Orleans in 1971. The "wearable chair" was his ingenious response to a fourth-year sketch problem.

After graduating in 1976, Bonner returned to Dallas to begin his professional architectural career, working for Paul E. Pate and Associates and Beran and Shelmire. The next year, after the "wearable chair" won the second prize in the International Chair Design Competition, Bonner stopped working in order to produce the prototype of his design. He moved to Chicago in 1978 and began working for the architectural firm of Booth, Nagle and Hartray Ltd. In July 1979 he opened his own practice in architectural, interior, and product design.

Collaborating with Scott Himmel, Bonner has completed the following Chicago projects: the renovation of an old spaghetti factory into "Off-Center," a six-story shopping center at 300 West Grand Avenue, featuring a mural by Richard Hass; some residential remodeling; the "Polo by Ralph Lauren" store at 906 North Michigan Avenue; remodeling of the Stanley Korshak store at 920 North Michigan Avenue; and the renovation of an office building at 205 West Wacker designed by D. H. Burnham and Company. They also collaborated on a dental clinic in Manhattan, Kansas, and a modular dental treatment support unit for Dentmodule Inc. In addition, Bonner's work has been published in many American and international periodicals. For one so young, Bonner has achieved notable success both in his architectural practice and in his experiments in product design.

145. Weighing only fifteen pounds, Henninger's chair is light enough to be carried in one hand with ease.

146. Henninger's chair is also multipurpose: with the back down, it can serve as a table.

147. Henninger's chair fully open.

148. A schematic drawing of Darcy Robert Bonner Jr.'s "wearable chair" in various positions.

"Wearable Chair," 1976

Bonner's design (Fig. 149) brings the concept of portability to its logical conclusion. The jury which awarded the chair second prize in the 1977 International Chair Design Competition recognized Bonner's important innovation: "The concept of a structural support that one could sit on that was worn as an item of clothing . . . is an entirely new concept—the first really new concept in seating in many years . . . the highly mechanized parts of the structure obviously represent the work of someone who is thinking out this completely fresh idea with very fresh details."[6]

Bonner's patent specifications describe the innovative mechanism: "With the lower member of the chair strapped to the calf, a spring presses the upper member against the thigh. As the user squats, the released compression bar pushes the leg of the chair to an extended position, thereby supporting the body. When the user rises, the lower member is retracted by a spring to its original position where it will not interfere with the user's movements." As of 1980, the wearable chair had not been put into production.

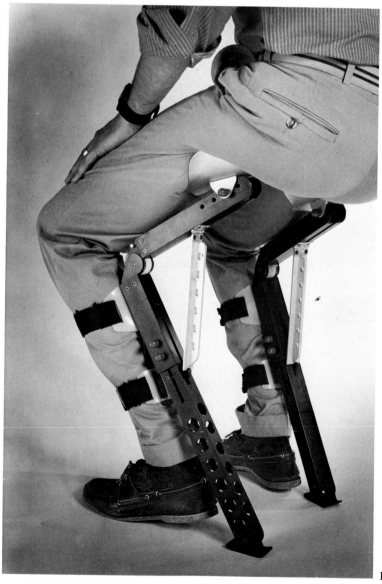

149

149. "Wearable chair," Darcy Robert Bonner Jr., Chicago, Ill., designed 1976. Aluminum tubing, canvas straps. 29½ (74.9 cm) long (strapped to leg); tubing width 1½ (3.8 cm). This design is so portable that it need not be carried and requires no manipulation to assume its seating form. Patents 4,138,156, February 6, 1979, and D249,987, October 24, 1978. Lent by Darcy Robert Bonner Jr.

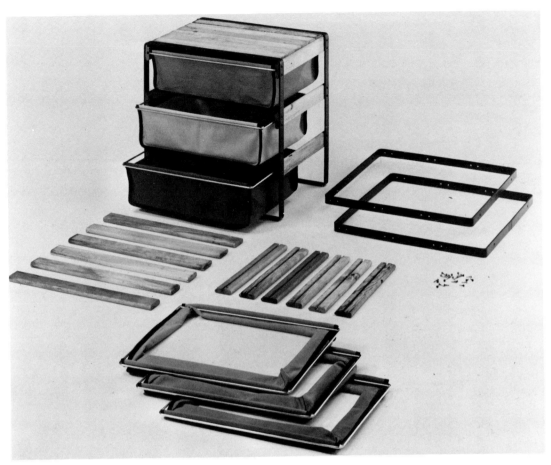

150

150. Storage system ("Northridge"), Jerry Johnson, Los Angeles, Calif., design introduced 1977. Wooden and metal frame, canvas drawers. 72 x 24 x 17½ (182.9 x 61 x 44.5 cm). Johnson's light, portable "knock-down" storage system is shown here disassembled. Patent 4,118,089, October 3, 1978 (furniture drawer); patent 256,305, August 12, 1980 (collapsible drawer). Manufactured by the Landes Manufacturing Company. Lent by the manufacturer.

JERRY JOHNSON (b. 1927)

Jerry Johnson, whose furniture designs have received recognition throughout the country, was born in Grand Rapids, Michigan, at the time of its greatest importance as the American furniture capital. After graduating from Michigan State University with an engineering degree in 1950, he spent two years learning the basics of furniture design at John Widdicomb Inc. in Grand Rapids when Robsjohn-Gibbings headed the design department, and created some furniture on his own as well. In 1952 he moved to Los Angeles and shortly thereafter began working for the Landes Manufacturing Company in Gardena. He has also designed for other major manufacturers.

In 1954, he was honored with a Gold Key award from the National Home Fashions League for a unique brass-frame canvas sling chair, selected for the first California Design exhibition at the Pasadena Art Museum that same year. His work has appeared in most of the California Design shows since then. In 1968, he won the top "Poly" award in the first juried show sponsored by the Society of Plastics Industries and the American Furniture Mart in Chicago, for his polyvinylchloride plastic outdoor furniture—the "Idyllwild Collection." Six years later he again received the "Poly" award for his plastic casegoods. His designs were exhibited at Eurodomus in Italy in 1972 and 1973 and at the Cologne Furniture Fair in 1973.

Among the design elements which he pioneered are canvas slings to replace webbing, springs, or strapping in seating pieces; puffy cushions filled with shredded foam; collapsible drawers for assemble-it-yourself furniture; the colorful canvas drawers used in his "Northridge" system; and extruded plastic.

During his tenure as president of the California Furniture Designers Association, Johnson worked to obtain legal protection for furniture comparable to that provided by literary or musical copyright. For years, design patents (as distinct from mechanical patents) were lightly regarded by manufacturers. In 1978 a violation of a design patent found legal remedy in a landmark federal court decision, which awarded double damages based on visual similarity between the original and the copy. Appropriately, it was handed down in behalf of a Johnson design for Landes.

The hallmark of Johnson's work is the creative use of a technical development or medium. Although mainly interested in technical innovation and other forms of experimentation, he says: "Very often solving a technical problem suggests the aesthetic consideration. It is the ultimate extension of the principle of form following function."[7]

Storage System ("Northridge"), 1977

The Northridge system is multipurpose as well as eminently portable. Shipped disassembled, with its canvas drawers packed flat (Fig. 150), it can be easily put together with a screwdriver. Each of the patented "knock-down" modular units consists of a steel-band frame with wood side rails and top, and a choice of three drawers or shelves. The modules combine horizontally or vertically in endless ways—as free-standing room dividers, wall units, or adjuncts to other forms of furniture. The canvas drawers are available in eighteen colors, including earth tones and a rainbow of bright pastels and primary hues. Prototypes for the system may be seen in the work of Charles Eames and George Nelson (Fig. 169).

151

151. Johnson's modules can be combined in numerous ways to fit individual requirements. The design is more than convenient: bright primary colors and self-supporting sculptural forms add aesthetic pleasure as well. Photograph courtesy of the Landes Manufacturing Company.

MULTIPLE FUNCTIONS

In the nineteenth century there developed among furniture makers and designers a tremendous interest in convertible forms. As Siegfried Giedion explained the phenomenon, "Patent furniture consists of types evolved by the middle brackets for their own urgent needs. Wealthy people had no call for a lounge convertible into a cradle, or a bed convertible into a wardrobe. They owned both the space and the means to satisfy their needs in other ways. The patent furniture arose, in America, at least, from the demands of an intermediate class that wished, without over-crowding, to bring a modicum of comfort into a minimum of space."[1]

While the concept of multipurpose furniture did not originate in the nineteenth century, the rage for convertibility was clearly symptomatic of an era in which an expanding, upwardly mobile population paid new attention to household decoration and the accumulation of material goods.

Most patented multipurpose furniture involved quite simple combinations—sofas which became beds, or tables which could be used in a variety of ways. In the latter part of the century, however, some of the more imaginative inventors suggested less plausible combinations. Bruschke and Ricke of Chicago, for example, felt that their combined sofa and bathtub (Fig. 152) was the "common sense invention of the age." Charles Hess was particularly creative in his "convertible bedroom piano," a curiosity if not a thing of beauty (Fig. 153). In addition to genuinely multipurpose designs we encounter pieces which were false fronts for other forms: closets disguised as desks, beds concealed in wardrobes, desks, and pianos (Fig. 154). Beds, it seems, because of their bulk, were the most likely candidates for concealment in other, less space-consuming forms.

Few, if any, of the more eccentric convertibles of the nineteenth century have survived the test of time, but some multipurpose forms of that and earlier centuries have indeed proved functional. Windsor writing-armchairs (Fig. 155) can be viewed as the forerunners of modern school desks; and sofa beds, in their many different forms and styles, are still undergoing changes today—modern advertisements continue to tout "improvements" on this theme which would appear to have long since been exhausted. Steps which convert into seating furniture are a common household article, particularly in the kitchen. While the Wooton desk (Figs. 167 and 168) is no longer in production, compact modern office equipment with file cabinets and drawers owes much to Wooton's design.

Some nineteenth-century multipurpose furniture included numerous functions in one form, such as the "combined wardrobe, bureau, looking glass, washstand, towel rack and toilet shelves" made by Ambrose E. Barnes and Brother. Less familiar than those mentioned above, such pieces are directly related to furniture designed for railroad sleeping cars.

Although the craze for convertible furniture has abated today, multipurpose designs are here to stay: kitchen "islands" that serve as both work space and storage units for pots, pans, and gadgets; the combined changing tables/bureaus found in babies' rooms; elaborate all-in-one "entertainment centers" featuring stereo, TV, and bar. It is unlikely that such multipurpose furniture will ever go out of fashion. (P. T.)

Combined Sofa and Bath Tub.

THE COMMON SENSE INVENTION OF THE AGE.

Is Practical, Convenient, Economical, Comfortable, Portable, Complete and Cheap.

In presenting this valuable combination to the public we are supplying a long-felt want, and placing a household necessity within the reach of all. It is not only a handsome and desirable piece of household furniture, but combines with it the best of bathing facilities. A full-sized Bath Tub, with water tank of 18 gallons capacity, the most improved Heating Device and complete Waste Water Attachments.

There is also provided a large rubber apron, that buttons on to the inside of outer edge of Bath Tub, folding over the front and covering the carpet one yard, thereby forming a perfect protection to the upholstery and carpet.

The combination can be upholstered appropriately for any room, and the bath used as satisfactorily as if taken in the most modern of bath-rooms.

For full particulars, as to styles of Upholstering, Prices, etc., address,

BRUSCHKE & RICKE,

Sole Manufacturers,

257 Division Street, Chicago, Ill.

152

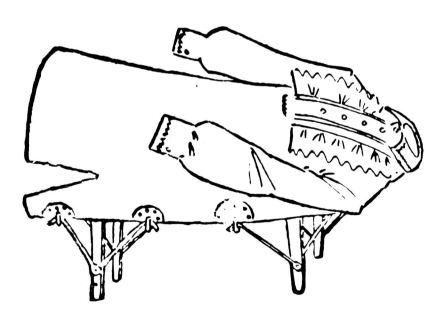

153

152. Combined sofa and bathtub, Bruschke and Ricke, Chicago, Ill. Multipurpose furniture was often carried to ridiculous extremes. This combination was evidently taken seriously by its manufacturer. From an advertisement in *Decorator and Furnisher*, December 1883.

153. "The Klondike Combined Folding Bed and Night Shirt," a cartoon ridiculing the craze for multipurpose forms. Although the enthusiasm of designers and furniture buyers occasionally reached humorous proportions, convertible forms were of major importance in the development of innovative nineteenth-century American furniture. From *The Furniture Worker*, January 10, 1898.

154. Patent drawing of "Convertible bed room piano," Charles Hess, Cincinnati, Ohio. Ink on paper. 19¼ x 14¾ (48.9 x 37.5 cm). This amusing example of multipurpose furniture, an upright version of the piano bed, was actually manufactured. Patent 56,413, July 17, 1866. Lent by The National Archives.

Charles Hess.

PATENTED
JUL 17.1866

Convertible bed room piano.

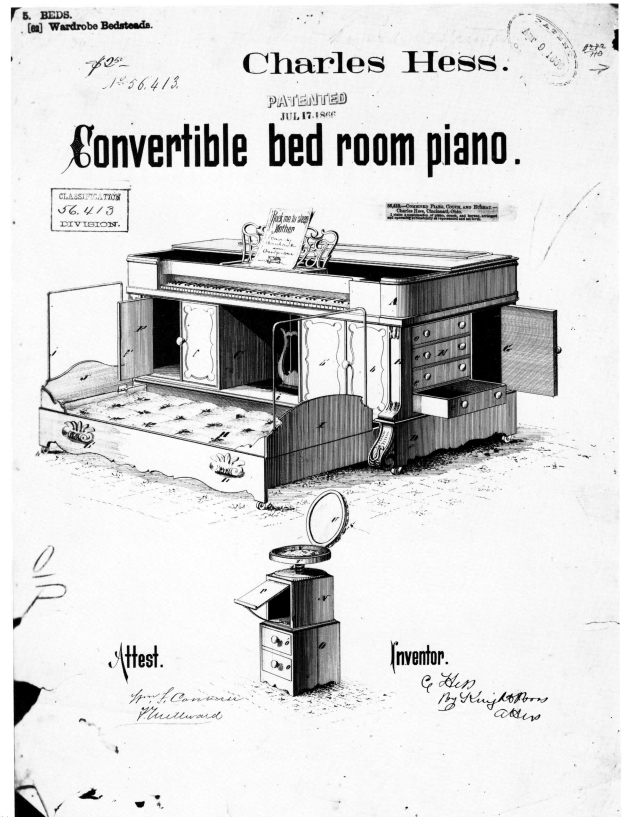

Attest.

Inventor.

154

Comb-back Windsor Writing Chair, mid-1800s (designer unknown)

Generally thought to have become popular in Philadelphia in the second half of the eighteenth century, Windsor desk chairs are early examples of furniture fulfilling more than one function. Most of these chairs used the comb-back form seen in this example (Fig. 155), which was modified by the addition of a large paddle-shaped writing surface attached to the right arm. Below this flat extension is a drawer to store writing implements. Under the seat is another drawer, making the chair totally functional for the student or clerk working in a limited space or having only modest financial means.

Desk chairs were popular through the nineteenth century; this example was probably made in the mid-1800s, as suggested by the attenuated turnings and flat seat. School desks of the twentieth century, common in high schools and colleges throughout the United States, have taken the lead directly from the Windsor design, implying the longevity of forms which have proved adaptable to new uses and environments.

155. Comb-back Windsor writing chair, designer unknown, mid-nineteenth century. Ash, maple, beech, leather. 40½ x 37 x 33 (102.9 x 94 x 83.8 cm). A combined desk and chair, this form has continued to the present in the design of schoolroom desks. Lent by the Cooper-Hewitt Museum, the Smithsonian Institution's National Museum of Design, gift of George A. Hearn.

AUGUSTUS ELIAERS (working 1849–1865)

First listed in the Boston city directory of 1849, Augustus Eliaers was a French émigré who opened a drawing school at 475 Washington Street with his countryman August Gassiot in that year. In 1851 Eliaers described himself as a cabinetmaker, working at 419 Washington Street. He reached national prominence in 1853 with his entries in the New York Crystal Palace Exhibition, a carved rosewood pier table and a rosewood sideboard of massive proportions in the Renaissance style.

With Eliaers's success at the Crystal Palace, he became known as the cabinetmaker to patronize if one wanted the finest furniture in Boston. His expertise was not limited to furniture, however: he was also a noted stair builder and architectural carver, creator of vast staircases reminiscent of those in French palaces. His work could be found in the most elegant houses in the developing Back Bay section of Boston.

Despite his reputation as the period's finest cabinetmaker, he is best known today for a different specialty. During the 1850s and 1860s he devoted much of his energy to inventions, many of which resulted in patents. The best-known is his library stairs which, when closed, become an elaborately carved armchair (Fig. 156); it is based on an eighteenth-century prototype. Other patents were for barber's chairs; extension chairs with attachable writing and reading tables; a seat for overnight railroad passengers who wished to sleep without being jostled into a neighbor's lap by the motion of the train; and a widely advertised reclining chair for invalids, with adjustable extensions.

From 1853 until his name disappeared from Boston city directories in 1865, he was listed as a "stair builder" and a "sofa manufacturer." His last address was at 367 Washington Street. That he left Boston is not certain, but a reference several years later in *Ballou's Pictorial* states that he returned to France. No proof of his residence in Paris has been located. It is known, however, that he stopped submitting patent applications after 1865 and was no longer mentioned in local sources. His years in business produced a considerable legacy of innovation and creativity.[2] (P. T.)

Library Chair and Patent Model, 1853–1865

Conceived in response to the growing importance of private libraries in the eighteenth century, library steps were used by leisured gentlemen to reach large folios on high shelves. The steps were meant to remain out of sight when not needed. Thus cabinetmakers and inventors alike produced designs for convertible library furniture. The notables among them include Thomas Chippendale, who built steps that folded into a case for Harewood House (1770–1775); Benjamin Franklin, who attached a stepladder to the bottom of his library chair (circa 1780); and Thomas Sheraton, whose two known sets of library steps converted into tables.[3] Surviving American examples of steps-and-table combinations suggest that the form was popular on this side of the Atlantic, too.

Like Benjamin Franklin, however, Augustus Eliaers decided to couple his steps with a handsome chair, in this case one combining elements of both the rococo and the Renaissance styles (Fig. 156). Five Eliaers examples of this type, plus a patent model, are known to survive, and, curiously, each is slightly different, suggesting the degree of freedom available to a patent owner in the completion of his product.

Even more significant are the differences between the patent model (Fig. 159) and the full-scale chairs. While the proportions and basic design elements are the same, the model is not upholstered and has a square rather than an ovoid back, a flat rear horizontal slat, and an undulating crest rail. In each of the five completed chairs, the back, seat, and armrest are upholstered. But the finished chairs differ in the number of steps (some have three, others five), the wood used (oak or mahogany), and the type and quality of carved ornament in the "ears" on either side of the crest rail and in the center of the seat rails. The treatment of the stretchers also varies.

It is the combination of elegant carving with a patented device that makes this group of chairs unusual. While much of the patent furniture of the mid-nineteenth century was innovative in terms of function, few cabinetmakers achieved the degree of sophistication in their finished products that Eliaers attained in his monumental design. (P. T.)

156

156. Library chair, Augustus Eliaers, Boston, Mass., c. 1853–1865. Mahogany and oak. 37⅜ x 24½ x 25 (94.9 x 62.2 x 63.5 cm). One of Boston's leading cabinet shops, known for its fine rococo-revival furniture, the Eliaers firm is famous today because of the survival of five of these labeled and patented multipurpose library chairs. Patent 10,151, October 25, 1853. "A. ELIAERS/PATENT" stamped on crest rail; "A. ELIAERS/PATENT" stamped on one side of fourth riser, "12 CORNHILL/BOSTON" on the other. Lent by the Museum of Fine Arts, Boston, Hezekiah Bolles Fund.

157. The Eliaers chair in the process of being converted into library steps.

158. The Eliaers chair ready for use in reaching high bookshelves.

159. Patent model of Eliaers's convertible library chair. Mahogany. 7 x 4½ x 4½ (17.8 x 11.4 x 11.4 cm). Unlike the extant full-size examples of the design, the model is unembellished with carving. Lent by the Museum of Fine Arts, Boston, Hezekiah Bolles Fund.

157

158

159

160

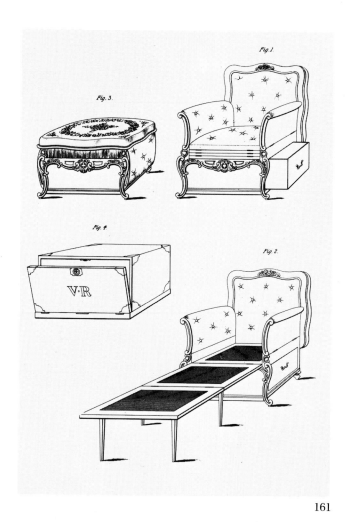

161

DUNCAN FORBES (working 1861–1872)

Duncan Forbes, born in Scotland, was first listed in a Chicago directory in 1861 as a ship's carpenter, boarding at 78 West Washington Street. In 1863, having changed professions, he was listed in the furniture business, at 57–59 West Madison.

One directory listing differs from the others. In C. W. Bailey's *Chicago City Directory* for 1867–68, Forbes is described as a manufacturer of "spring bed bottoms." It was in 1868 that he received a patent for an improved folding lounge which most likely incorporated the technology he used in making bedsprings.

In 1870–1871 Forbes was in partnership with John Cochran, also from Scotland, at 179 Madison Street. Listed under "retail furniture," the firm employed one man and one woman in what was clearly a small business. In 1872 both Forbes and Cochran disappeared from the city directories. (P. T.)

Patent Model of Folding Lounge, 1868

Beds disguised as other forms of furniture by day were by no means the invention of the nineteenth century. As early as the 1600s, beds had been concealed in trunks and chairs. An eighteenth-century Queen Anne-style wing chair found in Ellsworth, Maine, and press beds of the same period which could fold inside two cupboard doors, exemplify the desire to

160. Library steps and table. From Thomas Sheraton, *The Cabinet-Maker and Upholsterer's Drawing Book* (London, 1793), Plate 5.

161. "Portable Bed-Chair and Ottoman Seat," from Blackie and Son, *The Victorian Cabinet-Maker's Assistant* (London, 1853), Plate XCV.

162. Patent model of folding lounge, Duncan Forbes, Chicago, Ill. Walnut, upholstered. 5⅞ x 11¾ x 6⅜ (15 x 29.8 x 16.2 cm). A familiar form in the twentieth century, the sofa bed or "folding lounge" has been in existence from at least the 1600s. This patent model is an early example both of Chicago furniture and of the sofa bed form. Patent 83,949, November 10, 1868. Lent by the National Museum of History and Technology, Smithsonian Institution, transfer from the U.S. Patent Office, 65.470.

"economize room, owing to the size of [the purchasers'] families and sometimes owing to their modest-sized houses."[4]

If patent records are any indication, the need for dual-purpose furniture persisted in the nineteenth century, producing a stream of sofa beds and other multipurpose furniture designs, particularly after 1850. Hundreds of furniture makers claimed improvements on existing sofa beds and asserted that theirs was the best on the market.

While early convertible beds tended to be extremely narrow, like the one illustrated in *The Victorian Cabinet-Makers Assistant* (Fig. 161), later designs were usually made to fold out from sofas. A typical, simple device involved a two-layer mattress that folded out on springs, thus doubling the depth of the sofa frame to create a large flat surface for sleeping.

Other, later sofa beds were not so elementary. Duncan Forbes claimed that his 1868 design (Fig. 162) was a "novel combination of a two-part bolster with a peculiarly arranged spring-top, the whole being an improvement on the ordinary folding lounge."[5] The metal-framed bolster and the concealed drawer beneath the mattress distinguished Forbes's sofa from others and made it patentable. Other patented sofa beds include Philipp Frank's 1872 version in which the back folded down, and Ferdinand Braun's complicated version of a bed lounge, patented in 1874, which featured a side rail and head rest. One of the

162

better-known sofa beds of the period was that patented by George J. Henkels and featured at the Philadelphia Centennial Exhibition of 1876; it sold for $35.

The most famous of the twentieth-century versions of the sofa bed is the Castro Convertible, a trade name which has almost become synonymous with the form. The modern examples usually combine a low-arm rectangular frame with a collapsible metal spring which supports a folding mattress.

Successive patents have changed and "improved" the earliest sofa beds. Duncan Forbes's relatively early multipurpose form typifies the continuous effort to innovate in behalf of increased comfort, better use of space, and greater mechanical efficiency. (P. T.)

163. Forbes's patent model in its opened form.
164. The label for the table shown in Fig. 165 notes its usefulness for games, cutting, drawing, and reading. Projected over a bed, it served the needs of the invalid as well. Photograph courtesy of the Smithsonian Institution.

163

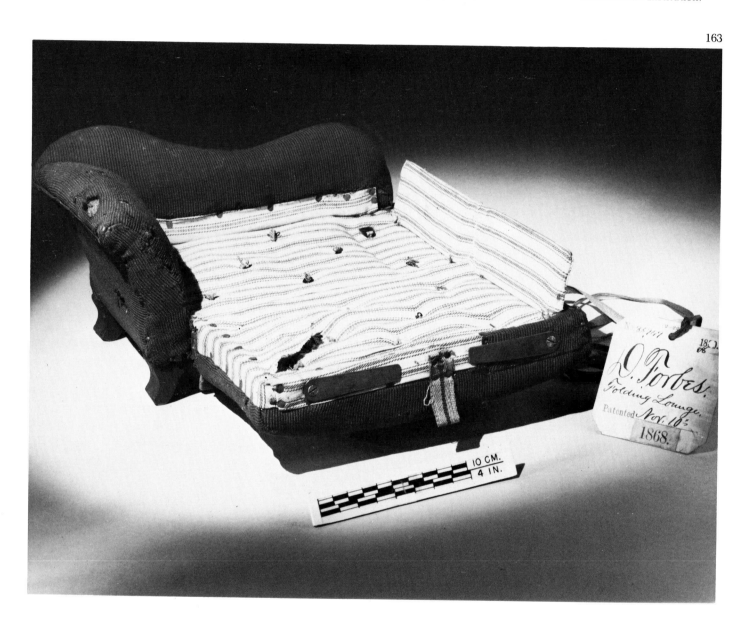

164

CLOWES AND GATES MANUFACTURING COMPANY (listed 1883)
GEORGE W. GATES (working 1876–1909)

All evidence points to George W. Gates as the craftsman and inventor in the Clowes and Gates Manufacturing Company, makers of the "Work, Study, Card, or Office Table" (Fig. 165). It was in Gates's name that the 1877 patent for the table was entered, and he was described as a table maker in the years before and after his partnership with George H. Clowes.

Gates was first listed in the Worcester, Massachusetts, city directory in 1876, producing "ladies' work tables" at 169 Chandler, his home as well as his shop. The retail outlet for his merchandise was located at 368 Main Street. By 1878 Gates's products were described as "folding tables," made at 131 Centre Street. The name change no doubt corresponds to the recently awarded patent for a folding table which was apparently Gates's most successful model. In 1880 he moved his shop to 80 Hanover, and in 1883 to 47 Foster. It was here that he was joined by Clowes, whose home was listed as Waterbury, Connecticut. In that year the Worcester directory lists "Clowes and Gates, table manufacturers," with Clowes most likely the "capitalist" in the firm.

By 1884 Clowes was no longer listed and Gates had moved to Philadelphia, where he remained for the rest of his life. One might assume, therefore, that the table shown here was made in 1883, the one year in which Clowes and Gates were partners. This thesis is tenuous, however, because an identical design, sold by Gates after he moved to Philadelphia, bears a label with the name "Clowes and Gates Mfg. Co." as well as the individual name of "George W. Gates, Washington Ave. and 17th Street (ex. Waterbury, Conn.), Philadelphia, Pa."[6]

Evidently Clowes was the "silent partner," and may well have been involved with Gates for longer than the year when he was listed in the directory. Clearly George Gates was the more active of the two, particularly since the location of the manufactory of the tables moved from Worcester to Philadelphia when he did.

Gates was listed in the Philadelphia directories from 1885 until 1909, first as a table maker at Washington Avenue near South 17 Street, and later at 120 Exchange Place. He was variously described as "president," "manufacturer's agent," "cabinetmaker" and "carpenter," but the word "tables" was the most frequent designation, indicating his consistent involvement with this specialty. (P. T.)

Work, Study, Card, or Office Table, 1877

Meeting the need for a small, multipurpose folding table, George W. Gates joined the ranks of inventors of patent furniture in 1877 with what he claimed in his paper label was the "best

165. Work, study, card, or office table, Clowes and Gates Manufacturing Company, Worcester, Mass. Mahogany, cherry, iron. 34 x 32 x 24 open (86.4 x 81.3 x 61 cm). This functional piece was embellished with turned and carved supports, a contrast to its simple unadorned tabletop. Patent 192,252 (issued to George W. Gates), June 19, 1877. Paper label in drawer (now removed): white ground, blue and black ink (restored). Lent by the National Museum of History and Technology, Smithsonian Institution, Anonymous Gift Fund R (300529.1).

165

work, study, card or office table ever manufactured" (Fig. 164). So adaptable was the table that it was "equally entitled to a place" in the sitting-room, library, office, or sickroom.

The table's adjustable rotating supporting column could be folded or closed together with the legs and the top (Fig. 166). Capable of achieving three different heights, the form could be adapted for children, or function as a desk for reading, drafting, and office work. The neatly carved legs, turned pedestal, and stenciled decoration on the column helped make the table a welcome addition to any room.

The Gates table was a particularly successful attempt at a versatile piece of furniture that was both functional and aesthetically pleasing. This combination of good design and usefulness typified a large proportion of the patent furniture of the late nineteenth century. Recognizable adaptations of the form—for example, Stacor's drawing table with basswood top and Victorian-style iron base, illustrated in the *New York Times,* June 5, 1980—are still available. (P. T.)

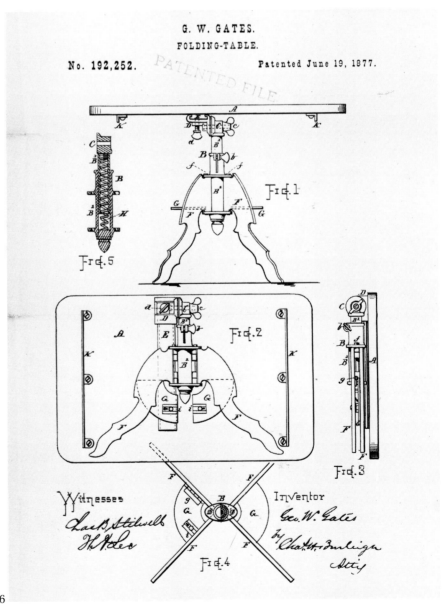

166. Patent drawing of "Folding-Table" (side elevation, plan, and details), George W. Gates, Worcester, Mass. Ink on paper. 18½ x 14 (47 x 35.6 cm). The schematized drawing demonstrates the mechanical folding devices. Patent 192, 252, June 19, 1877. Lent by the U.S. Department of Commerce, Patent and Trademark Office.

166

WILLIAM S. WOOTON (working 1874–1897)

A Quaker who spent his early years in Terre Haute, Indiana, William S. Wooton, founder of the Wooton Desk Company, worked in Richmond for three years before moving to Indianapolis. In Richmond, Wooton had been a partner of George H. Grant and Company, manufacturers of "school furniture, office, and court supplies," a specialty which he pursued when he started Wooton and Company in Indianapolis in 1870. From the start his firm specialized in school, office, and church furniture; the business was worth $18,500 in its first year of operation.

Although already the owner of two patents for school furniture, Wooton did not achieve prominence in Indianapolis until 1874 when he was awarded a patent for a "Patent Cabinet Office Secretary"—"a secretary in three parts, two of which are together equal in width to the other, each part being provided with compartments or pigeon-holes suitable for storing books, papers, etc. . . ." (Fig. 168).[7] In November of that same year Wooton formed a partnership with John G. Blake and Harmon H. Fulton in the name of the Wooton Desk Company. Rapid production of the patented secretary ensued, and soon the company was well known throughout the United States.

By 1876 the rage for the Wooton "cabinet office secretary" had spread to Europe, in part due to its display at the Centennial Exhibition in Philadelphia. Advertisements in newspapers, trade journals, and magazines touted the desk's "compactness, convenience, and utility," and it was featured in the company's second annual catalog, along with the newly patented "rotary office desk," a smaller and less expensive version of the original model (Fig. 167). Possessing a Wooton desk in 1876 was a status symbol, and the list of its owners reads like a Who's Who of American businessmen—Jay Gould, Joseph Pulitzer, and John D. Rockefeller among them. The desk was also to be found in prominent public buildings. The one in the White House, made for Ulysses S. Grant, had an eagle on its cornice; the Smithsonian Institution's model was purchased in 1875 and used by Spencer Baird during his tenure as Secretary of the Smithsonian from 1878 to 1887 (Fig. 168).

167. "Wooton No. 8 Rotary Desk" (small-scale model, probably a salesman's sample), William S. Wooton, Indianapolis, Ind. Walnut with burled walnut veneer on drawer fronts and pedestal panels. 13 x 8 x 7½ (33 x 20.3 x 19.1 cm). The rotary desk exemplifies the ingenuity of the nineteenth century. When closed, it was simple in appearance and took up only limited space in the office or library; when open, it was virtually an office in itself. Patent 172,362, January 18, 1876. Lent by Mr. and Mrs. David J. Baer.

167

Despite Wooton's patents, several similar desks began to be seen on the market after 1876. Joseph A. Moore, formerly Wooton's general manager, took out patents in 1878 and 1882 for desks which, though somewhat different in form, were obvious derivatives. Moore's Combination Desk Company remained in business until 1894.

In 1880 William Wooton moved to Danville, Indiana, having already left the company he founded (he is no longer listed as an officer after 1876). By that time the firm, which remained in Indianapolis, was known as the Wooton Desk Manufacturing Company. The following year Wooton filed his last patent, for a modification in the secretary which made "the writing table and the pigeon-hole space about equal in width to the combined width of the door portions and their extensions."[8] Three years later the last advertisement for the Wooton Desk Manufacturing Company appeared. The firm apparently went out of business in 1884 or 1885, for in February 1885 the Wooton desk was advertised as being manufactured by Haynes, Spencer and Company of Richmond, the successor to George H. Grant and Company, where Wooton had started his career. The desk continued to be made by a series of firms until 1898, when the last reference to it is found, as a product of the Indianapolis Cabinet Company. By that time the proliferation of business records resulting from the use of typewriters and duplicating machines created a need for more filing space; not surprisingly, numerous patents for file cabinets were issued during the 1890s. The tremendous popularity of the Wooton desk during the 1870s and 1880s, however, suggests that this remarkable invention had for a time thoroughly satisfied the public's desire for multipurpose furniture that was both solidly constructed and beautiful.[9] (P. T.)

Wooton No. 8 Rotary Desk, 1876

Less well-known today than Wooton's "cabinet office secretary," the rotary desk was nonetheless an important and popular model sold in a variety of styles and grades by the Wooton Desk Company. Its rotating device, patented in 1876, was described in the firm's *Illustrated Catalogue* the same year: "This is an ingenious device, a perfect model of convenience, the main features of which may be attached to all grades of desks constructed with piers . . . it will be seen that the space of the lower part is brought forward to the operator by rotating cases, pivoted substantially, so as to revolve with perfect freedom."

The design filled the need for a smaller and less expensive version of the secretary for "those whose business does not require the capacity of the Cabinet, and being sold at as favorable prices as the old inconvenient styles, brings them within the reach of all. . . ."

The form was available in twelve styles, including a single and double pedestal variety, with either a flat or a slanted top writing surface. The No. 8 model (Fig. 167) was described as a standard grade, double-pier countinghouse desk, four feet eight inches wide when closed, and two feet wider when open.

Wooton's ingenuity and creativity are apparent in several features of the rotary desk. When closed, it occupied a limited space and provided a comfortable writing surface. In its open form, however, it revealed file drawers, a place for ledgers and standing files, as well as room for supplies—a miniature office. The concept of multipurpose furniture is here stretched to its limits, without reaching the extremes of some of the more bizarre examples of nineteenth-century inventiveness, such as the combination bed and piano, or bathtub and sofa.

The purpose of the miniature version of the desk shown here has not been ascertained, but the conjecture that it served as a salesman's sample is most probable. Wooton desks were sold by many agents in cities across the United States as well as in foreign cities such as Glasgow, London, and Rio de Janeiro.[10] It seems highly likely that the Wooton company would have prepared a model to show potential customers. (P. T.)

GEORGE NELSON (b. 1908)

Trained as an architect, George Nelson has also been a furniture designer, teacher, and writer. He was born in Hartford but has spent most of his life in New York City. At the end of his professional study at Yale, where he received a B.A. in 1928 and a B.F.A. in 1931, he won a national competition for the Rome Prize in Architecture and spent two years studying in Italy, which resulted in his writing the first series of articles to appear in the United States on the pioneering modern architects of Europe. These brought him an invitation to join the staff of *Architectural Forum*, one of the most prestigious magazines in the field at that time. He later became managing coeditor with Henry Wright.

In association with William Hamby, Nelson opened an architectural office in 1936, receiving a number of commissions, primarily residential. With the outbreak of World War II, architectural work had to be put aside and the next few years were taken up with a variety of activities—editorial work, a book (*Tomorrow's House*, 1945, written in collaboration with Henry Wright), and industrial design commissions.

The "Storagewall," forerunner of the storage system shown here, was an offshoot of the book and received wide publicity through a feature in *Life* magazine. This novel design replaced the conventional partition by a set of units that functioned both as a wall and as storage space for household items. *Life's* publication of the design led to Nelson's association with the Herman Miller Furniture Company and in 1946, after the death of Gilbert Rohde, he became the firm's design director, bringing in many young innovative designers, including Charles Eames and Alexander Girard. In the course of his work for Herman Miller in 1945–1946, he found time to produce an important controversial article on the furniture industry which appeared in *Fortune* magazine, January 1947. At the end of 1947 he opened an architecture and industrial design practice in New York.

His office has designed products, graphics, restaurants, shops, and office interiors. It was responsible for the design of the United States National Exhibition in Moscow in 1959, the first major American display under the U.S.-Soviet cultural exchange agreement. Other projects have included space planning and interior design for large office facilities and hospitals, as well as equipment specifications for the latter; visual identification and graphic communications projects for corporations and government agencies; and the design of business equipment.

Nelson is the author of numerous articles published in the United States and abroad. His book *Problems of Design*, 1957, has been translated into Japanese and Russian. *How to See*, an illustrated commentary on our environment, appeared in 1977. *George Nelson on Design*, an essay collection, was published by the Whitney Library of Design in 1979.

Nelson continues in business in New York today as president of George Nelson and Company and a partner in Nelson and Chadwick, Architects.

168. Wooton cabinet office secretary, William S. Wooton, Indianapolis, Ind. Patented in 1874, this design made Wooton a celebrity among furniture makers. Its owners included some of the period's most prominent figures, among them President Ulysses S. Grant. Photograph courtesy of the Smithsonian Institution.

Comprehensive Storage System (section), 1959

The comprehensive storage system, or CSS (Fig. 169), is an example of multipurpose furniture *par excellence*. The initial design goes back to 1945 when Nelson and Henry N. Wright produced the prototype for his "Storagewall," which was publicized that year in *Life* magazine in conjunction with an exhibition at Macy's department store, New York. The system was an answer to a growing problem of American lifestyle: more acquired objects and smaller living spaces. Nelson conceived that most household items could be stored in depths of ten inches or less, and that connecting storage components—shelves, cabinets, and desk—could be erected against unused walls and changed according to need. Thus the system fulfilled the functions of numerous pieces of furniture, from breakfronts to bookcases.

A development of earlier designs (Figs. 170 and 171), the system contained twenty-two basic components, including a desk, drawers, and space for files and books. As with Nelson's earlier designs, the system could be expanded both vertically and horizontally, and the storage elements—for example, the drop-front desk—which were supported by poles and brackets, could be either mounted against the wall or used as free-standing ceiling-to-floor dividers. Each adjustable aluminum pole, which was pressure-fitted between ceiling and floor, contained a continuous track. This gave CSS tremendous flexibility, as its sixteen storage elements or shelves could be placed at any height on the poles. CSS not only was less expensive than built-in carpentry work but it could be "knocked down" and transported.

Introduced by Herman Miller in May 1959, CSS was discontinued in 1973. Today, numerous storage units based on Nelson's innovative system are available in a variety of styles—wall-mount or free-standing, with closed or open cases for storage or partitions.

169

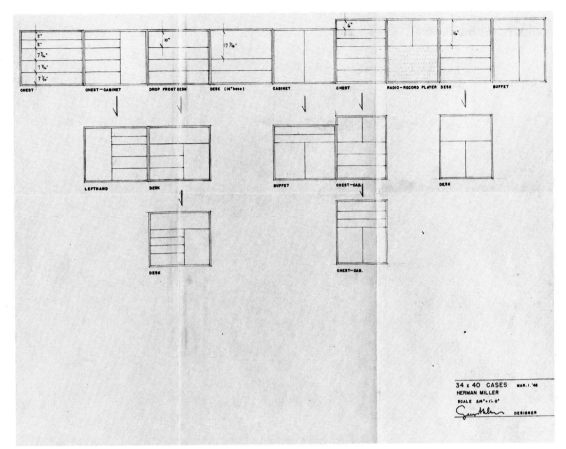

170

171

169. Comprehensive storage system (section), George Nelson, New York, design introduced 1959. 75³/₁₆ x 32 x 10 (191 x 81.3 x 25.4 cm). Aluminum poles, wooden compartments. A solution to a growing problem for American households, this modular system takes advantage of unused wall space. It can also be set up as a room divider. The units fulfill both storage and furniture functions. Manufactured by Herman Miller Inc. Lent by the Herman Miller Inc. Resource Center.

170. Drawing of storage cases (front elevation), George Nelson, New York, March 1, 1946. Pencil and pen on tracing paper. 18⅝ x 23¾ (47.3 x 60.3 cm). The inscriptions under the elevations indicate desks, chest-cabinets, buffets, and a radio–record player. At lower right: "34 x 40 CASES MAR. 1, '46/HERMAN MILLER/ . . . /George Nelson [signature] DESIGNER." Lent by the Herman Miller Inc. Resource Center.

171. Drawing of storage system (front and side elevations), George Nelson, New York, 1949–1950. Pencil on tracing paper. 18⅜ x 29¾ (46.7 x 75.6 cm). An earlier version of the comprehensive storage system (Fig. 169), the drawing shows various combinations of the modular units, with specification notes. Inscribed in lower right: "GEORGE NELSON 20 WEST 55th St., NEW YORK 19, N.Y./ . . . HERMAN MILLER FURNITURE COMPANY/ . . . 8-1-49/ . . . Revisions/ 8-19-49 . . . 9-15-50 . . . / Drawing No./182/Revised." Lent by the Herman Miller Inc. Resource Center.

Lenders to the Exhibition

Atelier International Ltd.
Mr. and Mrs. David J. Baer
Darcy Robert Bonner Jr.
Dr. and Mrs. Milton L. Brindley
Cooper-Hewitt Museum, The Smithsonian Institution's National Museum of Design
Gold Medal Inc.
Ralph W. Henninger
Herman Miller Inc. Resource Center
Eleanor K. Johnson
Margot Johnson
S. C. Johnson and Sons Inc.
Knoll International
Landes Manufacturing Company
Mrs. Robert Augustus Leighey
Elinor Merrell
The Metropolitan Museum of Art
Museum of Fine Arts (Boston)
John H. Nally
The National Archives
National Museum of History and Technology, Smithsonian Institution
Davis J. Pratt
Smithsonian Institution Furnishings Collection
Thonet Industries Inc.
U. S. Department of Commerce, Patent and Trademark Office
Anonymous lenders

Objects in the Exhibition of Innovative Furniture in America

Designers and Manufacturers of Objects in the Exhibition (chronologically arranged)

Samuel Gragg (1772–?1855)
John Henry Belter (1804–1863)
Heywood Brothers and Company (1826–1897)
American Chair Company (1829–1858)
Gasper Gadone (working 1830–1870)
George J. Hunzinger (1835–1898)
Samuel G. McCullough (1843–1927)
Wakefield Rattan Company (1844–1897)
Allen and Brothers (1847–1902)
Thomas E. Warren (working 1849–1852)
Augustus Eliaers (working 1849–1865)
Lalance and Grosjean (working 1852–post-1900)
Duncan Forbes (working 1861–1872)
Gardner and Company (working 1863–1888)
Frank Lloyd Wright (1867–1959)
Isaac I. Cole (working 1870s)
Cevedra B. Sheldon (working 1873–1877)
William S. Wooton (working 1874–1897)
George W. Gates (working 1876–1909)
Marks Adjustable Folding Chair Company (1877–1897)
Clowes and Gates Manufacturing Company (listed 1883)
Troy Sunshade Company (1887–   )

Gold Medal Inc. (1892–   )
Gilbert Rohde (1894–1944)
Heywood-Wakefield Company (1897–   )
Royal Metal Manufacturing Company (1900–1962)
Charles Eames (1907–1978)
George Nelson (b. 1908)
Eero Saarinen (1910–1961)
Steelcase Inc. (1912–   )
Harry Bertoia (1915–1978)
Florence Schust Knoll (b. 1917)
Davis J. Pratt (b. 1917)
Edgar Bartolucci (b. 1918)
Paul Tuttle (b. 1918)
Jack Waldheim (b. 1920)
Herman Miller Inc. (1923–   )
Jerry Johnson (b. 1927)
Frank O. Gehry (b. 1929)
Ralph W. Henninger (b. 1935)
Don Chadwick (b. 1936)
Knoll International (1939–   )
Peter J. Danko (b. 1949)
Darcy Robert Bonner Jr. (b. 1952)
Landes Manufacturing Company (1953–   )

Notes

AUTHOR'S PREFACE

[1]*Mechanization Takes Command: A Contribution to Anonymous History* (New York: Oxford University Press, 1948), p. 390.
[2]*Ibid.*, p. 365.
[3]Though many such manufacturers are known by name, it could be said that their fame is frequently the result of chance survivals of archive materials. One satisfaction in the study of patent furniture is that the designer's name and geographic location may be discovered through the patent specification. The designer of high-style furniture is often known only when the piece is labeled or by some other documentation.
[4]"Styling, Organization, Design," *Arts and Architecture*, August 1947, p. 24.
[5]A chronological list of the designers and manufacturers of objects in the exhibition appears on page 190.
[6]Reyner Banham, "The Chair as Art," in *Modern Chairs, 1918–1970* (Boston: Boston Book and Art, 1970), p. 19.
[7]Banham, *ibid.*, pp. 20–21, traces the concept's origin to William Morris and the English arts and crafts movement at the end of the nineteenth century.
[8]*Illustrated London News*, August 23, 1851, p. 250.

NINETEENTH-CENTURY AMERICAN PATENT FURNITURE

[1]The classic work on patent furniture remains Siegfried Giedion, *Mechanization Takes Command: A Contribution to Anonymous History* (New York: Oxford University Press, 1948), in which he shows in the section on "The Constituent Furniture of the Nineteenth Century," using artifacts and records of the 1800s, especially furniture patents, how motion, comfort, and convertibility in furniture were approached "in a manner completely new to the century." Giedion's work is one of the few examinations of "non-'artistic' furniture" and what it can tell us about the vigor, inventive urge, and functional approach of Americans during the "Decades of Patent Furniture, 1850–90." Also using patents as a source for the study of society, Peter C. Welsh explores "the changing contemporary interests" they reflect in "United States Patents 1790 to 1870: New Uses for Old Ideas," Paper 48 in *Contributions from the Museum of History and Technology (United States National Museum Bulletin 241)* (Washington, D.C.: Smithsonian Institution Press, 1965), pp. 109–52.
[2]The best introduction to the patent records is Nathan Reingold, "U.S. Patent Office Records as Sources for the History of Invention and Technological Property," *Technology and Culture* 1, no. 2 (Spring 1960): 156–67. See also "Patents, The Law of," *Encyclopedia Americana, International Edition* (New York: Americana

Corporation, 1976); Robert C. Post, "The American Genius," in *The Smithsonian Book of Invention* (Washington, D.C.: Smithsonian Exposition Books, 1978), pp. 22–31; Morgan Sherwood, "A Patent Madness," in *ibid.*, pp. 156–59.
[3]U.S. Patent Office, *United States Patents of Invention, 1790–* (microform) (New Haven, Conn.: Research Publications, 1973–).
[4]For the history of the models and their dispersal, see Donald W. Hogan, "Unwanted Treasures of the Patent Office," *American Heritage*, February 1958, pp. 16–19, 101–3; William and Marlys Ray, *The Art of Invention: Patent Models and Their Makers* (Princeton, N.J.: The Pyne Press, 1974); Jan Greenberg, Jessica Hagemann, and William Schinsky, *American Patent Models 1836/1880* (Fullerton, Calif.: The Art Gallery, California State University at Fullerton, 1977); Eugene S. Ferguson and Christopher Baer, *Little Machines: Patent Models in the Nineteenth Century* (Greenville, Del.: The Hagley Museum, 1979).
[5](Washington, D.C.: Government Printing Office, 1874; repr. New York: Arno Press, 1976).
[6]See, for example, "Convertibility," in Giedion, *Mechanization Takes Command*, pp. 423–38; and Peter Thornton, *Seventeenth-Century Interior Decoration in England, France and Holland* (New Haven, Conn.: Yale University Press, 1978), p. 169.
[7]U.S. Patent Office, *Women Inventors to Whom Patents Have Been Granted by the United States Government, 1790 to July 1, 1888* (Washington, D.C.: Government Printing Office, 1888); U.S. Patent Office, *Women Inventors to Whom Patents Have Been Granted by the United States Government, July 1, 1888, to October 1, 1892* (Washington, D.C.: Government Printing Office, 1892); U.S. Patent Office, *Women Inventors to Whom Patents Have Been Granted by the United States Government, October 1, 1892, to March 1, 1895. Arranged Chronologically and by Classes* (Washington, D.C.: Government Printing Office, 1895).
[8]Rodris Roth, "A Patent Model by John Henry Belter," *Antiques* 111, no. 5 (May 1977): 1038–40.
[9]Robert C. Post, " 'Liberalizers' versus 'Scientific Men' in the Antebellum Patent Office," *Technology and Culture* 17, no. 1 (January 1976): 24–54.
[10]Rodris Roth, "Seating for Anyplace: The Folding Chair" (paper presented at "Furniture in Victorian America" symposium, Philadelphia, 1978), forthcoming.
[11]During his entire career Palmer was in a partnership, first as Palmer, Owen and Company at 207, 209, 211 Canal in 1869, then as Palmer, Embury and Company at 207 Canal in 1872, and at 46 Elizabeth in 1873. In 1877 the name was changed to Palmer and Embury and the address to 185 Canal. For the remainder of the century the firm was located at 185 and 187 Canal and at Water and Gouverneur, in addition to being listed at 20 East 18 Street in 1884, at 18 East 18 in 1890, and at 38 Union Square West in 1895. The next year the name was once again changed to Palmer and Embury

Manufacturing Company. Business continued in this century at 42 East 20 Street in 1900. See also Ellen and Bert Denker, *The Rocking Chair Book* (New York: Mayflower Books, 1979), p. 85, Figs. 74 and 75.

[12]All directory references are from the microform *City Directories of the United States, Segment 1. Through 1860; . . . Segment 2. 1861–1881; . . . Segment 3. 1882–1901* (New Haven, Conn.: Research Publications, 1966).

[13]All quotations from judges' reports are from U.S. Centennial Commission, *Reports and Awards*, ed. Francis A. Walker (Washington, D.C.: Government Printing Office, 1880–84), Vol. IV, Group VII, Furniture.

[14]I am indebted to Regina Lee Blaszczyk for bringing the advertisement in *Baldwin's Directory* to my attention. For an account of Hunzinger's activity, see the Materials section.

[15]Patent 211,159, January 7, 1879, was for an improvement in the manufacture of chair frames "in which the wood is strengthened by metal strips drawn upon the same." Hunzinger's specifications further noted: "the metal bars become ornaments to the wooden chair-frame, as well as strengthening the same." In short, the metal was more trim than functional. This is true of the Smithsonian chair, catalog 1980.446.1, gift of Mrs. Mary Jean Alexander.

[16]Kenneth Ames, "Gardner & Company of New York," *Antiques* 100, no. 2 (August 1971): 252–55. See also the Technique section.

[17]The Collignon address in 1871, the first year the New York office was listed, was 35 Park Place; in 1873 it was 83 Bowery, and in 1874, 181 Canal, the final location for the remaining period the Collignons were in business. The firm name varied over the years, too. N. Collignon and Brothers was changed in 1877 to Collignon Brothers, in 1885 to Claudius O. Collignon, and in 1892, following the death of Claudius, to Peter C. Collignon. No entry for Collignon chairs is listed in the New York City directory after 1896.

[18]Patent 110,220, December 20, 1870.

[19]Patent 94,617, September 7, 1869, granted to Charles P. Lenz, Poughkeepsie, N. Y.

[20]Patent 107,215, September 13, 1870, granted to Melvin Bancroft, Montague, Mass., assignor to George F. Richardson and Company, of same place.

[21](New York: D. Appleton and Company, 1850; repr. New York: Dover Publications, 1969), p. 428.

[22]*The New York Times Magazine*, June 22, 1980, carried five advertisements (pp. 4, 10, 14, 44, 57) for sofa beds, also called convertibles. One featured a "patented . . . mechanism" and another the absence of "heavy metal rods and springs" as reasons to select their products.

[23]Patent 130,290, August 6, 1872, granted to Philipp Frank, New York, N. Y.

[24]First listed in the city directories at 101 East 12 Street in 1861, Werner gave his occupation as furnishings; the following year it was upholsterer. He moved to 100 Third Avenue in 1864, to 103 Third Avenue in 1867, to 88 Third Avenue in 1868, and 405 Fourth Avenue in 1870. That year he gave his occupation as decorator, the next year as upholsterer, and then as "furniture," while from 1875 to 1877 he listed it as clothier at 10 Walker. He moved again to 102 West 42 Street in 1878, to 225 West 46 in 1886, and finally to 255 West 26 in 1890, the last year his name appears. (I am indebted for this information to Debora Fillos and her Smithsonian museum internship paper, "An Examination of Eleven Models of Sofa Beds and Lounge Beds, Patented Between 1868 and 1876, and Their Inventors," December 1979.)

[25]Knell was first listed in the Philadelphia city directory in 1856 as an upholsterer at 176 Shippen. He changed addresses frequently, moving to 47 Coates in 1857, 330 Garden in 1858, 1120 Division in 1859, 6 Clarissa Place in 1860, 1103 Locust in 1861, 459 York in 1863, 130 Market in 1869 (listing his business as furniture), and 155

North Fourth in 1872. Four years later the firm's name was changed to George Knell and Son, appearing thus in the 1877 directory, when upholstery again was listed along with furniture. The company moved to 228 South Second in 1885 and to 628 North Sixth in 1890. No listing appears after 1893.

[26]Philadelphia city directories show that Hover was first working as an upholsterer at 7 Julianna in 1843, moving to 7 Chatham in 1844. His name disappears between 1846 and 1849. He is listed again in 1850 as an upholsterer at 205 North Third, moving to 132 South Second in 1851 and to 126 South Second in 1852. His furniture shop was at 230 South Second from 1858 until 1886, when it was listed at 232 South Second. The business terminated that year or next because of Hover's death. (I am grateful to Olive Graffam for tracing part of this directory listing.)

[27]Patent 180,694, August 1, 1876, granted to Henry York, Philadelphia, Pa. First listed as a cabinetmaker in 1862, York moved in 1864 to 920 South Third and in 1866 to 261 South Second, his last address. He was in partnership first as Moore and York from 1871 to 1874, next as Moore, York and Howell from 1875 to 1878, and finally as York and Eastburn from 1879 to 1883. (I am indebted to Debora Fillos for tracing part of this directory listing.)

[28]The only patent pertaining to a bed listed for Hover between 1855 and 1882 was a reissue, number 4,713, January 16, 1872, granted to Elisha E. Everitt, assignor to Henry F. Hover, both of Philadelphia, for a spring bed bottom. The English and French patents have not been checked.

[29]Betty Lawson Walters, *The King of Desks: Wooton's Patent Secretary*, Smithsonian Studies in History and Technology No. 3 (Washington, D.C.: Smithsonian Institution Press, 1969), pp. 2, 5, 20, 24.

[30]"A New Folding Chair," *The Cabinet Maker and Art Furnisher* (London), June 2, 1890, pp. 329–30. (I am indebted to David Hanks for bringing this article to my attention.)

[31]"American Furniture in London," *The Trade Bureau*, October 1, 1881, p. 14.

[32]*Ibid.*

TECHNIQUE: BENDING AND LAMINATION

[1]Nikolaus Pevsner, "The History of Plywood up to 1814," *Architectural Review*, September 1939, p. 129.

[2]Siegfried Giedion, *Mechanization Takes Command: A Contribution to Anonymous History* (New York: Oxford University Press, 1948), pp. 507–8.

[3]The technical notes are based on Bryan Westwood, "Plywood," *Architectural Review Supplement*, September 1939, pp. 133–41.

[4]"Samuel Gragg: His Bentwood Fancy Chairs," *Yale University Art Gallery Bulletin* 33, no. 2 (Autumn 1971): 31.

[5]*A List of Patents Granted by the United States from April 10, 1790, to December 31, 1836* (Washington, D. C., 1872), p. 67.

[6]Charles F. Montgomery, *American Furniture, The Federal Period* (New York: Viking Press, 1966), p. 469, No. 431.

[7]Clare Vincent, "John Henry Belter: Manufacturer of All Kinds of Fine Furniture," in *Technological Innovation and the Decorative Arts* (Winterthur Conference Report, 1973), ed. Ian M. G. Quimby and Polly Anne Earl (Charlottesville, Va.: The University Press of Virginia, 1974), pp. 207–34.

[8]See Rodris Roth, "A Patent Model by John Henry Belter," *Antiques* 111, no. 5 (May 1977): 1038–40.

[9]"Gardner & Company of New York,," *Antiques* 100, no. 2 (August 1971): 252–55. We have drawn on this article for some of the information included here and in the discussion of the Gardner platform rocker, below.

[10]Gardner and Company catalog, *Perforated Veneer Seats. . . .*

(New York, 1884) (Winterthur Museum).

[11]Ellen and Bert Denker, *The Rocking Chair Book* (New York: Mayflower Books, 1979), pp. 106–10.

[12]See "Design for Living House," *Architectural Forum* 59, no. 1 (July 1933): 53.

[13]*The National Cyclopedia of American Biography* (New York: James T. White and Company, 1949), p. 224.

[14]*A Modern Consciousness: D. J. De Pree, Florence Knoll,* exhibition catalog (Washington, D.C.: Smithsonian Institution Press, 1975), pp. 7–8.

[15]Quoted in Arthur Drexler, *Charles Eames: Furniture from the Design Collection,* exhibition catalog (New York: The Museum of Modern Art, 1973), p. 5.

[16]Letter from Peter Danko to the author, November 18, 1979.

[17]Suzanne Slesin, "Sizing Up the Furniture at the Chicago Show," *New York Times,* June 19, 1980.

MATERIALS

[1]John F. Pile, *Modern Furniture* (New York: John Wiley and Sons, 1979), p. 148.

[2]Joseph Aronson, *The Book of Furniture and Decoration: Period and Modern,* rev. ed. (New York: Crown, 1941), pp. 242–43.

[3]Pile, *Modern Furniture,* p. 88.

[4]James, Kirtland and Company, *Illustrated Catalogue of Ornamental Ironwork,* reprint (Princeton, N.J.: Pyne Press, 1971 [1870]).

[5]U. S. Centennial Commission, *Official Catalogue of the International Exhibition* (Philadelphia: Centennial Catalogue Company, 1876), pp. 37–39.

[6]The biographical information included here is drawn primarily from Richard W. Flint, "George Hunzinger, Patent Furniture Maker," *Art & Antiques* 3, no. 1 (January-February 1980): 116–23.

[7]The history of the company is drawn mainly from *A Completed Century, 1826–1926: The Story of Heywood-Wakefield Company* (Boston: The Marymount Press, 1926).

[8]Quoted in *Antiques from the Civil War to World War I* (New York: American Heritage, 1969), p. 168.

[9]Roosevelt's chair is pictured and discussed in *19th Century America, Furniture and Other Decorative Arts* (New York: The Metropolitan Museum of Art, 1970), No. 260. On the basis of this source, many horn chairs have subsequently been attributed to Associated Artists, Tiffany's first decorating firm, disbanded in 1884. While such chairs may indeed have been the work of Associated Artists or its successors (Tiffany Glass and Decorating Company and Tiffany Studios), the glass ball foot with four-pronged brass casters, considered a hallmark of Tiffany's firms, was also used by Wenzel Friedrich and probably others.

[10]Craig Gilborn, "Rustic Furniture in the Adirondacks, 1875–1925," *Antiques* 109, no. 6 (June 1976): 1213.

[11]Peter F. R. Donner, "The Lure of Rusticity," *Architectural Review,* January 1943, p. 27.

[12]"Garden Decorations," *Godey's Lady's Book,* July 1857, p. 30.

[13]An exception was the "Andrews Metal Chair," specialty of the A. H. Andrews Company of Chicago, which sold a variety of steel-rod office chairs, many with adjustable backs and seats. The company's most popular item, however, according to its 1896 furniture and fitings catalog, was the "curtain" desk of quarter-sawed oak.

[14]Aluminum furniture for porches and out-of-doors became increasingly popular in the late 1940s and the 1950s and remains so today: see the designs by Robert Briers Wemyss in *U.S. Industrial Design 1949-50* (New York: Studio Publications, 1949). The Barwa chair itself was still in production in 1980.

[15]Letter to the author, July 11, 1980.

[16]See Edgar Kaufmann Jr., *Prize Designs for Modern Furniture from the International Competition for Low-Cost Furniture Design* (New York: The Museum of Modern Art, 1950), pp. 24–25.

[17]*What is Modern Design?* (New York: The Museum of Modern Art, 1950), p. 11.

[18]*The Herman Miller Collection,* 1952, p. 4.

[19]Charles Eames, "Biography of a Chair," *New York Times Magazine,* July 17, 1966, p. 4.

[20]*A Modern Consciousness: D. J. De Pree, Florence Knoll,* exhibition catalog (Washington, D.C.: Smithsonian Institution Press, 1975), p. 23.

[21]Aline Saarinen, ed., *Eero Saarinen on His Work, 1947–1964,* 2d ed. (New Haven and London: Yale University Press, 1968), p. 66.

[22]Helena Heyward, ed., *World Furniture* (London: Hamlyn Publishing Group, 1965), p. 301.

[23]Quoted in *Modern Chairs, 1918–1970* (Boston: Boston Book and Art, 1970), No. 29.

[24]"Bertoia: His Sculpture—His Kind of Wire Chair," *Interiors* 112, no. 3 (October 1952): 119.

[25]*New Furniture* 11 (1970):9.

[26]Patent 4,067,615, January 10, 1978.

[27]*Ibid.*

[28]Much of the information above is from Eudorah H. Moore, *Paul Tuttle, Designer,* exhibition catalog (Santa Barbara, Calif.: Santa Barbara Museum of Art, 1978).

COMFORT

[1]"The Evolution of the Easy Chair," *Architectural Review,* March 1942, pp. 59-62. Pevsner notes, however (p. 59), that Loudon's *Encyclopedia* contained the "missing links" between the semi-Grecian type and the Victorian easy chair.

[2]"New Developments in Chair Manufacture," in *Modern Chairs, 1918–1970* (Boston: Boston Book and Art, 1970), p. 14.

[3]"Styling, Organization, Design," *Arts and Architecture,* August, 1947, p. 24.

[4]*Victorian and After* (New York: Walker and Company, 1968), p. 52.

[5]John H. White, *The American Railroad Passenger Car* (Baltimore, Md.: John Hopkins University Press, 1978), p. 117.

[6]Franklin Institute, *Twentieth Annual Exhibition* (Philadelphia, 1850), p. 17.

[7]*Victorian and After,* p. 52.

[8]*A Completed Century, 1826–1926: The Story of Heywood-Wakefield Company* (Boston: The Marymount Press, 1926).

[9]Quoted in Ellen and Bert Denker, *The Rocking Chair Book* (New York: Mayflower Books, 1979), p. 82.

[10]*Manufacturers and Manufactories of Pennsylvania in the Nineteenth Century* (Philadelphia: Galaxy, 1875), p. 22.

[11](Philadelphia: J. B. Lippincott and Sons, 1861), p. 348.

[12]Letter to the author, July 1980.

PORTABILITY

[1]"Interior Decoration, 1940," *Pencil Points,* July 1940, p. 440.

[2]Edgar Kaufmann Jr., *Prize Designs for Modern Furniture from the International Competition for Low-Cost Furniture Design* (New York: The Museum of Modern Art, 1950), p. 8.

[3]A fuller history of the "Hardoy" chair and a source of some of the information above is Peter Blake and Jane Thompson, "A Very Significant Chair," *Architecture Plus,* May 1973, pp. 73–79.

[4]Letter to the author, June 1980.

[5]*The 1977 International Chair Design Competition,* exhibition catalog (Balboa Park, Calif.: Fine Art Gallery of San Diego, 1977), p. 26.

[6]*Ibid.,* p. 22.

[7]Quoted in a letter to the author from Martin R. Liebhold, September 12, 1979.

MULTIPLE FUNCTIONS

[1]*Mechanization Takes Command: A Contribution to Anonymous History* (New York: Oxford University Press, 1948), p. 395.

[2]This biographical account draws primarily on research by Jan Seidler, assistant curator of the Decorative Arts Department, Museum of Fine Arts, Boston.

[3]Illustrated in Sheraton's *Cabinet-Maker and Upholsterer's Drawing Book* (London, 1793), Plates 5 and 22. See Fig. 160, below.

[4]Wallace Nutting, *Furniture Treasury,* Vol. III (New York: Macmillan, 1933), p. 221.

[5]Patent 83,949, November 10, 1868.

[6]This table was sold in Chadds Ford, Pa., in 1975.

[7]Wooton's specifications for patent 155,604, October 6, 1874.

[8]Wooton's specifications for patent 247,979, October 4, 1881.

[9]Much of the information above derives from Betty Lawson Walters, *The King of Desks: Wooton's Patent Secretary,* Smithsonian Studies in History and Technology No. 3 (Washington, D. C.: Smithsonian Institution Press, 1969).

[10]*Ibid.*

Selected Bibliography

American Chairs: Form, Function and Fantasy. Exhibition catalog. Sheboygan, Wis.: John Michael Kohler Arts Center, 1978.

Ames, Kenneth. "Gardner & Company of New York." *Antiques* 100, no. 2 (August 1971), pp. 252–55.

"Architecture and Design." In *Masters of Modern Art*, edited by Alfred H. Barr Jr., pp. 214–27. New York: The Museum of Modern Art, 1954.

Aronson, Joseph. *Book of Furniture and Decoration: Period and Modern*. 2d rev. ed. New York: Crown, 1952.

Banham, Reyner. *Theory and Design and the First Machine Age*. New York: Praeger, 1960.

Baroni, Daniele. *The Furniture of Gerrit Thomas Rietveld*. New York: Barron's, 1978.

Bel Geddes, Norman. *Horizons*. Reprint. New York: Dover, 1977 [1932].

Benton, Tim, and Charlotte and Dennis Sharp, eds. *Architecture and Design*. New York: Whitney Library of Design, 1975.

[Bertoia, Harry.] "Pure Design Research Transforms Abstract Sculpture into New Forms for Architecture and Furniture." *Architectural Forum* 97, no. 3 (September 1952): 142–47.

"Bertoia: His Sculpture—His Kind of Wire Chair." *Interiors* 112, no. 3 (October 1952): 118–21.

Bishop, Robert. *Centuries and Styles of the American Chair, 1640–1970*. New York: E. P. Dutton, 1972.

Buchwald, Hans H. *Form from Process—The Thonet Chair*. Cambridge, Mass.: Harvard University Press, 1967.

Bush, Donald J. *The Streamlined Decade*. New York: George Braziller, 1975.

Caplan, Ralph. *The Design of Herman Miller*. New York: Whitney Library of Design, 1976.

Cheney, Sheldon and Martha. *Art and the Machine, An Account of Industrial Design in 20th-Century America*. New York: Whittlesey House, 1936.

Chermayeff, Serge, and René D'Harnoncourt. "Design for Use." In *Art in Progress*, exhibition catalog, pp. 190–201. New York: The Museum of Modern Art, 1944.

A Completed Century, 1826–1926: The Story of Heywood-Wakefield Company. Boston: The Marymount Press, 1926.

Donner, Peter F. R. "The Lure of Rusticity." *Architectural Review*, January 1943, pp. 26–27.

Downs, Joseph. "Design for the Machine." *Pennsylvania Museum Bulletin*, March 1932, pp. 115–19.

Drexler, Arthur. *Charles Eames. Furniture from the Design Collection*. Exhibition catalog. New York: The Museum of Modern Art, 1973.

Dreyfuss, Henry. *Designing for People*. Reprint. New York: Viking Press, 1974 [1955].

Eames, Charles, and Herbert Bayer. "Design, Designer and Industry." *Magazine of Art*, December 1951, pp. 320–21.

"Eames Celebration." *Architectural Design*, September 1966, pp. 432–42.

Flint, Richard W. "George Hunzinger, Patent Furniture Maker." *Art & Antiques* 3, no. 1 (January-February 1980): 116–23.

For Modern Living: An Exhibition. Exhibition catalog. Detroit: Detroit Institute of Arts, 1949.

Frankl, Paul T. *Form and Re-form: A Practical Handbook of Modern Interiors*. New York: Harper, 1930.

———. *Machine-Made Leisure*. New York: Harper, 1932.

———. *New Dimensions: The Decorative Arts of Today in Words and Pictures*. New York: Payson, 1928.

Gaines, Edith. "The Rocking Chair in America." *Antiques* 99, no. 2 (February 1971): 238–40.

Giedion, Siegfried. *Mechanization Takes Command: A Contribution to Anonymous History*. New York: Oxford University Press, 1948.

———. *Space, Time and Architecture*. 5th rev. ed. Cambridge, Mass.: Harvard University Press, 1967.

Gloag, John. *The Chair: Its Origins, Design and Social History*. New York: A. S. Barnes, 1964.

———, ed. *Design in Modern Life*. London: Allen and Unwin, 1934.

———. *The Missing Technician in Industrial Production*. London: Allen and Unwin, 1944.

———. *Plastics in Industrial Design*. London: Allen and Unwin, 1945.

———. "The Rocking Chair in Victorian England." *Antiques* 99, no. 2 (February 1971): 241–44.

———. *Victorian Comfort: A Social History of Design, 1830–1900*. New York: St. Martin's Press, 1973.

Goldwater, Robert, and René D'Harnoncourt. *Modern Art in Your Life*. Exhibition catalog. New York: The Museum of Modern Art, 1953.

Good Design: An Exhibition of Home Furnishings. Exhibition catalogs. New York: The Museum of Modern Art, twice yearly 1950–55.

Good Design Is Your Business. Exhibition catalog. Buffalo, N.Y.: Albright-Knox Gallery, 1947.

Herman Miller Furniture Company. *The Herman Miller Collection: Furniture Designed by George Nelson, Charles Eames, Isamu Noguchi, Paul László*. Zeeland, Mich.: The Company, 1948.

Heyward, Helena, ed. *World Furniture*. London: Hamlyn Publishing Group, 1965.

"Industrial Design." *Architectural Review*, October 1946, pp. 91–122.

"The Institute of Design: A Laboratory for a New Education." *Interiors* 108, no. 3 (September 1948): 134–39.

An International Exposition of Art in Industry. Exhibition catalog.

New York: R. H. Macy and Company, 1928.

"Inventions in Furniture." *Interiors* 113, no. 4 (November 1953): 78–101.

Janes, Kirtland and Company. *Illustrated Catalogue of Ornamental Ironwork.* Reprint. Princeton, N.J.: Pyne Press, 1971 [1870].

Johnson, Philip. *Machine Art.* Exhibition catalog. New York: The Museum of Modern Art, 1934; W. W. Norton, 1934.

Joy, Edward. *Pictorial Dictionary of British 19th-Century Furniture Design.* London: Antique Collectors Club, 1980.

Kane, Patricia E. "Samuel Gragg: His Bentwood Fancy Chairs." *Yale University Art Gallery Bulletin* 33, no. 2 (Autumn 1971): 27–37.

Kaufmann, Edgar, Jr. "Chairs, Eames and Chests." *Art News* 49, no. 3 (May 1950): 36–40.

———. "The Department of Industrial Design." *The Museum of Modern Art Bulletin* 14, no. 1 (Fall 1946): 1–14.

———. "Furniture [the Morris chair]." *Architectural Review,* August 1950, pp. 127–29.

———. "New Directions in Design." In *New Directions in Prose and Poetry 1938,* pp. 87–92. Reprint. New York: Kraus Reprint Corporation, 1967 [1938].

———. *Prize Designs for Modern Furniture from the International Competition for Low-Cost Furniture Design.* New York: The Museum of Modern Art, 1950.

———. *What Is Modern Design?* New York: The Museum of Modern Art, 1950.

———. *What Is Modern Interior Design?* New York: The Museum of Modern Art, 1953.

Knoll Associates Inc. *Knoll Index of Designs.* New York: Knoll Associates Inc., 1950.

———. *Knoll Index of Designs.* New York: Knoll Associates Inc., 1954.

Kouwenhoven, John A. *The Arts in Modern American Civilization.* New York: W. W. Norton, 1967. (Originally published as *Made in America* [Garden City, N.Y.: Doubleday, 1948].)

Kron, John, and Suzanne Slesin. *High-Tech: The Industrial Style and Source Book for the Home.* New York: Clarkson N. Potter, 1978.

Logie, Gordon. *Furniture from Machines.* London: Allen and Unwin, 1947.

Loudon, J. C. *Encyclopedia of Cottage, Farm, and Villa Architecture and Furniture.* Reprint. Watkins Glen, N.Y.: American Life Foundation, 1968 [1833].

Lynes, Russell. *The Tastemakers.* New York: Harper, 1954.

Made with Paper. Exhibition catalog. New York: The Museum of Contemporary Crafts, 1967.

Mang, Karl. *History of Modern Furniture,* translated by John William Gabriel. New York: Harry N. Abrams, 1979.

Meadmore, Clement. *The Chair.* New York: Van Nostrand Reinhold, 1970.

———. *The Modern Chair: Classics in Production.* Van Nostrand Reinhold, 1979.

Meikle, Jeffrey L. *Twentieth Century Limited: Industrial Design in America, 1925–1939.* Philadelphia: Temple University Press, 1979.

Modern Chairs, 1918–1970. Boston: Boston Book and Art, 1970.

A Modern Consciousness: D. J. De Pree, Florence Knoll. Exhibition catalog. Washington, D.C.: Smithsonian Institution Press, 1975.

Moholy-Nagy, Laszlo. "Art in Industry." *Arts and Architecture,* October 1947, p. 28.

———. *The New Vision,* 3rd rev. ed. New York: Wittenborn, 1946.

Moore, Eudorah H. *Paul Tuttle, Designer.* Exhibition catalog. Santa Barbara, Calif.: Santa Barbara Museum of Art, 1978.

Nelson, George. "The Furniture Industry." *Fortune* 35, no. 1 (January 1947): 107–11, 171–81.

———. *Living Spaces.* New York: Whitney, 1952.

———. *Storage.* New York: Whitney, 1954.

Neutra, Richard. *Survival through Design.* New York: Oxford University Press, 1954.

The 1977 International Chair Design Competition. Exhibition catalog. Balboa Park, Calif.: Fine Art Gallery of San Diego, 1977.

Noyes, Eliot. "Charles Eames." *Arts and Architecture,* September 1946, pp. 26–44.

———. *Organic Design in Home Furnishings.* Exhibition catalog. New York: The Museum of Modern Art, 1941.

"Organic Design at the Museum of Modern Art." *Interiors* 101, no. 3 (October 1941): 38–39.

Pevsner, Nikolaus. *An Enquiry into Industrial Art in England.* London: Cambridge University Press, 1937.

———. "The Evolution of the Easy Chair." *Architectural Review,* March 1942, pp. 59–62.

———. "The First Plywood Furniture." *Architectural Review,* August 1938, pp. 75–76.

———. "The History of Plywood up to 1814." *Architectural Review,* September 1939, pp. 129–30.

———. *The Sources of Modern Architecture and Design.* New York: Oxford University Press, 1968.

———. *Victorian and After.* New York: Walker and Company, 1968.

Pile, John F. *Modern Furniture.* New York: John Wiley and Sons, 1979.

"Prophetic Plastics." *House & Garden* 78, no. 4 (October 1940): 26–31, 72.

Ray, William and Marlys. *The Art of Invention: Patent Models and Their Makers.* Princeton, N.J.: The Pyne Press, 1974.

Richards, Charles. *Industrial Art and the Museum.* New York: Macmillan, 1927.

"The Rocking Chair, America's Contribution to Furniture Design." *Interiors* 102, no. 11 (June 1943): 46–47, 71–74.

Ross, Isabel. *Taste in America.* New York: Thomas Y. Crowell, 1967.

Roth, Rodris. "A Patent Model by John Henry Belter." *Antiques* 111, no. 5 (May 1977): 1038–40.

Saarinen, Aline, ed. *Eero Saarinen on His Work, 1947–1964.* 2d ed. New Haven and London: Yale University Press, 1968.

Schaefer, Herwin. *Nineteenth Century Modern: The Functional Tradition of Victorian Design.* New York: Praeger, 1970.

Schwab, Frances T. "Victorian Prototypes of the Present." *Architectural Record,* September 1945, pp. 70–75.

Stephenson, Sue. *Rustic Furniture.* New York: Van Nostrand Reinhold, 1977.

Teague, Walter Dorwin. *Design This Day: The Technique of Order in the Machine Age.* New York: Harcourt, Brace, 1940.

Temko, Allan. *Eero Saarinen.* New York: George Braziller, 1962.

Victorian Ironwork: The Wickersham Catalogue of 1857, introduction by Margot Gayle. Philadelphia: The Athenaeum of Philadelphia, 1977.

Vincent, Clare. "John Henry Belter: Manufacturer of All Kinds of Fine Furniture." In Ian M. G. Quimby and Polly Anne Earl, eds., *Technological Innovation and the Decorative Arts* (Winterthur Conference Report, 1973), pp. 207–34. Charlottesville, Va.: University Press of Virginia, 1974.

Waldheim, Jack. "The Chairs." *Arts and Architecture,* June 1949, pp. 26–27, 52.

White, John H. *The American Railroad Passenger Car.* Baltimore: Johns Hopkins University Press, 1974.

Wright, Mary and Russell. *Guide for Easier Living.* New York: Simon and Schuster, 1951.

The following periodicals contain useful information about past and current developments in furniture design: *Architectural Forum; Architectural Record; Architectural Review* (London); *Arts and Architecture; Good Furniture; House & Garden; House Beautiful; Interiors; New Furniture.*

Index

Photographic Credits

About the Author

David A. Hanks, whose museum career began in the Department of Education of the Saint Louis Art Museum, has been Associate Curator of Decorative Arts at the Art Institute of Chicago; Curator, Department of American Art, Philadelphia Museum of Art; and Guest Curator at the Smithsonian Institution and The High Museum of Art in Atlanta. While at the Art Institute of Chicago he organized two major exhibitions, "American Art of the Colonies and Early Republic" and "The Arts and Crafts Movement in America, 1876–1916." Among Mr. Hanks's publications are articles on Chicago silversmith Robert Jarvie and Gothic-revival furniture in Philadelphia for *Antiques* magazine. His first book, *The Decorative Designs of Frank Lloyd Wright*, appeared in 1979.

THE COLLIGNON BROS. MANUFACTORIES P.

WAREROOMS 181 CANAL ST. N.Y.

FOLDING CHAIRS NEAR CLOSTER, BERGEN CO. N. J.

ILLUSTRATED CIRCULARS MAILED FREE.